BULLETS OVER
BOMBAY

BULLETS OVER BOMBAY

Satya and the Hindi Film Gangster

UDAY BHATIA

HarperCollins *Publishers* India

First published in India by
HarperCollins *Publishers* 2021
A-75, Sector 57, Noida, Uttar Pradesh 201301, India
www.harpercollins.co.in

2 4 6 8 10 9 7 5 3 1

P-ISBN: 978-93-5422-785-1
E-ISBN: 978-93-5422-793-6

Typeset in 12/15.7 Adobe Devanagari at
Manipal Technologies Limited, Manipal

Printed and bound at
Replika Press Pvt. Ltd.

MIX
Paper from
responsible sources
FSC
www.fsc.org   FSC® C016779

To the films, filmmakers and film viewers of the '90s

Contents

1. The Moment of Satya   1

2. Ten Scenes   15

3. The Hindi Film Gangster   43

4. Bombay on Film   80

5. Getting the Team Together   105

6. Making the Film   136

7. After Satya   185

Bibliography   217

Index   225

Acknowledgements   241

About the Author   243

1

The Moment of Satya

'There is really only one possibility – failure.'

– Robert Warshow, 'The Gangster as Tragic Hero'

In 1964, while promoting his film *Bande à part*, Jean-Luc Godard repurposed a line from American cinema pioneer D.W. Griffith. *What do filmgoers want? A girl and a gun.* Like the French director's other famous aphorism – cinema is truth 24 times per second – it was glib, but it stuck. Guns and girls, danger and beauty – there, apparently, for the gratification of the boys on screen and in the audience. This adage certainly applies to Indian commercial cinema, whose practitioners know the value of a thrill introduced for thrill's sake – except here it's a girl and a gun and a song and a mother and a god.

Let's look at one Indian film in particular. There's a girl, not the Godard kind, but naïve and warm. There's a gun in the hands of her lover. The film is about him, but it all started with a similar girl in a book. And it was named for a girl. To this, we add one more thing: Mumbai.

A girl, a gun, a boy and a city. *Satya*.

—

August 1997. Independent India turns 50. Sachin Tendulkar scores back-to-back Test centuries against Sri Lanka. Word is getting around that Kajol is the killer in *Gupt*. Everyone's talking about *The God of Small Things*, which will go on to win Arundhati Roy the Booker Prize. The market is holding itself together even as Asia collapses. Two months after 59 people die in a fire during a screening of *Border* in Delhi's Uphaar cinema, moviegoers continue to frequent theatres. And Ram Gopal Varma, with goodwill left over from *Rangeela* but knowing he's messed up *Daud*, sets out to make a film on the Mumbai underworld.

Eleven months later, *Satya* opens to critical acclaim and modest business. Did anyone then guess it would be relevant two decades later? All anyone could talk about in 1998 was *Kuch Kuch Hota Hai*. Karan Johar's film, a college romance which catches up with its central characters later in life, unfolds in a fantasy India where students wear designer clothes and are totally insufferable in ways that must have seemed cool to us back then. It canonised the pairing of Kajol and Shah Rukh Khan, launched Rani Mukerji's career and became, for a spell, the third-highest-grossing Indian film ever. Like everyone else in the country, I watched it in the theatre when it released, and again when it played on TV. I can't sit through 10 minutes of it now, let alone the whole three hours. I suspect it's the same with a lot of people my age.

Several other big releases of 1998 were romantic dramas too. Three films that year had *pyaar* (love) in the title: *Pyaar To Hona*

Hi Tha, *Pyaar Kiya To Darna Kya* and *Jab Pyaar Kisise Hota Hai*. There was also Mani Ratnam's haunting *Dil Se* (From the Heart) and Feroz Khan's *Prem Aggan* (Burning Love), one of the daftest Hindi films ever. Bobby Deol had a hit with the action film *Soldier*, as did Amitabh Bachchan and Govinda with the slapstick *Bade Miyan Chote Miyan* and Aamir Khan with the *On the Waterfront* remake *Ghulam*. *Dil Se* is the only one of this lot worth revisiting, though at the time it eluded both critics and viewers. The biggest surprise was a no-budget indie called *Hyderabad Blues*, made by a former engineer named Nagesh Kukunoor for 17 lakh rupees (a million is 10 lakhs; a crore is 100 lakhs) in two-and-a-half weeks. It was mumblecore before the term existed, and one of the first proto-'Hindies' after the Arundhati Roy-scripted *In Which Annie Gives It Those Ones* (1989).

Change was afoot, even if it seemed like cinema was in a rut. This was the year Hindi film was deemed an industry by the government. This meant that makers could apply for loans from financial institutions instead of trying to secure them from builders and jewellers, many of whom used movie productions to offload their 'black' money. Film editing was poised to go digital – songs and promos were being cut on Avid, and the trusty Steenbeck machines would soon be put out to pasture. DVDs were trickling into the market, first as luxury items, then as cheap knockoffs in seedy shops. PVR opened India's first multiplex in Delhi's Saket neighbourhood in 1997. With all the nostalgia associated with single-screen theatres today, it's easy to forget how we welcomed multiplexes when they started out. Their pricing was, and still is, prohibitively expensive for the urban poor, but they dramatically improved viewing conditions for those who could afford them. For my generation, old enough to have grown up watching movies in single-screens but not so old as to have a sentimental attachment to them, it was a gleaming new world.

As PVR expanded and competitors entered the market, multiplexes started to have an impact not just on how we were seeing movies but on the kinds of movies that were being made. Multiple screens meant less pressure to carry a single saleable film. You could run something like *Hyderabad Blues* one show a day for a week, while also screening whatever mainstream commercial product was in circulation then. For a brief period, these smaller, bolder releases were referred to as 'multiplex films'.

—

After making his first original Hindi film, *Rangeela* (1995), with Aamir Khan, and his second, *Daud* (1997), with Sanjay Dutt, Varma wrong-footed everyone by hiring a bunch of nobodies for his next project. *Satya*'s credits read like an honour roll today. In 1997, an average moviegoer would have been hard-pressed to recognise more than three names. There was Anurag Kashyap, in his mid-twenties, all restless energy and no screen credit to show for it. Saurabh Shukla, with two acclaimed, little-seen films under his belt in a two-film-old career. Manoj Bajpayee, going stir-crazy after months of bit parts and TV work, hungry for a chance to explode onscreen. Vishal Bhardwaj, building a reputation as a composer, nursing a dream of directing one day. Makarand Deshpande and Apurva Asrani, Sandeep Chowta and Aditya Srivastava, all standing around on the ground floor, waiting for the elevator.

It's perfect, this moment. *Satya*, before it was a film, before the accolades, a cloud of possibility and potential. Everyone at the start of their careers, drinking cheap alcohol in one-room apartments, complaining, plotting their takeover of Bollywood.

The film opened on 3 July 1998. For the first day or two, collections weren't encouraging. The newcomers gulped. Varma, too, must have wondered if he was headed for his second failure in a row after *Daud*. He'd already moved on to *Kaun*, following the ancient showbiz maxim which says you book your next gig before a release, not after. Would he be able to continue making Hindi films if *Satya* wasn't successful, or would this mean a return to Telugu cinema?

To everyone's relief, business started picking up. People read the reviews over the weekend, went to watch it, came back and raved to their friends. Word got around that an unusually gritty Hindi film was in theatres. I remember a friend's mother recommending it to my parents, with the caveat that it might not be suitable for our 14-year-old sensibilities (it wasn't, but we watched it anyway). Shobha De wrote about it, which meant the film had become small talk in fancy Mumbai parties. The actors started getting recognised on the street. It wasn't a huge hit, but it ran steadily for a couple of months, celebrating a silver jubilee in Mumbai. More importantly, at a time when Hindi cinema was spinning its wheels, it showed the way forward.

The immediate influence of *Satya* was on the gangster film. Hindi cinema had looked at the lives of landless farmers, rickshaw-pullers, army doctors, circus clowns. Somehow, in all this, no one had thought of seriously exploring the life of the workaday urban criminal. Sure, there'd been gangsters in Hindi films, but they'd mostly been exceptions – either camp, like the mob bosses played by Ajit and Prem Nath, or psychotic, like Nana Patekar's Anna in *Parinda* (1989), or the larger-than-life Amitabh Bachchan antiheroes. Few filmmakers considered the possibility of an ordinary criminal. And yet, that's what they usually were – nondescript-looking people who'd simply stopped playing by the rules of society. 'He could be anyone', Suketu Mehta wrote of a shooter in Dawood Ibrahim's organisation in *Maximum City*, 'the lift man, the peon in my uncle's office, any one of the people walking on the sidewalk as I pass in my car.'

Satya imagined what a day, a week, a month might be like for a gangster. It treated them as it would normal people, catching up with them not just when they were on the job but also when they drank and argued with their wives and went on dates. Two years earlier, in *Is Raat Ki Subah Nahin* (1996), Sudhir Mishra had shown gangsters as family men – one of the best scenes was Ashish Vidyarthi trying to talk business while being interrupted by his father, sister and brother. *Satya* took this idea and went further. Varma's film wasn't stylised – the photography was unadorned, the language rough. Much of it was shot in actual locations. All of this encouraged the perception that this was the real thing.

Varma wasn't interested in the moral fallout of organised crime; he was only trying to show the ins and outs of a cruel and charismatic world.* Others soon followed suit. *Vaastav* (1999) was the first to arrive – similarly tough-minded but closer to the mainstream. Anurag Kashyap's *Black Friday* (2004) was an extension of the documentary aspects of Varma's film. Vishal Bhardwaj's *Maqbool* (2003) added some poetry. Varma returned to the genre himself with *Company* (2002) and *Sarkar* (2005). For the next few years, crime films kept coming, many of them Varma's own productions and protégés. Having only made a handful of genuine gangster films in its first century, Hindi cinema made up for lost time in the 2000s. *Satya* was the catalyst, but *Company*, loosely based on the Dawood Ibrahim–Chhota Rajan split, was also an influence in its weaving of fact and legend. Films like *D* (2005), *Shootout at Lokhandwala* (2007) and *Once upon a Time in Mumbaai* (2010) drew from the lives of

---

*   Varma disdained intellectual analysis, once telling journalist and author Manu Joseph, 'When do I know a guy is bullshitting me? When he comes to me and says he wants to make a film on the psychological conflict in Indian society.'

famous Mumbai dons – like *Deewar* (1975) and *Dharmatma* (1975) had in their time. Other films used the genre as a jumping-off point, venturing into politics (*Sarkar*) and literature (*Maqbool*). There were romantic dramas (*Gangster*, 2006), even comedies (*Munna Bhai M.B.B.S.*, 2003) set within the underworld. With the waning of the Mumbai mafia, the gangster film moved out of the city (*Omkara*, 2006; *Rakta Charitra*, 2010; *Gangs of Wasseypur*, 2012), returning as period spectacle (*Bombay Velvet*, 2015). The torch is now being carried by Tamil and Malayalam cinema, whose directors seem to reinvent the gangster film every few years, and by streaming shows like *Sacred Games* and *Mirzapur*, which bypass the censorship of the big screen.

———

Satya changed Hindi cinema in profound ways, but its legacy also includes those who worked on it, benefitted from its success and went on to change Hindi cinema themselves. Anurag Kashyap has directed a dozen features and made, in *Gangs of Wasseypur*, perhaps the best Hindi film of the last decade. Saurabh Shukla remains one of the most underrated character actors in the country. With his Shakespeare trilogy of *Maqbool*, *Omkara* and *Haider* (2014), Vishal Bhardwaj created an enduring work of Indian art. Apurva Asrani wrote the National Award-winning *Shahid* (2012) and *Aligarh* (2015). Manoj Bajpayee inspired a generation of actors with his performances in *Satya* and *Shool* (1999), and another generation with *Gangs of Wasseypur*.

Like American kids in the '60s who heard The Velvet Underground and started their own bands, a generation of Indians saw in *Satya* a call to arms. Rajkummar Rao watched it and spent the next decade trying to become Manoj Bajpayee; the two ended up acting together in *Gangs of Wasseypur*, *Chittagong* (2012), *Aligarh* and *Love Sonia*

(2018). Performers like Kay Kay Menon, trying to break into the industry, found the doors were now ajar ('If it were not for Manoj's brilliant performance in *Satya*, actors like Irrfan and me might still be staring at the ceiling and waiting to be accepted,' he said years later). Varma's production house would get 20 scripts a week from young writers convinced they'd written his next project. Actors with bit parts dreamed of doing what Sushant Singh had managed – to go from two scenes in *Satya* to the third lead in *Kaun* mere months later. Delhi University theatre troupes, where Kashyap, Bajpayee, Shukla, Singh, Bhardwaj and Aditya Srivastava got their start, suddenly seemed like a viable first step to a film career.

For Varma, who began by making films in his native Telugu, *Satya* opened up the Hindi industry. *Rangeela* had been a bigger hit, but its success could be attributed to leads Aamir Khan and Urmila Matondkar, and A.R. Rahman's music. But *Satya* was all Varma. He'd shown he could make a film without stars, item songs (at least item songs that didn't have grimy bearded men) or a happy ending. Having delivered a sleeper hit, he could have cashed Bollywood's cheques, cast Khans and Kapoors. Instead, he bet the house on new talent. For a short while in the 2000s, Varma was practically a parallel industry unto himself. In his films, and through his productions, he gave breaks to a series of unheralded actors, directors, writers and technicians. Sriram Raghavan, Hemant Chaturvedi, Jaideep Sahni, Randeep Hooda and Shimit Amin all worked for him at the start of the careers. Out of his production setup, dubbed The Factory, came hard, exciting films: *Shool*, *Ab Tak Chhappan* (2004), *Ek Hasina Thi* (2004). He worked fast, with one ear to the ground, churning out genre cinema like an Indian Roger Corman. For a while, even his missteps seemed like inspired rolls of the dice.

—

Once I started speaking to people who worked on *Satya*, it became clear just how chaotic the production had been. Scenes were rewritten at night and handed to the actors in the morning before filming. They couldn't always get permission to shoot, so Varma and the cameraperson and a few actors would often go in guerrilla-style, get what they needed and scram before the cops showed up. Most of the crew was young and enthusiastic, which meant that Varma always had someone coming up to him with suggestions. Expectations were low, which freed everyone up to experiment with naturalistic sets, lighting and performances – things that would have been impossible on a prestige production, with financiers worried about making back their money and stars concerned about denting their image.

It's a measure of how early in their careers *Satya* happened that most of its cast and crew are still full-time professionals (it's also a testament to their talent that they're in demand over 20 years later). Schedules had to be worked around – my regular job as a newspaper critic and theirs as actors, directors, cinematographers. Secretaries and PR agents were cajoled (and, if they were unhelpful, silently cursed). Over many months, I met the *Satya* team in offices and homes, coffee shops and country clubs. One of my first conversations was over Skype with Gerard Hooper, the American cinematographer who shot this one seminal film and never worked in India again. A year later, I was on the Indian Institute of Technology (IIT) Bombay campus, talking to *Satya*'s other cinematographer, Mazhar Kamran (Hooper left after a few months), trying to understand how a film shot by two camerapersons could look so cohesive.

Often, I had to nab my interviewees between shooting or editing or production schedules – or during them. Everyone besides Chakravarthy, Bhanodaya and Hooper lived in Mumbai, but I still needed some luck. I'm convinced I only got hold of Anurag Kashyap because I caught him at a weak moment: sick, eyes watering, wiping his nose on the bedspread, the sheet and his shirt as we spoke in his bedroom. Vishal Bhardwaj was busy with a film, a play, and then another film, and it was after many, many months that I finally got an entertaining 45 minutes with him.

It took about a year and a half to speak to everyone. Somewhere along the way, I began to realise that multiple accounts did not necessarily mean more clarity. In my darker moments, I imagined *Satya* alums colluding to each tell me a slightly different version of what went down. Kamram said there were frequent breaks in the production; assistant director Barnali Ray Shukla didn't recall any. The opening monologue was attributed to five different people by five separate interviewees. The killing of music baron Gulshan Kumar happened in the second week, on the first day and before shooting started, depending on which account you believe. 'Goli Maar Bheje Mein' was shot by Varma in one recollection, by Kamran in another, by Steadicam operator Nitin Rao in yet another; though my favourite scenario is the one where Chakravarthy is the choreographer.

I met Varma in early 2018. His Lokhandwala office was a singular experience. Above the front entrance, giant rust-coloured letters spelt out 'Company'; to its right, mounted on the outer wall, was a pistol the size of a camel. The waiting room had a poster of a naked girl licking the ground and another of Bruce Lee with the words 'I care a fuck about circumstances, I create my own opportunities'. I was ushered into Varma's spacious office. 'Those who cannot hear my music will not like my dance' was painted on the floor. There was a sofa-bed in the corner and what appeared to be mirrors on the ceiling. There were sculptures, if that's the word, of a chameleon and a bulldog. Potted plants. A pair of boxing gloves. Several posters: Amitabh Bachchan in *Sarkar*; Steven Spielberg saying, 'I dream for a living'; a naked woman sitting on a lion with the words 'Real power is in thought'; another Bruce Lee. And a stack of books: *Ayn Rand and the World She Made*, *Sex Sells!*, *Manhunt: The Ten-Year Search for Bin Laden*, *Martin Scorsese in Ten Scenes*, *Saddam Defiant*, *The Godfather* and an Indira Gandhi biography.

Initially, Varma wasn't keen to talk about himself or *Satya*. He told me he was bored of repeating the same stories and suggested I'd find answers to all my questions in his autobiography, *Guns & Thighs*. We kept talking. I played him scenes from the film on my laptop. From time to time, he'd get a phone call and we'd break for five, 10 minutes. Lunch was brought in. Afternoon turned to evening. After a series of monosyllabic answers, I decided to call it a day and turned off the recorder. This seemed to cheer him up. He spoke a while longer, ending with a bemused recollection of a review where the critic called him irresponsible for making gangsters look human.

Inevitably, there were some people I couldn't get hold of. The closest I got to speaking to Urmila Matondkar was when her secretary told me to submit questions that she may or may not answer. Later, even that offer was rescinded. If the idea of reading a book about *Satya* without the voice of its biggest (and only) star is unacceptable to you, this is where we must part. Bhanodaya, one of the film's editors,* also proved elusive, as did actor Makarand Deshpande and score composer Sandeep Chowta.

With each successive account, the story of the film's making grew bigger and more convoluted. I had, perhaps unreasonably, expected detailed accounts of weekly activities from 20 years earlier. Instead,

---

* This was a film made by pairs. Two editors (Apurva Asrani, Bhanodaya), writers (Anurag Kashyap, Saurabh Shukla), cinematographers (Gerard Hooper, Mazhar Kamran). Even the music was divided between Vishal Bhardwaj (songs) and Sandeep Chowta (score).

I got dozens upon dozens of fragments that refused to fit together. Patently false information was related with supreme confidence. No one had anything as useful as a production diary with actual dates and numbers. It felt like I was assembling a jigsaw with pieces that didn't all belong to the same puzzle.

In telling the story of how the team and the film came together, I hope I've managed to convey to some small extent the excitement that existed on that set. Every person I spoke to had fond memories of making *Satya*. They didn't expect it to be a hit, or even run for more than a few weeks, but there was a growing feeling that they were working on something special. 'All of us were very charged – we were doing our first big work,' Kamran said. Before a scene, Varma would solicit opinions from anyone around – actor, key grip, set designer – but once they were ready to shoot, he knew exactly what he wanted. This openness was mentioned again and again, usually prefaced with 'I don't know about now, but Ramu then ...'

Varma's career over the last decade has been one of the more dramatic downward trajectories in Hindi cinema. He still keeps busy; when I met him, he appeared to be working on four or five projects simultaneously. Yet, it's been a long time since he's made worthwhile cinema. He's out of favour in Bollywood, so he works in Telugu film, in shorter formats and online. Maybe he just had that many years as a vital artist, and we should be grateful for the extraordinary 13-year run from *Siva* (1989) to *Company*, where even his bad films were intriguing and his good films changed Indian cinema.

Hindi film wasn't the same after *Satya*. Suddenly, the older directors seemed very old indeed. New voices began to emerge – Kashyap, Bhardwaj, Rajkumar Hirani, Dibakar Banerjee, Sriram Raghavan. Their films didn't look like *Satya*, but they'd imbibed its lessons, finding ways to make them the way they wanted while staying within the ballpark of popular cinema. Bollywood remains a dynastic industry, always eager to give chances to the children of various royal filmic lineages – Kapoors, Bachchans, Bhatts, Khans. Varma challenged the industry to bet on unknown young talent by doing so himself. It was as crucial a prod to Indian film as *Satya* or *Rangeela* or *Company*.

Satya has in its DNA two separate strands of cinema. The first is the gangster film, whose genealogy I'll trace in the third chapter – an exercise complicated by the fact that the genre only existed in fits and starts in Hindi cinema before the 1980s, and only came into force after *Satya*. The other is a more expansive tradition – that of the city film. It's the cumulative effect of these two traditions that makes *Satya* the film it is. Varma could have made a gangster film with similar characters and situations set in Delhi or Kolkata or Chennai, but he could only have made *Satya* in Mumbai. It's a film about people in *this* city as much as it is about the underworld. That *Satya* melds the gangster film and the city film isn't surprising – these two worlds have always overlapped in the movies. 'The gangster is the man of the city', Robert Warshow wrote in a famous 1948 tract, 'with the city's language and knowledge, with its queer and dishonest skills and its terrible daring …' So, perhaps unwisely, I'll also try and map the broad contours of the Bombay street film.* But before that, for the benefit of those whose memories of *Satya* are hazy or non-existent, I'll narrate the film, as it were, through 10 scenes.

It's been over 20 years since *Satya* released, which seems a reasonable gap to be able to start talking of the film in terms of a classic. What kind of classic, though? It would surprise me if 20 years later, Varma's film is spoken of in the same breath as *Sholay* (1975) or *Dilwale Dulhania Le Jayenge* (1995). It's not that *Satya* isn't their

---

* Bombay was renamed Mumbai in 1995. In this book, I'll refer to the city pre-'95 as Bombay and thereafter as Mumbai.

equal, but those were big-banner films and huge, popular successes. *Satya* was closer to an indie in spirit and execution. Its roots went deep, not wide. A possible parallel for its impact might be *Easy Rider* shaking up Hollywood in 1969 – a young rebel crew infusing a complacent industry with rude energy. Perhaps *Satya* will join the ranks of that handful of films which are genres unto themselves. If they're making films like *Satya* in another 20 years, if '*Satya*-like' requires no explanation, then its legacy is secure.

2

Ten Scenes

'*Kya danger story hai! Kya danger film hai!*'

– Bheeku telling Satya and Vidya about *Jurassic Park*

MUMBAI

The first image in *Satya* is of a funeral pyre. It's past twilight. The sky is a muddy brown, factory chimneys just about visible in the distance. We hear something ticking, too fast for a clock. A long-haired man reads something in the newspaper, throws it aside violently, grabs a gun and shoots at it. We hear the clatter of a train. Fire flashes on screen again. Suddenly, we're looking at the ocean.

With the first shots of boats bobbing on the sea, the credits start to roll. 'Bharat Shah presents … A Ram Gopal Varma film … *Satya*' – the title in blood red, painted with thick strokes, like the lettering in a Kurosawa film. Then we're back in the city – traffic, rain. And a voice says, 'Mumbai'.

Aditya Srivastava's voiceover describes a city that never sleeps but can't stop dreaming when it's awake; that has sparkling heights and dark, silent depths. We see ordinary Mumbaikars walking flooded streets, drying clothes, playing cricket. As the words 'Mumbai underworld' are spoken, Saurabh Shukla appears, points a gun at the camera and shoots – a split-second image that reaches all the way back to 1903 and *The Great Train Robbery*.

More scenes of everyday life follow, interspersed with cops hunting down gangsters. Sandeep Chowta's piano-and-flute theme is aching and elegiac, linking it to the sombre credits of other Indian gangster films. In Mani Ratnam's *Nayakan* (1987), the haunting 'Thenpandi Cheemayile' is sung as a young Velu Naicker walks out of Victoria Terminus, as Satya (Chakravarthy) does here. And in the opening credits of Vidhu Vinod Chopra's *Parinda*, static aerial images of Bombay at dusk are accompanied by Aaron Copland's 'Fanfare for the Common Man' – a rare instance of a Western classical composition starting a Hindi film.

Satya's credits end with a shot of Victoria Terminus (renamed Chhatrapati Shivaji Terminus, or CST, in 1996) seen from a distance. We briefly glimpse Satya standing beside one of the pillars. '*Kahin se ek aadmi aaya, yeh uski kahaani hai*' (From somewhere came a man, this is his story). As these words are spoken, the camera abruptly pulls out; we only see the crowd now. It zooms in on Satya a few seconds later, but that movement away is key. It's an instinctively democratic gesture; a way of saying that, in another film, we could be following a lawyer or a coconut-seller out of here instead of a would-be gangster. As Robert Warshow put it, one must emerge from the crowd or else one is nothing.

Anurag Kashyap was put in charge of the second unit filming Satya's arrival in Mumbai. It was the first time anyone had sent the young man to shoot something by himself. Full of ideas, he headed to 'Town' – the local term for south Mumbai – with Mazhar Kamran, Chakravarthy and a small crew. It was a disaster. When Varma saw the footage, he exploded – *who shot this?* Kashyap tried to explain that he couldn't get his ideas across to the crew. 'They're my seniors,' he said. 'They know better'. 'No one knows better,' Varma fired back. Kashyap returned to the location and, this time, got the shots.

The film was supposed to start more prosaically – no montage or narration, just Satya walking out of the station. But Gerard Hooper had been going out by himself, walking the streets and shooting on the fly. He'd amassed a lot of documentary footage that didn't fit the main narrative but made for great filler. Someone had the bright idea of stringing these images together. Apurva Asrani claimed credit; Varma too said it might have been the editor's idea. One scene, shot by Steadicam operator Nitin Rao, was of the wreckage of Poonam Chambers in Worli, a building collapse in which 15 people died. Shooting had barely started when Varma found out about the accident and sent his fixer, Sabir Masani (who plays Yeda, the man in the opening montage), to see if he could get some authentic tragedy on film.

On top of the documentary-like images, Varma added voiceover. He'd always liked the narration in adventure films like *The Guns of Navarone* (1961) and Westerns like *Mackenna's Gold* (1969). Kamran encouraged him to try it – he too was a fan of voiceovers, though in French New Wave films. Varma says he wrote the words himself in English, and got them translated. Asrani says he came up with a draft which Srivastava and Kashyap polished. Kashyap vaguely remembers Manoj Bajpayee or Makarand Deshpande writing it. Only Saurabh Shukla seems to have had nothing to do with the voiceover.

Satya goes from the station to his first home in Mumbai, a cowshed. He's accosted by a local goon (Sushant Singh) who asks for a 'donation'.

Satya refuses and, threatened with a knife, slashes the man's face. The victim's boss, a pimp named Jagga (Jeeva) – whom Satya has already had a run-in with – sends men to beat him up. Later, Satya attacks Jagga, who gets him thrown in jail. Meanwhile, a hit on a film producer sees gangster Bheeku Mhatre (Manoj Bajpayee) placed in the same jail. Satya and Bheeku clash, but then become friends.

SATYA MEETS THE GANG

Long takes are the closest a film comes to approximating live performance. More than any other piece of cinema craft, they can make you feel the presence of an organising intelligence – someone orchestrating all those moving parts. An extended take also changes something in the alchemy of a viewer's experience, whether or not they're even aware the scene is unfolding without cuts.

There are a couple of excellent one-ers in *Satya*, but for sheer fluency and watchability, it's difficult to improve on the scene where Satya is introduced by advocate Mule (Makarand Deshpande) to the rest of the gang (Bheeku's still in prison). It begins as the two climb a staircase and enter a crowded flat (Hooper recalled the challenge of adjusting from natural light to the dingy atmosphere inside). There's a cut, followed by an unbroken shot, the camera trailing Mule as he unhurriedly winds his way through the room, greeting some of the men, spraying them with perfume, kissing Bappu (Rajesh Joshi) on the cheek, telling the taciturn Yeda, 'My only wish in life is to see you smile', recommending Shabu, his regular in the Pila House brothel, to anyone in earshot. The camera takes a quick tour of the adjoining room – we catch a glimpse of Chander (Snehal Dabi), eager as always to tell a joke – before settling on a portly man behind a desk, speaking into a red phone. This is Kallu Mama (Saurabh Shukla), who runs

Bheeku's organisation.* We stay on him until the conversation ends. Mule and Satya enter his cabin, and the shot ends.

All of this lasts 65 seconds – not a particularly long take. Still, it captures perfectly the boisterous energy of a gang headquarters – and, one imagines, of the *Satya* set. Because the shot is unbroken, it imparts a breathless rhythm which tells us what this bustling den of thieves must look like to a fresh pair of eyes like Satya's. A straw poll of elaborate one-take scenes in gangster films will fetch you '*Goodfellas* Copacabana' nine times out of 10. And with good reason – few single-shot scenes are more intricate or attuned to the mood of the film than Scorsese's magical choreography of Henry, Karen and a nightclub. The *Satya* shot is much less complicated, but the governing principle is the same: the new kid is thrust into an exciting, dangerous world. You could do the scene with cuts and it wouldn't have the same exhilaration.

Varma says most viewers have no idea when they're watching a single-shot scene. 'But', he added, 'for the people who realise it, I think it makes a lot of difference'. *Satya* wasn't the first time he'd tried a one-take introduction. There's a wonderful unbroken shot in his first film, *Siva*, where a car pulls up, a man alights, walks up a flight of stairs, enters a house, walks through rooms and up another staircase before he finally reaches crime boss Bhavani (the idea came from the scene in *Ardh Satya* (1983) where Om Puri's cop meets gangster Rama Shetty for the first time).

---

* A literary cousin to Kallu Mama is Otto 'Abbadabba' Berman, right-hand man to mobster Dutch Schultz in E.L. Doctorow's novel *Billy Bathgate*. Like Schultz, Berman was a real-life underworld figure in the 1920s and '30s who, legend has it, was fond of saying, 'Nothing personal, it's just business' – words that Mario Puzo later put in Michael Corleone's mouth in *The Godfather*.

After Satya is introduced, a builder named Malhotra is sent in. A bit of playacting ensues, with Kallu Mama putting on a scary face and threatening the real estate man with dire consequences if he doesn't cough up the money he owes them in 10 days. This was inspired by the owner of a bar in Borivali that Varma wanted to use as a location. In their first meeting, the man, who was either part of, or connected to, the underworld, kept large wads of cash lying on a mattress. The sight of all that money made the director feel uneasy; he interpreted it as the man 'sending a subconscious or conscious signal to me that he didn't need to be scared of anyone because of who he was'. But then Varma met him again and he was much friendlier, almost a different person. That first meeting was an act, a tough-guy pose. Varma was struck by this adoption of a dual personality, and wrote it into the disposition of Kallu Mama.

Satya is shown the one-room apartment Bheeku has arranged for him. He meets Vidya (Urmila Matondkar), who lives with her parents across the hall. Vitthal (Sanjay Mishra), the gunman who killed the producer and then got trapped under his own scooter while trying to get away, is presented in court. He's pressed to implicate Bheeku as the instigator of the hit, but he won't talk.

MAMA, KALLU MAMA

As Mule and Vitthal frustrate the prosecution, we hear the opening bars of something like a tango. The scene shifts from the courtroom to an underlit den. Whatever light there is comes from a small window and a couple of hanging bulbs. You can almost smell the sweat and the cigarette smoke. And then, this:

Goli maar bheje mein
Ke bheja shor karta hai
Bheje ki sunega to marega, Kallu
Arre tu karega doosra bharega, Kallu

(Put a bullet in the head
Because the voices inside it won't stop
You listen to your head, you die, Kallu
You slip up, someone else will pay, Kallu)

In India, songs have always arrived in advance of the film. Often, they're what draw audiences to theatres. For half a century, until television took its place, radio was almost as crucial a delivery device for Bollywood as cinema. In the '90s, song promos could get a month or two of airtime before films opened. Every entertainment channel – not just the music-focused ones – had a countdown show; I remember recapping *Superhit Muqabla* and *Philips Top 10* like they were cricket matches on the bus ride to school. MTV and Channel V had newly arrived, so the star choreographers – Saroj Khan, Farah Khan, Shiamak Davar, Ahmed Khan – took that aesthetic and mixed it with the Bollywood style. The mid-to-late '90s was a truly creative time for the musical sequence in Hindi film. You had the MTV-ish flash zooms and pop art colours of 'Sundra Sundra' and the mad exuberance of 'Chaiyya Chaiyya', but also the Dev Anand charm of 'Rooth Na Jaana' and the moments in *Yes Boss* (1997) where Shah Rukh Khan, under the instruction of Farah Khan, achieves a Gene Kelly-like fluency.

It's difficult to explain just how disruptive 'Goli Maar' looked and sounded when it first landed on our television screens. Who were these unkempt men? Why weren't they moving in step? What self-respecting lyricist begins a song with '*Goli maar bheje mein*'? (Imagine our shock when we found out it was Gulzar, responsible for some of the most finely wrought songwriting in Hindi film.) What kind of refrain is '*Mama, Kallu Mama*' (Uncle, Kallu Uncle)? Did they forget to turn on the lights on set?

It was weird, it was catchy. And so a film that started off song-less ended up owing its initial popularity to something that sounded like a Bollywood version of a Tom Waits number.

Even today, its directness is startling. Singer Mano's voice is harsh. The chorus is loud, lusty. The language, even untranslated, is abrasive to the ear – '*kharochna*', '*dabochna*', '*khopdi ki jhopdi*'. The actors look drunk; Bajpayee says they really were. Certainly they look like they're having the greatest on-set party a mid-budget film could afford.

If Bajpayee and Masani have their timelines right, there was actual cause for celebration: it was the last day of the shoot.* The gang assembled at the bungalow that stood in for Kallu Mama's den. 'You all do something,' Varma told them as he headed out for some work. 'I'll come back and see.' And so the actors and Mazhar Kamran and the assistants did something. Choreographer Ahmed Khan wasn't around, so they worked out their own steps. Assistant director A.K. Feroz suggested Masani enter with a police siren. Kamran lit the room with a few hundred-watt bulbs and nothing else. Varma returned a couple of hours later, reviewed the footage, shot some more.

---

* Kashyap writes in a blog post that when this sequence was shot, the song hadn't yet been written, and the popular Madhuri Dixit dance number 'Mera Piya Ghar Aaya' was the temp music used. This seems patently incorrect, as you can see the actors lip-sync and perform actions that match the lyrics. Vishal Bhardwaj also confirmed to me that the song was composed before the scene was shot.

The song was a huge hit, selling the rough aesthetic of the film
to the public better than any trailer could. Maybe the imperfection
made it seem more real. As low-down musical numbers went, it
was less Amitabh Bachchan proclaiming 'Main Hoon Don', more
a combination of Pran dancing awkwardly to 'Daru Ki Botal Mein'
in *Majboor* (1974) and the angry young men led by Sunny Deol in
Arjun (1985) running in the streets singing 'Goli Maaro'. It made
Saurabh Shukla a fan favourite – to this day, strangers call out 'Mama'
or 'Mamu' to him on the street.

It was a team effort – Bhardwaj's music, Mano's wild vocal, the
abandon of the actors and Kamran's use of an enclosed space and
minimal light. But the greatest credit belongs to Gulzar. Not only
did he put his reputation as a serious poet on the line with this
song, he also saved Varma and Co. from trying to inject a bit of
class where none was needed. Nearly everyone – Varma, Kashyap,
Shukla – thought '*Goli maar bheje mein, ke bheja shor karta hai*' was
ridiculous, and wanted to use Urdu-inflected temp lyrics written by
Bhardwaj. No one, however, could summon up the courage to tell
Gulzar – after all, he had some 30 years of cinema experience on them.
Finally, it was decided that Kashyap, as the youngest in the brain trust
and therefore the one with least to lose, would speak to him. At a
'sitting' with the master, silently egged on by Varma and Bhardwaj,
he hesitantly broached the topic. Gulzar shooed him away, telling
him to first learn how to pronounce the Urdu word *gham* (which
figured in Bhardwaj's version) before talking to him about lyrics.

Years later, Gulzar told author and filmmaker Nasreen Munni
Kabir why he'd chosen such a direct idiom. 'I wrote a song ... for
a character who is a violent man, a man who listens to no one and
shoots people who contradict him or come in his way. He decides
to sing a song when he is drunk. The gangster cannot sing a Ghalib
ghazal like "Dil-e-Naadaan, Tujhe Hua Kya Hai?" (O Innocent Heart,

What Has Come Over You?). How can he express sentiments like that? So what will he sing? "*Goli maar bheje mein, bheja shor karta hai.*"

Bheeku gives Satya a gun, drops him at the bar where Jagga is. Satya goes inside and shoots Jagga in the head – his first kill.

THE GANGSTER'S WIFE

By his own admission, Shukla was a reluctant writer coming into *Satya*. He didn't really consider himself a writer at all – *Satya* was his first non-acting screen credit outside of TV. Still, he had a rare knack of inventing scenes on the spot. When they first met, Varma narrated the scene where Satya carries out his first hit and is brought home by a proud Bheeku. 'We can twist this,' Shukla suggested. He started improvising the sequence of events that follows the murder.

Bheeku reaches home in an expansive mood, chattering to Satya as his wife, Pyaari (Shefali Shah), opens the door. We know that she isn't cowed by her husband's outsized personality; earlier in the film, when she brings their two kids to meet him in prison, she gives him a talking-to. Now, with no children present, and with him drunk and unrepentant for not coming straight home from the lockup, she parks herself at the door and starts yelling. '*Iske bheje ka top gaya*' (She's blown her lid), Bheeku jokes to Satya. 'I just got out of prison,' he complains. 'You're not doing me a favour,' she yells back.

Bheeku continues to talk over her scolding, then suddenly slaps her. Pyaari is shocked into silence. Once Satya is sent off and the door closes, Bheeku's barely opened his mouth to try and make things right when Pyaari slaps him back. Short of breath, they glare at each other for a few seconds, then start laughing.

Satya looking on with a mulish expression as Bheeku and Pyaari go at one another is a confounding element in an otherwise electric scene. Varma takes responsibility for this, admitting that he never had a fixed idea of what Satya was like as a character, which resulted in conflicting signals for Chakravarthy. Years later, in Reema Kagti's *Talaash* (2012), Aamir Khan and Rani Mukerji, playing husband and wife, have an exchange that's almost as heated as the Mhatres'. That scene, though, is stolen by the onlooker, Rajkummar Rao, playing Khan's subordinate, whose exquisite embarrassment is as deft as Chakravarthy's is stolid.

This, incidentally, was the first scene Shah shot for the film. She remembers getting her lines and asking if she could add a couple of Marathi words. Varma told her to do whatever she felt like. Bajpayee says they improvised, which is entirely believable. There was a discussion about a possible love scene with Bheeku and Pyaari to follow their making up. It never happened, and, as Shah points out, it wasn't needed. 'When you see these two people, you can make out the sexual energy, the tension that is there,' she said. 'It comes out in a different form, but you know they are just waiting to tear each other apart.'

It's a rare acting showcase in a non-indulgent film – just a static camera and two performers going at each other. It's over in three whirlwind minutes, but there's a wealth of detail – Bheeku's sheepish drunk grin when he walks in; the subtle hardening of his tone until he snaps; the slaps foreshadowed by Pyaari grabbing Bheeku's face in anger, and him trying to grasp hers playfully. You could take this scene out and *Satya* would remain, for all practical purposes, the same. I'm thankful it exists. *Satya* broke with Hindi film tradition by making its gangsters seem entirely human. And Bheeku is at his most human when he's with Pyaari.

Vidya brings over some prasad for Satya. Later, he's teased by Bheeku and Chander, who see him walk out of the building with her. Collecting their dues from builder Malhotra at an under-construction building, the gang is ambushed by rival shooters. Bheeku and most of his men survive, and capture one of the attackers.

TORTURE

We see a pair of legs, feet bare, dangling just off the ground. The camera pans up slowly to reveal the man Satya had restrained Bheeku from killing during the shootout. Given the bloodied condition we now find him in, he might have preferred going out in a hail of bullets. 'Pain can only be withstood to an extent,' Satya says to him. 'Tell us who sent you.' Yeda brandishes a heated spike.* Bheeku viciously shoves his fingers up the man's nose, then grabs the spike and holds it inches away from his eyeball. The mask has fallen. Gone is the jocular *mawaali*. In his place is a gangster scary enough to command respect in prison and rule a small fiefdom outside. 'Manoj was like a possessed guy,' Varma said of that scene. Spare a thought for the junior artist playing the torture victim, staring terrified at the spike and the lunatic holding it.

I asked Bajpayee if he thought Bheeku would have gone ahead and pierced the eye. Absolutely, he replied.

Whether Bheeku would go that far and still retain a measure of audience sympathy we'll never know, for the terrified prisoner chooses this moment to give up the name of Guru Narayan, a rival gang boss and Bheeku's once-friend. Just then, Chander notices

---

* If you look closely, the spike emits wisps of smoke. Barnali Ray Shukla and the other assistants were told that Ramu wanted the *sariya* orange-hot. They heated rods of different thickness, but couldn't get the desired molten look. After a while, art director Krishna intervened, saying 'I'll show you truth for camera.' The effect was achieved with a painted room-temperature rod and a concealed *agarbatti*.

Vidya on the street outside. Satya slips out to meet her, accompanied by ribbing from the gang. The teasing continues when he returns, until Bheeku puts a stop to it (the expression on his face when Satya leaves the room to meet Vidya is curiously stricken). A decision is taken to kill Guru. Kallu abruptly shoots the prisoner, making everyone jump and prompting Bheeku to yell at his lieutenant to give him some warning next time – an inspired ad lib from Bajpayee.

Part of the reason this scene works so well is the change of tone when Vidya turns up outside. The mood before that is grisly; Bheeku in particular looks transported with rage. Chowta contributes one of his subtler themes, a low drone, like classical musicians warming up – and for once, the volume is kept low. But then Satya leaves the room, promoting one of the funniest exchanges in the film. Chander refers to Vidya as Satya's *chhaavi* (crush, or someone looking fine) and a 'piece', says he saw them cooing to each other outside their building. Bappu marvels at how Satya's barely been in the city four days but has still managed to *patao* (woo) a girl. '*Yeda ban ke peda khaya hai, tu bhi kha le*', is Kallu Mama's hilarious – and untranslatable – response.

This shift from serious criminal business to comedy and back bears the imprint of a director who came to define American cinema in the '90s. In *Reservoir Dogs* (1992) and *Pulp Fiction* (1994), Quentin Tarantino offered a new way of stretching out a tense scene: not through film craft, as Hitchcock and Leone did, but with funny, profane chatter. There's an echo here of the infamous *Reservoir Dogs* torture scene, with Michael Madsen dancing to 'Stuck in the Middle With You' before cutting off a cop's ear – savage violence mixed up with comedy, and brought to an end by a sudden shooting (of the torturer in *Reservoir Dogs*, and the tortured in *Satya*).

Varma, always happy to debunk a theory, told me he hadn't watched *Reservoir Dogs*. He did admit that the image of Bheeku with the spike came from *Raiders of the Lost Ark* (1981). Sure enough, there's a scene in Steven Spielberg's first Indiana Jones movie in which a glowing-hot rod is held threateningly near Karen Allen's eyes.

The violence, both implied and apparent, is made more vivid by the mundanity that surrounds it. Kallu Mama spends most of the scene eating lunch; he has to put his plate down to pick up his revolver and shoot the man. 'The juxtaposition is something I liked,' Varma said. 'Someone's being tortured, but they're also looking at a girl like any other guy would look. That those guys can torture and kill someone in cold blood – suddenly, that becomes real.' The audience is also being made complicit, whether or not they're aware of it. By keeping the hanging man in the foreground for most of the scene, even when the gang is joking around with Satya, the film forces us to examine what it means to laugh with and care about these men who can so casually commit acts of violence.

Vidya meets composer Runu Sagar (Neeraj Vora), who, instead of auditioning her, indicates that she'll have to sleep with him to get the job. Back home, Vidya unburdens herself to Satya. With some help from the gang, Satya scares Runu into hiring Vidya. Guru Narayan returns to Mumbai. Bheeku is all set to ambush him on the highway when a last-minute call from politician Bhau Thakurdas Jhavle (Govind Namdev), mentor to both gang leaders, scuttles the plan. Bhau brokers a truce. Later, Satya convinces Bheeku it's in his interest to take out Guru anyway.

THE KILLING OF GURU NARAYAN

The extended sequence that culminates in the killing of Guru Narayan is one of the most effective conflations of city film and gangster film in Hindi cinema. On the far side of a drab residential complex, a red van pulls up. Our view is obscured by a woman sweeping and children on swings and slides. There's a quick downwards crane shot as Guru and his men emerge from an elevator and walk towards their car. We see Satya, gun at ready, in the red van. An infant waddles in the foreground. Suddenly, Bheeku and Yeda jump out of another van and start shooting. Guru's men return fire. The child ends up near Yeda, who grabs him with his right hand and keeps shooting with his left. Guru bolts, nearly barrelling into a young couple around a corner (didn't they hear the shots?), then across the play area, scattering kids.

A high-angle shot shows Guru running out of the building compound and into the streets, followed at some distance by Satya and Bheeku. There are several bystanders, yet both parties continue to shoot as they run through the lanes. Guru bounds up the stairs of a railway station overbridge, but his pursuers have almost caught up. Satya shoots him in the leg, and Guru goes down on the walkway. He begs for mercy, reminding Bheeku of their past friendship, which drives the already fuming gangster over the edge. '*Meri biwi isko rakhi baandhti thi, mere bachhe isko mama bolte the*' (My wife used to consider him a brother, my kids used to call him uncle), he yells, half-crazed with anger. Guru, seeing Bheeku distracted, lunges for his gun. He grabs it, but Satya notices just in time. He and Bheeku unload eight bullets into Guru as the camera gazes up at them in a disturbingly exhilarating moment.

Even after shooting him, Bheeku is so angry that he can't seem to leave Guru. He crouches over the body, babbling angrily – an image which recalls Joe Pesci's psychotic Tommy abusing the dead Billy Batts in *Goodfellas* (1990). As Satya tries to pull Bheeku away, a local train rattles past beneath them. Mazhar Kamran, who shot the scene, said they timed it so Bheeku's tirade coincided with the train passing. The implication is clear: shootouts notwithstanding, normal life will go on. Put another way, it's a gangster film in the foreground, a city film unfolding in the back.

The housing complex shoot was done with a small unit of five or six people. Varma had heard that during the bloody gun battle between gangster Maya Dolas and the police in Lokhandwala in 1991 (an incident which inspired the 2007 film *Shootout at Lokhandwala*), there were children playing in the vicinity, so he added some to his own scene. The chase and Guru's killing were shot with a similarly lean crew on a pedestrian bridge at either Mahim or Matunga station (as usual, accounts vary). 'The actors used to get out from the car and run, and the cameraman used to run behind them,' Varma said in an interview. 'It was shot in a very guerrilla style, and I think it is that sense of urgency that added a lot to the realism.' He didn't storyboard the scene, trusting himself and stunt director Allan Amin to figure out the action once they reached the location.

The scene was partially scripted – Raju Mavani wasn't a regular actor then, so Guru's lines were on page. Bajpayee was given a few broad points to cover and set loose. Varma and the crew watched in amazement as he ranted away about *rakhi*s and taking a bullet for Guru. It's some of the most feral acting he does in the film – and the ice-cold alertness of Satya is some of Chakravarthy's best work as well. Still, Varma wasn't sure how the scene would play. He liked Kashyap's idea of having Bheeku and Guru's entire history spew out in a few tense seconds. At the same time, he said, 'It's a slightly illogical thing. He's come to kill Guru Narayan, there's no reason for him to talk so much. I was very unsure if it might look ridiculous. But I just loved the intensity with which Manoj performed.'

'The energy during the scene was electric,' Kamran recalled. Bajpayee went further. 'It was an atmosphere I have never experienced after that. It felt like every one of us was gelling. As if we were all born in one room. Born to make this film.'

After this very public shootout, the existing police commissioner is
replaced by Amod Shukla (Paresh Rawal). Satya and Vidya grow closer,
but he still doesn't tell her who he really is. The rift between Bhau and
Bheeku deepens, but an appearance in person by the politician helps
patch things up. Shukla takes aggressive measures to control crime.
Many gangsters are killed, including Chander. Satya convinces Bheeku
to eliminate the commissioner, a decision Kallu Mama strongly protests.
Shukla is shot outside his home. Bhau wins the election.

STAMPEDE AT THE CINEMA

On 13 June 1997, almost exactly two months before *Satya* started
filming, a packed house was watching J.P. Dutta's war film *Border* at
Uphaar Cinema in Delhi. Around 5 p.m., smoke started to fill the
hall. The transformer, which had been repaired earlier that day, had
caught fire. As the film continued to play, panicked patrons stumbled
to the exits, which in those days weren't indicated by neon signs, but
found most of them bolted shut. Some suffocated, others died in
the crush of bodies or attempting to jump from the balcony. In all,
59 died that day.

Did Uphaar flash through viewers' minds as they watched the
theatre stampede in *Satya*? This is the point at which the film turns,
when the inevitable tragic undertow of the gangster genre starts
pulling at the narrative. Satya, relaxed after the twin successes of
Bhau's election win and Amod Shukla's murder, takes Vidya to see
a film: *Border*. During the intermission, while buying a cold drink,
he's recognised by Pakiya (Sushant Singh), the goon whose face he'd
slashed soon after arriving in Mumbai. He heads back to his movie,
and Pakiya calls the cops (there's a nice unbroken shot that follows
Singh as he pushes aside people in his hurry to get to an auto; the
camera travels with him even after the vehicle pulls away – one of

those nifty Varma touches). Khandilkar, perhaps rattled by the death of his mentor, shuts down the movie and tells everyone to leave from a single exit so the criminal among them can be identified.*

As Satya nears the door and certain detection, he fires his revolver into the ground. The audience panics and rushes en masse for the door. Satya and Vidya are swept along with the crowd, and manage to get out safely. This sequence is Varma at his most Eisensteinian – brutal fragmented images of people pushing each other, falling, getting trampled, blood stains on the floor and a stampede visual specific to India: abandoned chappals.

Varma said he didn't intend to reference Uphaar; they used the clip from *Border* because it was easily available (*Satya*'s financier, Bharat Shah, had also bankrolled Dutta's film). While the scene might have triggered memories of Uphaar, it also continues an existing motif in Varma's cinema – the tendency to use movie theatres as sites of disruption …

Siva. Asha, bored by the movie they're watching, won't stop talking. 'Don't be stupid', Siva whispers, 'stop it.' 'You stop it!' she snaps back loudly. The film freezes. Asha gets up, walks to the stage, strides across disdainfully, disappears behind the screen. Suddenly, she's *on* screen, transmuted into the cinema like Buster Keaton in *Sherlock Jr* (1924). The actors from the movie scene unfreeze and line up behind her. They break into a dance number, and are joined by Siva.

---

* Varma sees it as his own failure that Khandilkar's strategy wasn't smarter. No one else seemed to think so, or thought to mention it until the edit was almost done, at which point composer Chowta casually remarked that it was stupid of the police to announce their presence. 'Strangely, in the last 20 years, except for Sandeep Chowta, no one asked me that question,' Varma said. 'I always thought it was a major flaw.'

Raat. Mini is at the movies with her friends. It's a comedy, the audience is roaring with laughter. The camera zooms in on Mini's face as she closes her eyes for a second. When she opens them, she's alone in the hall. The screen goes blank. Though no one's there, Mini feels a malevolent presence. She runs out, frantically searches the building, but can't find another living soul. Finally, she sees someone on a swivel chair in an empty room. She turns it around. It's her – or someone who looks exactly like her. And like that, she's back in the hall, familiar surroundings restored.

Gaayam. A man stands in the wings in a crowded cinema hall, rifle raised. He misses the head he's aiming for, the bullet hitting the patron in front. Several people start shooting and the audience scatters.

Rangeela. Munna turns a visit to the cinema into street theatre, as he does any social occasion. After yelling at some unseen usher to switch on the fan, he hoists his leg onto the seat in front. Its occupant protests, prompting Munna to ask, '*Tu pair dekh raha hai,* picture *dekh raha hai?*' (Are you watching my foot or the movie?). Years later, in *Gangs of Wasseypur*, Ramadhir Singh summed up Munna and a million others like him across India: '*Sab ke dimaag mein apni apni* picture *chal rahi hai*' (Everyone has their own movie playing in their head).

I asked Varma why he keeps coming up with scenes that upend the theatre-viewing experience. 'It's kind of an obsession with me,' he replied. 'Obviously, I'm in love with cinema theatres, because that's where I watch films. To play around and make that a dream instead of a reality is, I think, an interesting concept.' He said the idea of using cinema halls as sites of unsettlement might have been seeded by the memory of horror films with theatres in them, like Wes Craven's *A Nightmare on Elm Street* (1984) and *Terror in the Aisles* (1984), a documentary that alternates scenes from scary movies with people getting spooked while watching them in a theatre.*

Khandilkar is pulled up for causing a stampede in which 21 people die. Like all the other scenes involving the police, it's awkward, and there to make a limited point: Khandilkar chose a risky method to flush out a criminal when he had other options.

MUMBAI KA KING KAUN?

He stands on a rocky outcrop overlooking the sea, framed against a blue sky, and asks one of the greatest rhetorical questions in Hindi cinema: 'Mumbai *ka* king *kaun*?' – Who's the king of Mumbai? If the gangster appears hubristic shouting his own praises at the ocean, he has good reason to be. His main rival is no more. He's back in Bhau's good books, and stands to benefit from his political ascension. Shukla is dead, Khandilkar is under a cloud. 'Is there anyone to challenge Bheeku in Mumbai?' he crows.

This is the moment most people remember *Satya* by – Bajpayee's ecstatic delivery of the famous line, the dramatic placement of his figure against the Mumbai skyline. The scene, shot at Bandstand in Bandra, then segues (a trifle awkwardly) into Satya's doubts about his future as a gangster and his desire to make a life with Vidya. Bheeku, realising the most stable relationship in his life is in danger of dissolving, tries to talk him out of it. But Satya is adamant – he'll

---

*   Corey Creekmur brings up a different sort of horror – academics' saying 'Brechtian' – in his wonderful observation about the stampede scene: 'In the sort of self-reflexive moment common to popular Hindi films but often only associated with "Brechtian" art cinema, the audience watching the Hindi film *Satya* in a cinema watches Satya in a cinema watching a Hindi film.'

tell Vidya the truth about himself and accept the consequences. Seeing how determined he is, Bheeku offers a better solution – don't tell her the truth, instead say you have a job in Dubai; he'll arrange everything.

This is Chakravarthy's big emotional scene, but it isn't the best we've seen from the actor. I've always found it tough to square the cold-blooded quick thinker from the stampede with the quavering worrier here. But Bajpayee's performance could hardly be improved upon – from the glee of his rant to his brief anger at Satya severing himself, followed by resignation and grace and, to save both of them the embarrassment of actual emotion, a bit of clowning (his admission that he's jealous of Vidya, though delivered laughingly, is in line with the gangster genre's penchant for intense homosocial bonds). Chakravarthy adds a nice touch by extending his arm around Bajpayee and clapping him once on the back – a concise, heartfelt gesture.

It's hard not to wish that the bit with Bheeku on the cliff had gone on longer. Bajpayee's performance had the sort of impact on a generation of Indian actors that Marlon Brando's turn in *On the Waterfront* did on American film. Had Bajpayee been allowed to yell some more, maybe Nawazuddin Siddiqui or Rajkummar Rao would have had a home-grown 'I coulda been a contender' to practice in front of the mirror. But the cliff scene is all of 30 seconds.* You could put this down to Varma's storytelling concision, but the real reason is Bajpayee probably wouldn't have lasted longer. 'I have a problem with heights,' he told me. 'I have major vertigo. And they wanted me to stand right on the edge.' During one of the takes, he says, the bulky

---

* The rocks at Bandstand were a popular setting for Hindi films of the '90s. Varma had himself used it earlier; in *Rangeela*, during the 'Pyar Yeh Jaane Kaisa Hai' number, Aamir Khan is briefly seen in front of the same rockface as Bheeku.

Shukla lay down on his feet so he'd feel enough at ease to wave his arms around. 'Ramu was instructing, Anurag was telling me things. When I say, "Mumbai *ka* king *kaun*", they wanted me in a long shot, so there I could not cheat. I didn't say the line, I yelled something like, "Mumbai *ka* … *kya kar rahe ho yaar*?" (What the hell are you doing?). The rest was dubbed in the studio.'

Kamran tried out several camera positions before he and Varma settled on one. Bajpayee was visibly nervous that day, he recalled. What stuck with him was the actor's willingness to power through the fear and perform in character. 'He was walking on the edge, and he's so scared of looking down, but then he just comes and stands and he's ready.'

The more you watch this scene, the more it gives back. One thing I hadn't reckoned with in my initial viewings, but which struck me as significant later on, is its placement in the larger narrative. We've just seen the stampede caused by Satya. It's quite a shock to go from ordinary citizens being trampled and the gloom of the police station in the next scene to the bright outdoors and Bheeku's manic laughter. His glee is infectious, but it's also cruel, especially when he tells Satya '*Sahi bawaal machaya tu* theatre *mein*' (You created a nice ruckus in the theatre). Though Bheeku is again humanised through his concern for his friend, it's possible to see this burst of callousness as Varma's way of lessening the viewer's affection for him just a bit, in time for his sudden death in the next scene. Don't get too attached to these guys, the film seems to be warning us, because they don't care about you.

From placement in the story to placement within the frame. In a paper on *Satya*, academic and film writer Mihir Pandya points out that Bheeku is not only looking at the Mumbai skyline but is positioned above it. The city is, quite literally, at his feet. No wonder he's feeling boastful. There's some irony in the idea that viewers in

1998 were seeing Mumbai, under the then-anti-immigrant Shiv Sena, at the feet of a Bihari actor. By the end of the scene, he's on level ground, Satya's decision to leave having brought him back to earth. Genre rules will soon impose themselves. 'The typical gangster film presents a steady upward progress followed by a very precipitate fall,' Warshow wrote in 'The Gangster as Tragic Hero'. We know Bheeku is marked for failure because, for that one moment on the rocks, he thinks he's invincible.

Bhau calls Bheeku and Kallu Mama over to celebrate his election victory. It turns out to be an ambush, as Bhau shoots the unsuspecting Bheeku in the back of the head. It turns out Mule, who's also present, knew of the plan. The police nearly nab Satya at his building, but he slips out. Vidya is interrogated by Khandilkar. Kallu Mama tells Satya about their boss's murder and that he's made arrangements for him in Dubai. Satya, though, won't leave without avenging Bheeku.

DEATH ON THE BEACH

Unlike Gerard Hooper's other documentary excursions, which were used in montages or as city-establishing shots, the Ganesh Chaturthi scenes were done with a specific purpose in mind. Varma wanted the fervour of the annual Girgaum Chowpatty *visarjan* – the city's biggest gathering of devotees immersing Ganesh idols – in his film. But getting permission to shoot on Chowpatty beach would have been impossible. So they devised another plan – shoot from the roof of a sea-facing building across the street using long lenses. As he did many times during the production, Sabir Masani bluffed his way into getting permission. 'We're from BBC Channel 4,' he told the owner, gesturing to the only Caucasian in the team, Hooper. 'We're making a documentary on Ganapati.'

The *visarjan* scenes were shot in early September, less than a month after production began. Three cameras were used – Hooper across the road, shooting the sweep of the festivities, and Kamran and an assistant on the ground. Varma and the writers hadn't figured at this stage that Satya would kill Bhau during the commotion on the beach. When it did arrive, though, the idea was a keeper. The symbolism was perfect – a knife through the heart of Mumbai. The *visarjan* was later recreated on a different beach across town in Juhu, with the actors and extras and a replica of the giant Ganesh statue. These scenes were matched with the ones shot months earlier.

In the film, we see thousands of devotees bidding a boisterous farewell to the elephant god, Ganesh. Bhau leads one group in prayer, with his bodyguard (Telugu actor Banerjee) nearby. Intercut with this are shots of Satya, his hand wrapped in a red cloth, making his way through the crowd to Bhau (both Varma and action director Allan Amin said it was their idea to have the camera follow a cloth-covered hand). The politician looks up and sees the man he'd hoped to kill along with Bheeku. There's a pause – a fraction of a second – and then Satya plunges the knife he's been concealing into Bhau's stomach, holding him in a deadly embrace (Chowta uses a version of the musical sting from *Psycho* here). Bhau splutters, but can't get the attention of his bodyguard. Finally, the man notices, tries to pull Satya off, shoots him – somehow, not fatally. Kallu Mama turns up out of nowhere with a gun, killing the bodyguard. The crowd scatters. Kallu drags a badly injured Satya to his car and they drive off. The last shot is a brilliant top angle, as if from the point of view of the statue. We see the tide lapping at, then turning over, the body of Bhau.

Initially, the sequence was more elaborate, with plans drawn up for Kallu Mama to enter with Holi colours on his face, and the camera panning to someone stationed in a building across the road.

Two days before the shoot, Varma changed his mind. 'I said, cut all that. At this point of time, I want to see him be killed. I don't want to go through the process of how he was killed. That becomes very technical and mechanical; I'd rather have an emotional aspect to it.' Like most of his gut decisions on the film, Varma was right. Logically, it would have been difficult for Satya to just walk up to Bhau and knife him. Yet, the way it's shot and edited and acted by Namdev and Chakravarthy (always more compelling when he doesn't have lines), it feels inevitable.

The intercutting of religious ritual and murder is a Coppola trick – you see it in the killings at the end of *The Godfather* (1972) and *Apocalypse Now* (1979). Writing about Bhau's death, academic Ravi Vasudevan points to another famous Coppola sequence – the assassination of Don Fanucci in *The Godfather: Part II* (1974). 'The red sheath bobs along in the crowd, reminding us of a similar scene … in which Vito Corleone moves through a street overwhelmed by festivities celebrating a Roman Catholic holy day to target the local gang leader.' There's a key difference, though. Vito killing the powerful Fanucci is a cold-blooded decision, entirely in keeping with his personality. Satya has the same practical approach to the crime business … until Bheeku's death. Everything he does after – attacking Bhau in full public view, visiting Vidya when he knows the cops are looking for him – is out of sync with the calculating personality we've spent two and a half hours with. Maybe the death of his only friend knocks something loose in him, just as Amod Shukla's death causes Khandilkar to unravel.

Though *The Godfather* was never far from Varma's mind in those days, the scene might be inspired by something closer home. At the end of *Agneepath* (1990), Mukul Anand's reworking of *Scarface* (1983), mafia don Vijay (Amitabh Bachchan) is ambushed by sword-wielding attackers. Both scenes take place on a beach during frenzied Ganesh Chaturthi celebrations. Anand blends documentary footage of a real immersion with scenes featuring his actors, just as *Satya* did eight years later. It's quite possible that Varma, one film old at the time of *Agneepath*'s release and a massive Bachchan fan, was taking notes.

In the car, Kallu Mama tells a barely conscious Satya that he's arranged for him to leave on a ship to Dubai. Satya insists on seeing Vidya one last time. He pulls a gun on Kallu, who reluctantly takes him to his building. Satya staggers up the stairs as the police arrive outside.

TEARS

The gangster must die. It was true in 1948, when Warshow wrote: 'There is really only one possibility – failure. The final meaning of the city is anonymity and death.' And it was true 50 years later, when Satya collapses at Vidya's feet. Back when Warshow was writing, there was pressure on Hollywood to pretend to not enjoy these Mafioso types so much. Tony and Rico could have all the fun they wanted as long as they paid with their lives in the last reel. The restrictions eventually lifted, but the tradition remained. It's still rare to have a gangster film where most of the major players survive.

Varma, always given to practical motives over polemical ones, said he killed Satya because he wanted to include a scene from a James Hadley Chase novel. It was an ending he'd already tried out in *Antham* (1992), where Nagarjuna's gangster dies after seeing his girlfriend – Urmila Matondkar! – one last time. Satya dying at Vidya's feet was the one thing that was in place from the start. It was decided before Satya was even a character, before there was a film.

Satya staggers up the stairs, badly wounded. As he gets closer to Vidya's room, images from his past flash onscreen: bright sunlight,

Vidya beckoning to him – Asrani's suggestion.* 'I just felt the film was going so dark', Varma said, 'that he should have a memory of those happier times.' Meanwhile, Kallu Mama dies an unceremonious death in his car, drawing his gun in desperation and getting shot by the cops. Khandilkar makes his way up the staircase. Satya yells at Vidya to open the door, but she won't. He throws his body against it. After several tries, it gives way. Vidya recoils, hunched in the far corner of the bed. Satya stares at her, swaying at the threshold. From down the hall, Khandilkar takes his shot. Three bullets hit Satya. He falls forward. As Vidya looks down, Satya's eyebrow moves, and then he's still.

Even for a gangster film, this is a bleak ending. Vidya has only just found out who Satya really is; there's no love for him in her eyes, only fear. Satya has gone from dreaming of a new life to seeing everything turn to dust in the span of a day. The last thing he sees is horror and confusion on the face of the woman he loves. Bheeku, Kallu Mama, Chander, Mule are all dead. Khandilkar will probably be transferred, and he'll have to live with the guilt of the stampede. Chowta's mournful flute theme reinforces the utter lack of comfort *Satya* leaves us with. No one gets what they want.

A quick montage follows – a crowd watching Satya's body being taken away; headlines announcing the end of Bhau and Bheeku, and calling Khandilkar the 'encounter king'; Yeda throwing the paper aside and shooting it, one of the images we started the film with. Finally, a note signed by the director:

---

* Asrani did something similar in Hansal Mehta's *Shahid*, a film he edited and co-wrote. Towards the end of the film, Shahid, who we know will die, seems to recall happy moments spent with his wife.

This film is an attempt on my part to reach out to all those people who took to violence as a means for their living. At the end, if even one of them out there looks into himself before he takes out his gun the next time, and understands that the pain he inflicts on others is exactly the same as he would suffer himself, I would consider this effort worthwhile.

My tears for Satya are as much as they are for the people whom he killed.

Satya mostly steers clear of that very Hindi film impulse to bring about the moral betterment of its audience. Yet, this is the sort of message you'd expect from a well-meaning National Film Development Corporation (NFDC) production, not from a hard-hitting gangster film. The last line, though, is revealing. Throughout his career, Varma has been fascinated by violent rebels: gangsters, street thugs, rogue cops, militants. He might sympathise with ordinary, lawful citizens, but he isn't interested in them. Specifying an equal volume of tears for outlaw and victim strikes me as an oddly defensive gesture, as if he felt he had to justify his strong feelings for Satya.

3

The Hindi Film Gangster

'Bhai banna tereko? Bhai banna tereko?'

– Bheeku breaking up a fight between Satya and another inmate

Great Bombay's population, 1.8 million in 1941, jumped to almost 3 million in 1951, aided by an influx of migrants before and after Partition. Unemployment and easy access to ports at a time of wartime controls led to an increase in crime. Initially, it was petty thievery and pickpocketing, mugging and the odd heist. This is reflected in crime films of the 1940s and '50s such as *Kismet* (1943, Ashok Kumar as a pickpocket), *House No. 44* and *Pocket Maar* (1955 and '56, Dev Anand as a pickpocket), *Sangram* (1950, Kumar as a casino owner), *Awara* (1951, Raj Kapoor as a small-time thief), *Shree 420* and *Baazi* (1955 and '51, Kapoor and Anand as cardsharps). The first street gangs were formed, some of them taking the names of their members' towns of origin: Allahabadi Gang, Kanpuri Gang, Rampuri Gang.

Prohibition was introduced in Bombay Province by the Congress government in 1939. This was soon reversed by the British, but after Independence the state dried up again with the implementation of the Bombay Prohibition Act of 1949, which outlawed the buying, serving and consumption of alcohol without a permit. 'Aunty bars' – speakeasies run by women – supplied the populace with illicit liquor, a tradition alluded to by Vikram Chandra in his novel *Sacred Games* through the figure of Kanta Bai, who runs a rough dive, makes *desi* moonshine and partners with up-and-coming gangster Ganesh Gaitonde. As in the US during Prohibition, gangs in Bombay started distributing liquor.

Legends began to take shape. Karim Lala, a nearly seven-foot-tall Pathan, opened 'social clubs' – gambling dens – and became a supplier of both money and muscle. Varadarajan Mudaliar, from the southern state of Tamil Nadu, maneuvered his way into the alcohol business. Haji Mastan started out as a dockyard worker and became the biggest smuggler in the city. Each of these gangsters was played, under a different name, in a hit film by a famous actor – Lala by Pran in *Zanjeer* (1973), Mastan by Amitabh Bachchan in *Deewar* and Mudaliar by Kamal Haasan in *Nayakan*.

In 1974, a young hood from Dongri named Dawood Ibrahim led a daring robbery of a taxi he was told was carrying Mastan's black money. The 4.75 lakh rupee heist – money belonging, it turned out, to Metropolitan Cooperative Bank, not Mastan – was one of the biggest of the decade, and put Dawood on the road to establishing a criminal empire. Rivals kept him on his toes – the Pathans; Manya Surve (played by John Abraham in *Shootout at Wadala*, 2013); Arun Gawli, now a politician (played by Arjun Rampal in 2017's *Daddy*, and by *Satya* alum Makarand Deshpande in the 2015 Marathi film *Dagdi*

Chawl). Eventually, Dawood was forced to leave India, operating by remote control from Dubai and Pakistan. His close friendship with his lieutenant Chhota Rajan and their violent severing was loosely adapted by Ram Gopal Varma as *Company*. Dawood has been portrayed, as himself or a recognisable version, by actors in at least 10 films, from a glowering, fit Randeep Hooda in *D* (2005) to a rotund Rishi Kapoor in *D-Day* (2013).

Hindi cinema's interest in the lives of gangsters was returned by the dons themselves. Mastan fell for Veena Sharma, a starlet who resembled '50s screen icon Madhubala. He financed films and began to be seen in public with politicians and stars. He was never a major player in the movies, but a precedent was set. By the '80s, underworld money was circulating in Bollywood. 'When Dawood Ibrahim entered the scene in the mid '80s, it was no longer only for glamour,' Smruti Koppikar wrote in *India Today*. 'Financing films became less romance, more serious business. Unheard of people became producers overnight: Hanif Kadawala and Samir Hingora, mere video pirates till Ibrahim's cash made them instant hits; Sudhakar Bokade, a former Air India cargo handler; Mukesh Duggal, a small-time garments trader; and Dinesh Patel, a clothes-shop owner.'

In the '90s, film folk also became soft targets for extortion. Subhash Ghai, the biggest director of his day, was threatened. Producer Rajiv Rai survived an attempt on his life. On 12 August 1997, a line was drawn in the sand when music magnate Gulshan Kumar, one of the major power brokers in Hindi cinema, was killed by mob hitmen in broad daylight – a murder which had a profound influence on *Satya*. The following year, producer Mukesh Duggal was killed by a gang, reportedly because he'd borrowed money from another.

The film world and the mafia were fascinated by each other. One of the most enduring flirtations any movie star has had with organised crime is Sanjay Dutt's association with various high-ranking gangsters. It began in 1992, when Hingora and Kadawala, who had links to D-Company, managed to land Dutt, then on a hot streak, for their production *Sanam* (it finally released in 1997). Dutt had been introduced to Dawood on a shoot in Dubai, where the don invited him to dinner. This wasn't unusual – many top Bollywood stars were hosted by Dawood in Dubai in the 1980s and '90s. But Dutt made a costly mistake in the aftermath of the 1992–93 Bombay riots, procuring an AK-56 gun and ammunition from Hingora and Kadawala, which were delivered to his house by Dawood's lieutenant, Abu Salem. Additional guns and hand grenades were also stored at Dutt's place by the terrorists. A month and a half later, serial blasts widely believed to be orchestrated by Dawood and carried out by Salem, Ibrahim 'Tiger' Memon and Yakub Memon claimed more than 300 lives and injured over a thousand in Bombay. Investigators traced a lead to the actor's house, and he was arrested.

Dutt may not have had sinister intentions but he was also, in the words of journalist Rajdeep Sardesai, 'happily flirting with the gangster sub-culture, like many other high-profile Mumbaikars of that period'. He was sentenced to five years in jail for illegal possession of a weapon under the Arms Act. Even as it complicated his life, he couldn't seem to let go of his fascination for the real-life versions of the heavies he'd played in *Hathyar* (1989), *Khal Nayak* (1993), *Vaastav* (1999) and so many other films. In 2002, an extraordinary phone conversation was tapped by the Mumbai police. On one end, in Karachi, was D-Company's Chhota Shakeel, one of India's most-wanted men; on the other were Dutt, directors Mahesh Manjrekar and Sanjay Gupta and producer Harish Sugandh. It's a relaxed, rambling chat, taking in everything from Dutt's request for something in rust-brown – shoes, perhaps, or a briefcase – to a possible hit on *chikna* (fair-skinned – code for actor Hrithik Roshan). The most revealing moments are when the gangster starts doling out film advice. He tells Manjrekar, 'You make good films, but you mess up sometimes … be careful about continuity, scenes getting cut … concentrate on the mixing.' Gupta tells Shakeel he wants to make a realistic film on his life. The don even narrates an imaginary sequence to Manjrekar, complete with dissolves and scene changes, based on a hit the gang had carried out. For a brief moment in time, the mob wasn't just financing Hindi films, it was getting them made in its own image, for its private amusement in a foreign land.

Satya may not have been mob-financed, but there weren't many degrees of separation between it and the Mumbai underworld. The film was made in violent times – more than a hundred people died in gang-related shootouts in the city in 1998. It was partly inspired by tales of the underworld related to Varma by Ajit Dewani, secretary to movie stars Mandakini and Manisha Koirala and a mid-level power broker with friends in low places. A few years after the film's release, Dewani was shot dead by hitmen. Bharat Shah, *Satya*'s financier, was arrested in 2001 for links to Chhota Shakeel and for allegedly funding *Chori Chori Chupke Chupke* (2001) with underworld money (he was convicted for withholding information on producer Nazim Rizvi's links with the underworld, though he was acquitted of more serious charges under the Maharashtra Control of Organised Crime Act). Shooting in an Agripada chawl required the tacit approval of local don Arun Gawli. The killing of Gulshan Kumar a few days into production changed Varma's entire approach to the film. The shadow of the mob was long then, and *Satya* grew in its shade.

———

You might find a portion of this chapter on the gangster in Hindi cinema lacking in, well, gangsters. The petty thief, the dacoit, the upper-class crime lord were quickly adopted by Indian films, but the bona fide gangster figure materialised over time. The genre was never as central here as it was in Hollywood. The simple reason was we didn't have the sort of organised crime here (unless the British Empire counts) that existed in the United States in the 1920s and '30s and inspired the classic gangster films of that era. It was only in the '50s, largely through the efforts of the Navketan banner, that the urban crime film became popular. It was a step closer to gangster cinema, but not quite there – the visual schema was borrowed from film noir, the criminals were usually street toughs and suave crime bosses. Black-and-white gave way to colour, but the idea of a fey crime lord and his henchmen stuck, continuing through the delirious Vijay Anand thrillers of the '60s and the Bachchan films of the '70s all the way up to Shakaal and Mogambo and other high-camp villains. It was only in the late 1980s, when the Mumbai underworld became visible and fractious, that a more realistic crime cinema began to emerge. By the end of that decade, India was finally making proper gangster films. But let's start at the beginning.

Since the majority of Indian cinema from the 1920s and '30s has been lost, and what little remains is mostly out of the reach of the average moviegoer, the crime film is usually traced back to a title from 1943 that's intact, available to watch and in relatively good shape. This is *Kismet*, a Bombay Talkies production directed by Gyan Mukherjee, starring Ashok Kumar as Shekhar, a pickpocket and smooth-talking conman. Though the criminal activity in *Kismet* is limited to a couple of chases and robberies, an anti-hero with a cigarette dangling from his lip was an illicit thrill for Indian audiences at the time. A fretting *Filmindia* review hints at how transgressive it must have seemed then: 'Bombay Talkies have produced *Kismet*, a picture which glorifies a handsome criminal all throughout, makes light of his pickpocketing crimes, lends humor to his petty thefts and ultimately restores him to a waiting fortune and parentage, not to mention the gift of the charming bride. Which young man would not like to be a criminal and a pickpocket after seeing Ashok Kumar achieve all this glory and popularity in *Kismet*?'

Kismet was hugely successful, running for three years uninterrupted at Calcutta's Roxy Theatre and becoming the first Hindi film to earn a crore (at a time when a movie ticket cost less than half a rupee). It made a star out of Kumar, who'd go on to feature prominently in the noir-influenced cinema of the 1950s and early '60s.* The one direct nod to the Hollywood gangster tradition in *Kismet* is when the inspector on Shekhar's case, played by Shah Nawaz, turns up looking like Al Capone, buried in a trench coat and hat, chewing on a cigar. The veiled homoeroticism of classic gangster films may have also inspired the scene where V.H. Desai and a disconcertingly youthful David touch cigars held in their mouths to light them. By including these touches, Mukherjee was simply using established filmic grammar. Hollywood had not only been making gangster movies for a decade and a half by then, but was starting to move past them into the more psychologically fraught terrain of noir cinema.

THE HOLLYWOOD GANGSTER

Like jazz and baseball, the gangster film was a uniquely American invention. Organised crime wasn't, though. 'Crime in America is an imported vice', wrote John Baxter in *The Gangster Film*, crediting

---

* *Kismet* has a memorable political footnote. One of its songs has the refrain '*Door hato ae duniya waalon, Hindustan hamara hai*' (Stay away, world, India is ours). It circumvented the British censors by name-checking the Japanese, then threatening India's borders, and the Germans. That the song might be a protest against India's resident occupiers doesn't seem to have occurred to the authorities. This subtext didn't escape the audience of the time, who greeted the number with 'tremendous applause and approbation', in the words of writer–director K.A. Abbas.

late 19th century migrations to the US with introducing 'many of the underworld elements of European cities ... the tightly organised street gangs of French and Italian cities, the violent political activists of Ireland and the Balkans, the blood-loyal mafiosi of Sicily.' The First World War had shaken up the country, and the decade-long run of Prohibition sparked off a wave of urban crime. Speakeasies and underground dives, many of them run by the mob, began to pop up in big cities in the 1920s. And as rivalries between gangsters intensified, the ones who survived and thrived became celebrities.

The movies were there, ready to print the legend. Just as earlier generations learnt about outlaws like Butch Cassidy and Billy the Kid through dime-store paperbacks, it was now the turn of crime bosses like Al Capone and Arnold Rothstein to have their stories turned into myth. Despite the disclaimers the films carried, big-screen mobsters like Tony Camonte in *Scarface* (1932) and Rico Bandello in *Little Caesar* (1931) had a rebellious charisma that was very American – Horatio Alger with a submachine gun. It made sense that the best gangster movie writers were former newspapermen (like Ben Hecht) and pulp novelists (like W.R. Burnett) – they knew the streets these men came from, the dives they frequented, the way they spoke.

The American gangster film was at its peak in 1931–32, with three iconic films – William Wellman's *The Public Enemy*, Mervyn LeRoy's *Little Caesar* and Howard Hawks' *Scarface* – releasing within months of each other. Yet, crime movies had been around long enough for the *New York Times* to wearily begin its review of *The Public Enemy* with: 'It is just another gangster film at the Strand, weaker than most in its story, stronger than most in its acting, and, like most, maintaining a certain level of interest through the last burst of machine-gun fire.' Josef von Sternberg's *Underworld* (1927) was arguably the first great gangster film, but this was a tradition that stretched as far back as D.W. Griffith's *The Musketeers of Pig Alley* (1912). In fact, you could go back even further, almost to the beginning of cinema, when the bandit in Edwin S. Porter's *The Great Train Robbery* fires his pistol at the camera. The action has been repeated in so many films – including *Satya* – that it's difficult to imagine what a shock it would have been for viewers barely used to moving images to see someone shoot straight at them.

For a few years in the 1930s, in America and wherever else Hollywood movies were shown, screens were overrun by violent, mother-fixated, sexually conflicted, gun-toting, sharp-dressing, wisecracking hoods. Some of the most memorable ones were played by James Cagney and Edward G. Robinson – pugnacious fellows, not handsome enough for the star roles, too interesting to restrict to bit parts. If *Satya* owes the classic Hollywood gangster anything, it's the freedom to cast tough-looking nobodies instead of pretty faces who would sell more tickets. At the time of the film's release, Bajpayee, Chakravarthy and Shukla were barely known. Their collective beauty wouldn't add up to one Sidharth Malhotra, but they had what Cagney and Robinson had – the ability to induce in the viewer the sensation of watching a real gangster and not some combination of make-up, stubble and dim lighting. There's a more elemental debt as well. The Hollywood gangster cycle of the 1930s established the grammar of the genre – the urban milieu, the fixations on clothes and cars and guns, the indictment of society over and above the criminal, the 'types' ranging from crusading district attorney to the young hothead whose death leaves the central figure unmoored. These strands have surfaced in the policier films of France, the yakuza sagas of Japan, films about the Hong Kong triads, the Italian mafia and the first wave of Hindi crime films in the 1950s. Though it may not be apparent, *Satya* has Wellman and Hecht, Cagney and Robinson in its DNA.

THE RISE OF HINDI NOIR

In 1949, three years after winning the Grand Prix at the inaugural
Cannes Film Festival with *Neecha Nagar*, Chetan Anand launched
his own banner, Navketan, with his younger brother, Dev. Their
first production, *Afsar* (1950), didn't draw crowds. But Dev, then
just becoming popular as a romantic star, knew someone promising
and in need of a break. A few years earlier, he'd become friends with
a choreographer and aspiring director named Guru Dutt; they met,
the legend goes, when the *dhobi* mixed their clothes up at Prabhat
Studios in Pune. Anand promised Dutt he'd give him his first
directing job. That turned out to be *Baazi* (1951), whose success
set Anand on a path to becoming the biggest star of the '50s along
with Raj Kapoor and Dilip Kumar, and launched Dutt's brief but
staggering directorial career.

Baazi was the first example of what would become the Navketan
style in the '50s. Like all good studios, they had a stock company: lead
actors Dev Anand and Kalpana Kartik; supporting players Rashid
Khan, Bhagwan Sinha and K.N. Singh; composer S.D. Burman;
lyricist Sahir Ludhianvi; cinematographer V. Ratra. Theirs were city
films, usually a sort of comedy-romance-thriller hybrid, indebted to
the American noir tradition, with some kind of underworld element.
You see this in *Taxi Driver* (1954), *House No. 44* (1955) and *Kala
Bazar* (1960) – films in which Dev Anand did, arguably, his most
interesting work, playing a series of laconic streetwise characters.
The Navketan style also reflected in Dutt's productions before he
turned to personal stories – his own *Aar-Paar* (1954) and Raj Khosla's
C.I.D. (1956).

Given its influence on black-and-white Indian crime films, it
might be useful at this point to consider what noir entails, and how it
differs from gangster film. The borders between gangster cinema and

noir can be blurry, especially since most noir films have an element of criminality. In India, 'noir' is applied with wild abandon (mostly by overenthusiastic critics) to any film with a gun and a couple of shadows. But there's a reason films like *Raakh* (1989) and *Is Raat Ki Subah Nahin* are noirs and *Satya* isn't. Gangster film is a self-evident genre. Noir informs other genres, from Westerns to melodramas. It is, in its most basic sense, a collection of stylistic choices and psychological conditions. You know a noir when you see it, whereas a gangster film simply is or isn't.

Since noir is defined by tone, not genre, what stripes or spots should you look for? For starters, shadows, lots of them. Light broken up into jagged shapes by window blinds or bars. Cigarette smoke. Mean streets. Hardboiled dialogue. Non-linear timeframes. Voiceover narration. Women with secrets. Men with hats. An all-pervasive fatalism.

Baazi didn't have the gloom of a true noir – Anand nearly always played incurable optimists – but with Ratra's shadowy photography, it looked like one. A young cardsharp, Madan (Anand), is hired by an unseen nightclub owner to hustle customers. He catches the eye of Leena, a bar singer played by Geeta Bali, but falls for doctor Rajani (Kalpana Kartik), who's treating his ailing sister. Rajani's wealthy father (K.N. Singh) doesn't approve of the union, a problem that's compounded when, in a twist which even in 1951 couldn't have come as a surprise, he's revealed to be Madan's mysterious employer.

Dutt and screenwriter Balraj Sahni lift the plot from the Rita Hayworth-starrer *Gilda* (1946). You can see Dutt and Anand's love for American film blend with the Hindi musical tradition in the 'Tadbeer Se Bigdi Hui' sequence. Dutt starts the song as pure noir, Anand and Rashid Khan entering a basement with a dangerous-looking man in a suit lounging by the stairs and Bali in the foreground strumming a guitar. The patrons exchange meaningful glances. A fight breaks out over a dropped wad of cash. It looks like a good place to get mugged, but just as Madan is about to bail, Bali starts singing – and how can you leave then? Anand puts on his best scowl, pulls a little trick out of the Brando/Dean playbook and chews his nails while Bali makes eyes at him. It's the best sort of I-don't-care gesture – almost a mockery of Raj Kapoor's I-care-too-much approach – and an example of how deft an actor Anand was before the mannerisms took over.

Baazi is more recognisably a crime film than *Kismet*. By revealing the heroine's father as Madan's employer – a suit-wearing, cigar-smoking kingpin who orders muggings and murders – the film ensures that all the plot strands circle back to illegality and danger. Even more crucial is the consistent atmosphere of vice that Dutt creates, moving the action in and out of shady clubs, gambling dens and police stations. This became the Navketan template over the decade – urban crime (not individuals, not too organised), two women (one 'modern', the other more traditional), a tough-talking hero in a hat, smoking a cigarette and not giving a damn. The trend was picked up by *Taxi Driver* (1954), a much-needed first hit for Chetan Anand. The film was a variation on *Baazi*, but a touch grittier, with knife fights, escorts and drunks (though no visible alcohol). Yet, it's also distinct from the other Navketan films because much of it was shot on location. As we'll see in the next chapter, this was the beginning of another subgenre – the Mumbai street film.

The Anands weren't the only ones remaking *Baazi* that year. Four months before *Taxi Driver* came *Aar-Paar*, Dutt's first noir film under his own banner, Guru Dutt Productions. He directed and starred as Kalu Birju, a laconic taxi driver pursued by two women and tangled up with criminals. You have to wonder whether Anand and Dutt ever discussed if it was wise for them to play essentially the same character in two not-dissimilar films releasing a few months apart. Then again, maybe it wasn't such a bad call – both films were commercial successes. Dutt is a more confident filmmaker here than in *Baazi*, and with V.K. Murthy behind the camera, there's a sublime fluency to some scenes – like the dramatic opening of 'Babuji Dheere Chalna', the camera following Shakila's feet as she descends a flight of stairs, then tracking her as she sashays across the nightclub (it was a similarly complicated shot in 'Suno Gajar Kya Gaye', a song from *Baazi*, which first brought Dutt and Murthy, then Ratra's assistant, together and initiated one of the great director–cinematographer partnerships).

Aar-Paar nudged Hindi cinema in the direction of organised crime as opposed to petty theft and gambling by having Kalu participate, reluctantly, in a bank heist. There's a sudden shift from romantic comedy (the charming 'Ye Lo Main Hari Piya', Shyama singing to Dutt while he drives) to suspense as Kalu drops ringleader Captain and three of his men, one at a time, at separate locations in Fort, south Bombay's financial district. As Captain watches from across the street, the others meet at the entrance of Allahabad Bank, where they smoke and check their watches. They look like they're set to rob the place, but then they suddenly bolt, jump in the taxi and are driven off by Kalu (a dog chases after them – a rare naturalistic moment in a Guru Dutt film). It's a neat bit of misdirection – not a robbery, but a rehearsal for one; the kind of joke Hitchcock liked.

In 1951, three years before *Aar-Paar*, a sensational bank robbery took place on Hornby Road, now Dadabhai Naoroji Road. In those days, banks would sometimes send surplus cash to the Reserve Bank of India (RBI). Lloyds Bank had received a large deposit from the Bank of Iran, and was planning to deliver 12 lakh rupees to the RBI. On 20 April, the taxi carrying the money and its guards was about to leave the bank when it was attacked by five men. The driver was shot, three employees were injured and the robbers made away with the cash, only to be apprehended a few days later. The papers reported that they had come up with the plan a month before, scoped out the area, even done dry runs. Legend has it the man who planned the heist, one Anokhelal Ranjit Singh, got the idea from a little-known Hollywood gangster movie, *Highway 301* (1950). The details of the case would have been fresh in the public's mind when *Aar-Paar* released; appeals by the robbers against the life sentences awarded were still ongoing in 1954. The mock robbery in the film takes place a stone's throw from where the real heist did – Captain even mentions Hornby Road when he's drawing out plans. Add to that the shared detail of a rehearsal, and it seems clear that Dutt was trying his hand at something American films did with great success in the '30s – take a well-publicised crime, dress it up and allow the viewing public to make the connection.

By the mid '50s, the house style for Navketan's noirs was so well-established that a new director simply had to come in and assemble the elements. M.K. Burman's *House No. 44* (1955) has Anand as a pickpocket compelled by poverty to work for a gang. Kartik's the female lead, K.N. Singh and Bhagwan Sinha are crooks, Ratra's behind the camera, Burman–Ludhianvi on the soundtrack. It isn't as polished a film as *Aar-Paar*, but there are brief, vivid flashes of style, like the sounds from rival dance-houses overlapping as the silhouette of a girl is cast onto the figure of a blissed-out Anand reclining drunk against a wall. And the quick, violent killing of a railway guard has a messy realism that's years ahead of its time.

C.I.D. (1956), directed by Guru Dutt's former assistant Raj Khosla and starring Anand, is arguably the best of the '50s noirs. With Murthy behind the camera, there's a Hitchcockian glide and economy to the opening sequence – an order to kill passed down from crime boss to intermediary (neither face is shown) to heavy (played by Mehmood!) over cryptic telephone exchanges. (Some things don't change – more than 40 years later, in *Satya* and *Company*, mob hits were still being coordinated over the phone.) The resulting murder of a newspaper editor who's about to expose the illegal activities of a prominent member of society is investigated by inspector Shekhar, an urbane, lawful version of the laconic street characters Anand had played in *Baazi*, *Taxi Driver* and *House No. 44*. The criminal mastermind turns out to be a *seth* and philanthropist – as with *Baazi*, the reveal comes around halfway through the film.

Though there are two murders – one on-screen and grisly, the other in jail and left to the viewer's imagination – and assorted criminal activities, there's a dreaminess to the narrative, a winking quality similar to Howard Hawks' classic 1946 detective noir, *The Big Sleep*. One of the best in-jokes has 'A. Alvi', 'P. Chakravorty' and 'O.P. Nayyar' – the film's writer, producer and composer – as some of the 'criminals' listed on a blackboard at the police station. Even the bits with real Bombay are like a waking dream – Worli Seaface is virtually empty for Anand, Shakila and two musicians to perform the unusual walking choreography of 'Leke Pehla Pehla Pyar'.

While the Hindi gangster film traces its origins back to these titles, they can't be called gangster films themselves. The genre is predicated on organised crime, which wasn't widespread in those days. The filmmakers didn't have much to draw on in terms of real-life material, and exploring the psychology of criminality wasn't of interest to directors (other than maybe Raj Kapoor). Still, seeds were being sown. In *Jaal* (1952), Dutt's second film, inspired by the Italian melodrama *Bitter Rice* (1949), Dev Anand plays Tony, a Goan smuggler. By Hindi film standards, Tony is a hardboiled character – a thief and cavalier heartbreaker who only redeems himself towards the end. The film is minor Dutt and minor Anand, but it made a big impression on screenwriter and lyricist Javed Akhtar, who, two decades later, came up with Hindi film's most famous smuggler, *Deewar*'s Vijay Verma. 'I think this fascination for the negative hero started with *Jaal*', he told Nasreen Munni Kabir, noting that Anand, when he played criminals in his own productions, was careful not to push the audience away, whereas in Dutt's film, he 'didn't care to be considered a good man'.

Meanwhile, Dev and Chetan Anand's brother, Vijay, who wrote *Taxi Driver* at 20, was showing signs of prodigious directorial talent. His second film, *Kala Bazar* (1960), was a stunner – commercial cinema executed with a lightness and command that must have made older directors weep. Raghu (Dev Anand) makes a living selling tickets at inflated prices to frantic moviegoers just as the show is about to begin – 'in black', as they say here. He gets into trouble with another street gang over ticket-selling territory. The film looks ahead to *Rangeela* and *Ghulam*, with their streetwise heroes. Yet, like other Navketan films, it's only partly concerned with crime. Much of the running time is taken up by a love story, with high-society girl Alka (Waheeda Rehman) being pursued by Raghu in the absence of her boyfriend, who's studying abroad. The Liberty Cinema montage (which cleverly intercuts footage of movie stars like Dilip Kumar, Nargis and Kishore Kumar arriving for the premiere of Mehboob's *Mother India* (1957) as Raghu and the other touts escalate ticket prices) is justly famous, but there are smaller miracles of framing and movement too – the play of glances in a train compartment in 'Apni Toh Har Aah Ek Toofan Hai', and the superimposed image of Dev on Waheeda's face, just as beautiful as when Jean Vigo did it in *L'Atalante* (1934).

Kala Bazar would be the last of the Navketan noirs. The Hollywood-influenced cigarettes-and-trenchcoats film was on its way out. Colour had arrived, and this meant a new kind of thriller – which Vijay Anand would be at the forefront of. But before we get to that, there's a few threads of noir-gangster cinema to be tied up.

Other studios had been looking at Navketan and Dev Anand and wondering why they didn't have a hardboiled hero of their own. Some went ahead and got one. Sunil Dutt is dapper in a fedora, suit and tie, playing a reporter in Nagina Films' *Post Box 999* (1958), a rip-off of the Jimmy Stewart-starrer *Call Northside 777* (1948). N.A. Ansari produced and directed for Sippy Films a noir comedy–thriller called *Black Cat* (1959), starring Balraj Sahni as a detective on the trail of a master criminal. Just as lively is Brij's *Ustadon Ke Ustad* (1963), which has hats, guns, genre mainstay Ashok Kumar, the imposing Sheikh Mukhtar as a genuinely menacing villain and some stunning noir photography.

There were also the urban crime films of Shakti Samanta. One of the underrated stylists of his era, Samanta was, at that time, a director in the Vijay Anand mould, with an eye for visual invention and an instinct for fun. Like the Anands, he too had a fondness for Hollywood gangster and noir film. In 1958, he directed *Howrah Bridge*, in which a businessman played by Ashok Kumar gets entangled with a smuggling syndicate over a missing heirloom, a small price to pay for being in the same room as Madhubala singing 'Aaiye Meherbaan'. Replace Kumar (looking not unlike Edward G. Robinson) with Anand, and it could almost be a Navketan production, Samanta peppering the film with gangster tropes before ending with a dash through the sewers – an idea likely swiped from Carol Reed's *The Third Man* (1949) – and a fight on the titular bridge, Calcutta's most recognisable landmark.

After the 1960 Indo-Malaya production, *Singapore*, a kind of Southeast Asian *Howrah Bridge* with Shammi Kapoor, Samanta returned to seedy, glamorous Calcutta. *China Town* (1962) might be the closest any film of that era got to appropriating the look and iconography of a classic Hollywood gangster film. The nighttime action sequence at the start, with local don Mike – a snarly, cigar-smoking Shammi Kapoor in hat, coat and tie – spotted at the waterfront, then in a car chase with the police, finally ending upside down, unconscious, arms flung out, could be out of *Scarface* or *The Public Enemy*. But then another Shammi Kapoor – Shekhar (moustache, muffler, checked shirt) – is in a bar singing '*taali ho*' and you know you're in a Hindi film. Pulled in on a police complaint, Shekhar is prevailed upon to impersonate Mike so the police can build a case against the kingpin, who's in jail. It's *Don* 16 years before *Don*, better-looking and arguably more fun.

Samanta's winking style is crystallised in a small, perfect scene. Still dressed up as Mike, Shekhar calls his love from a payphone. It's late. As they speak, we cut back and forth between them. His shadow on the wall looms over him; she's in her brightly lit home. Looked at another way, she's in a romantic comedy, he's in a gangster film. It's Samanta's way of saying he's perfectly aware he's mixing genres.

The noir style, with figures wreathed in shadows, framed in cigarette smoke, went on hiatus once black-and-white faded from Hindi cinema. But the upper-crust villain, dressed in a suit or *bandgala*, issuing commands to his henchmen, not only survived the move to colour, but thrived. In Vijay Anand's delirious thriller *Teesri Manzil* (1966), Prem Nath is a wealthy landlord who's revealed to be the antagonist; in Anand's *Johny Mera Naam* (1970), he's bad from the moment we lay eyes on him, but lives in a mansion, dresses like a *seth* and has the honorific 'Rai Bahadur' before his name. This figure would soon become campier, crazier – the influence of Bond movies, in which 007 was as constant as the North Star while the villains were distinguished by their weirdness. Brij's *Yakeen* (1969), with Dharmendra as both hero and surprisingly chilling blue-eyed villain, has a Bond-like outlandishness and sheen; so does the actor's 1968 spy thriller, *Ankhen*. Post *Jewel Thief* (1967), Vijay Anand's films also showed signs of being made in the age of Bond. In his 1973 thriller *Blackmail*, Italian mobsters looking to steal a 'formula for solar power' infiltrate an international golf championship.

SMUGGLERS AND DONS

By the '70s, Hindi cinema had mostly given up on maintaining any kind of consistent iconography for its dons. In the 1973 hit *Yaadon Ki Baaraat*, Ajit, as the evil Shakaal, initially turns up looking like a bandit in a Western: cowboy hat, jeans, mouth covered with a handkerchief. When we see him next, decades later, he's dressed like a Bond villain, in tie, waistcoat and oversized blue-tinted glasses. One of his henchmen wears a tight-fitting orange t-shirt. Another dresses like a '30s mobster and carries a Tommy gun in a guitar case. Gangster films had always fetishised clothes, but in the heyday of *masala* cinema, villainy had turned into fancy dress.

Hollywood, meanwhile, was moving on. Martin Scorsese showed with *Mean Streets* (1973) that it was possible to make a personal film, with its own preoccupations and rough poetry, about low-down hoods. The previous year, his friend Francis Ford Coppola reinvented the crime syndicate film with *The Godfather*, its gangsters like Chekhov characters. Over in Bombay, Vijay Anand was assembling a holy trinity of smarmy villainy – Prem Nath, Prem Chopra and Ajit – in *Chhupa Rustam* (1973), a film with all the inherent danger of a pillow fight. The Hindi film villain was stuck and the gangster was nowhere in sight.

A lanky inspector pushes Pran's chair away and growls, '*Yeh* police station *hai, tumhare baap ka ghar nahi* (This is a police station, not your father's house).' With this line, a lot of glowering and those long legs kicking out at the injustices of society, was born the legend of Amitabh Bachchan. *Zanjeer* (1973) wasn't a particularly sophisticated film, and Prakash Mehra wasn't a stylist like Ramesh Sippy or Chandra Barot, but that didn't matter. The script by Salim Khan and Javed Akhtar went off like a firecracker in every other scene, and Bachchan's brooding anger was something new for Hindi cinema. His incorruptible inspector Vijay has no qualms doling out vigilante justice after being dismissed from the police – a harsh new moral code that would define '70s action cinema. He's helped in his fight against the racketeer Teja (Ajit) by Sher Khan (Pran), a mid-level don who becomes his friend after Vijay shows up at his gambling house, unarmed and unaccompanied, and challenges him to a fight.

Despite the dry charms of Ajit, Teja wasn't significantly different from the camp '60s villain. Sher Khan was another matter. Gangster film has always depended, more than perhaps any other genre, on real-life figures for inspiration. Khan was based on Karim Lala, a strongman of Afghan descent, who ran gambling joints in Bombay. The resemblance ends there, as Salim–Javed leave out Lala's more serious crimes and make Khan a virtuous elder-brother figure for Vijay. Nevertheless, here, for the first time, was a Hindi film character based on an actual don – a significant milestone for the genre.

Salim–Javed borrowed again from the story of a real-life gangster for Yash Chopra's *Deewar* (1975). The Bachchan character in the film, again named Vijay, is a dockworker whose first act of rebellion is challenging the local heavy who takes a cut from everyone's salaries. He comes to the attention of a big-time smuggler, who takes him under his wing. Vijay soon takes over the business, which allows him to give his mother a comfortable life but puts him on a collision course with his brother, Ravi (Shashi Kapoor), a police inspector. Audiences at the time would have recognised in Vijay a sympathetic version of Haji Mastan, a celebrity don who started out working on the docks and challenged the local *hafta*-demanding heavy, before establishing his own thriving racket.

The film, more persuasively directed than *Zanjeer* and with even snappier writing, was a huge hit. It wasn't a faithful retelling of Mastan's life, but even the nods it makes in that direction would have been enough to make moviegoers feel like they and Vijay/Haji existed in the same Bombay. A couple of years later, in Prakash Mehra's *Muqaddar Ka Sikandar* (1978), Bachchan turned smugglers over to the cops ... for a fee. As we'll see in the next chapter, *Muqaddar's* most significant contribution from a genre standpoint was Amjad Khan's jailbird speaking authentic Bambaiyya – all thanks to writer Kader Khan, who'd used similar street slang with great success for Bachchan's Anthony Gonsalves in Manmohan Desai's *Amar Akbar Anthony* (1977). Bachchan also played a master criminal in the mould of The Jackal (and a lookalike sent to impersonate him) in Chandra Barot's stylish thriller *Don* (1978).

A less successful experiment in the year of *Deewar* was Feroz Khan's *Dharmatma*, which married *The Godfather* with the story of Rattan Khatri, the '*matka* king', who ran illegal betting in Bombay since the '60s, drawing lucky numbers for the day from a pack of playing cards placed in an earthen pot, or *matka*. Much of the gangster stuff is lifted wholesale from Coppola's film – the proposal by rival gangsters to team up and sell drugs, the attempt on the life of the old don in the hospital, the murder in the car. Khan is also working through some personal material here – he was a betting man himself, and his father was Afghani. But he's an inadequate Michael Corleone, and Prem Nath, in the Brando role, is stiff and stagey. The two main villains are high camp – one of them wears a neck brace and an eyeglass. Afghanistan is a pretty backdrop, but the time spent there among horses, sheep, goats and Hema Malini is too long a break from the gang stuff, which isn't too riveting anyway. Nevertheless, audiences ate it up.

By the start of the 1980s, crime bosses weren't just camp, they were deeply weird. In *Karz* (1980), Prem Nath is Sir Judah, a mute don whose taps on a whiskey glass are interpreted for visitors by an assistant. Bald, smirking Shakaal (Kulbhushan Kharbanda) in *Shaan* (1980) is a dead ringer for Telly Savalas as Blofeld, James Bond's most famous adversary, in *On Her Majesty's Secret Service* (1969); he catapults a hireling into a shark pool in a scene almost identical to the one in *Thunderball* (1965), where Blofeld electrocutes a minion in his chair. This trend of cartoon villains would peak some years later with Amrish Puri's Mogambo and his acid pits in *Mr India* (1987). Silly and psychologically inert, their popularity obscured the good work being done by other directors during the '80s to create grounded and compelling onscreen villains.

Hindi cinema in the '80s is usually dismissed as a cinematic wasteland separating the socially committed '70s and the youthful '90s. Yet, this was also a time when the city-centric parallel film was pushed to new heights by Saeed Akhtar Mirza, Govind Nihalani and Sai Paranjpye. Also around this time, a new generation of directors was starting out in commercial cinema. Many of them had been to film school, and had Kurosawa and Kubrick filed away in their heads. Subhash Ghai and N. Chandra and J.P. Dutta showed flashes of style beyond the capabilities of the workmanlike directors of the '70s. By the time the decade was over, they'd make the first bona fide Hindi gangster films.

REALITY BITES

You could see the genre growing in confidence over the decade. Finally, there were outright gangster films concerned with organised crime (*Dayavan, Parinda, Hathyar*); other films were gangster-adjacent (*Arjun, Tezaab*). More crucially, there was a change in tone from the '70s – a grounding in harsh reality that informed even the commercial films. Govind Nihalani's low-budget cop drama, *Ardh Satya* (1983), set the tone by showing how the Hindi gangster film, and the larger Bombay film, of the future might look – spare, shorn of glamour, engaged with the city at ground level, flawed characters negotiating an unsympathetic universe. Even pessimistic films like Yash Chopra's *Mashaal* (1984), in which Dilip Kumar goes from crusading newspaper editor to underworld boss and finally takes a bullet for a reformed thug, seemed old-fashioned in its wake. It also influenced the gangster film by introducing, in Sadashiv Amrapurkar's Rama Shetty, a new kind of criminal, watchful and amused instead of campy or psychotic. In the years to come, there'd be different iterations of the thinking gangster: Nana Patekar in *Parinda* (1989), Raghuvaran in *Siva* (1989), Kader Khan in *Angaar* (1992).

Ardh Satya is a harsh, incisive study of Indian male psychology. Anant Velankar (Om Puri) is a rule-bound Bombay sub-inspector, prone to bouts of violence and self-flagellation. His father (Amrish Puri), a violent bully and former constable, wants to get him married off. Anant takes a liking to Jyotsna (Smita Patil), a college professor, but proceeds shyly with her. His frustrations at work and in his personal life are seen by his father, and eventually by Anant, as a blot on his manhood. The film, adapted by playwright Vijay Tendulkar, uses the Hindi word *napunsak* (impotent) outside of a physical context: the inability to perform sexually is extended to an entire frustrated life.

Even today, *Ardh Satya* is discomfiting. How raw must it have seemed when it released? Nihalani shot it himself, and those familiar with his work will notice, in several scenes, his signature prowling camera movements. The world of the film is drab, the language rough – Velankar's speech is peppered with 'bastard' and '*haraami*', which is about as far as you could go in Hindi cinema in 1983.

There are shocking scenes of violence. A man set on fire falls by the roadside, screaming and writhing. Anant, drunk and at the end of his tether, delivers a fatal beating to a suspect in a police cell. There's ugliness wherever one looks – illegal trafficking and slum clearances, emotional violence and toxic masculinity.

As a progenitor of the gritty Mumbai crime film, *Ardh Satya* is a crucial forerunner of *Satya*. Kashyap said Nihalani's film had a 'very important role in Ramu's head', and Varma himself cited it along with *Arjun* and 1972's *The Way of the Dragon* as one of the inspirations for his first feature, *Siva*. Varma thought of getting Nihalani's screenwriter, Vijay Tendulkar, to write *Satya*. Some have even speculated Varma called his film *Satya* as a tribute to *Ardh Satya* (he actually named it for a girl he had a crush on in school). The closest Varma came to making his own *Ardh Satya* was *Shool* (1999), a film Kashyap wrote and he produced, which places a Velankar-like police officer, played by Manoj Bajpayee, in the Bihari heartland.

My first viewing of *Arjun* (1985) was on TV some afternoon home from school. The only thing that stayed with me was the angry musical number 'Mammaya Kero Kero', its tune and title borrowed, incredibly, from the 1937 Brazilian carnival song 'Mamãe Eu Quero', popularised by Carmen Miranda. Revisiting it decades later, the film seemed to me suspended between director Rahul Rawail's visual proficiency and Javed Akhtar's waning screenwriting powers. Sunny Deol plays Arjun, an educated but unemployed young man who takes on local goons, and soon gains a reputation as dependable muscle. He's hired by the outwardly respectable politician Shivkumar Chowgule (Anupam Kher) to clean up the city. Only towards the end of the film does it dawn on him that he's a tool to get rid of Chowgule's rival, a corrupt minister (Prem Chopra), and his hitman (Paresh Rawal).

The film's big confrontation cribs a visual from *Pyaasa* (1957): Arjun framed, Christ-like, in the doorway of an auditorium. But Rawail – like his contemporaries Pankaj Parashar, Mukul Anand and Ghai* – was just as interested in aping Spielberg and Coppola, lifting scenes from 1981's *Raiders of the Lost Ark* (Arjun waits for a man to finish showing off his nunchaku skills and then knocks him out) and *The Godfather* (an elderly female tenant on the verge of eviction is offered 'protection' by Arjun). The standout sequence – a murder committed amidst a sea of black umbrellas – carries an echo of a memorable assassination in Hitchcock's *Foreign Correspondent* (1940). Sword-wielding henchmen come after Arjun's friend. As rain pours down, he frantically pushes his way through a crowded gully, the phalanx of umbrellas obscuring our view of assailants and target. As they draw nearer, Rawail slows the action down, stretching out the doomed final moments. The scene was done with the help of Roy Scammell, stunt coordinator for *A Clockwork Orange* (1971) and *Alien* (1979). It is, quite simply, one of the great Bombay action sequences.

Arjun was essentially Akhtar giving his 'angry young man' template a dust-off and placing it on a new angry man's shoulders.

---

* I'm skipping over Subhash Ghai's action films of that period, but I'd like to mention in passing *Vidhaata*, a 1982 film in which Dilip Kumar's honest engine driver becomes a mafia don. Kumar, recently pulled out of retirement, is a rare restrained crime boss (that he resists the temptation to do a Brando imitation makes the performance even more impressive). If only there were more scenes like the unbroken shot towards the end which follows Kumar as he walks into a mansion, down a corridor, into the elevator, then out, down another corridor and into a room, where he shoots three men. It's a more ambitious version of the 50-second shot that opens Ghai's *Vishwanath* (1978).

The film was a hit, and captured the imagination of Varma, who was trying to break into the Telugu industry at the time. You can see its influence on *Siva*, both in the rawness of its action (there's a long bicycle chase in both) and the idea of a hot-headed youth taking on gangsters and corrupt politicians and becoming something close to a gangster himself. Paresh Rawal, a hitman in *Arjun*, is also the crooked politico with gang connections in *Siva*. More Varma connections emerge if you consider the Tamil remake of *Arjun*, made in 1988 (and released in a Telugu dub, as is common with films in these two languages). Crew members included actor Amala and composer Ilaiyaraaja, both of whom would work on *Siva*. It starred Kamal Haasan, whose beard and intense performance recall Chakravarthy in *Satya*. Then there's the title of the remake: *Sathyaa*.

A year before *Sathyaa*, Kamal Haasan starred in a seminal Tamil gangster film. Mani Ratnam's *Nayakan*, based on the life of real-life don Varadarajan Mudaliar, was miles ahead in technical sophistication and psychological complexity than the crime films Hindi directors were making. A Bombay-set film, it would've been squarely within this book's ambit had it been made in Hindi; readers will forgive me for not attempting (and inevitably failing) to map the gangster genre in other languages. *Nayakan* was remade in Hindi by Feroz Khan as *Dayavan* (1988). Though his film was almost a facsimile of Ratnam's, Khan wasn't right for this sort of material, and Vinod Khanna, in a tricky part that requires him to go from fiery community leader to grey-haired don, lacks the range Kamal Haasan brought to his portrayal of Velu Naicker.

Almost all '80s Hindi action cinema was Hollywood-inspired, but *Tezaab* (1988) was a veritable patchwork of American action movies. N. Chandra's film about a police-cadet-turned-gangster is remembered today for the incredibly popular Madhuri Dixit dance number 'Ek Do Teen'. Not many know this musical sequence is a frame-by-frame recreation of the opening musical number in Walter Hill's rock 'n' roll thriller, *Streets of Fire* (1984), from the motorcycle gang pulling up outside a concert to the singer's abduction at the close. There's an identical scene right after too: a girl from the concert writing to her brother to rescue the singer. A few scenes later, the brother (Anil Kapoor) disarms an attacker, hands him back his knife and tells him to try again – just as Michael Paré does in Hill's film.

Tezaab borrows from other American films as well. Two sequences are taken wholesale from Brian De Palma's *The Untouchables* (1987): the shootout on the stairs with the bouncing baby pram and the overhead shot where Al Capone is nicked by a barber. The expressionistic scene introducing Kapoor is straight out of a John Carpenter film. There's even a brief Sergio Leone moment, complete with Morricone whistling. But, like most '80s Hindi gangster films, the high style is hitched to ornate writing, which ends up sounding ridiculous in stories of urban crime. What's the use of a tense opening scene with knife-wielding toughs brandishing acid if they say '*dastakhat*' and '*dastavez*' like they've just come from Urdu class? Something had to give – and, a year later, it did.

———

We've made it to 1989, a pivotal year for representations of Bombay on film. It also marked the birth of the modern Hindi film gangster. J.P. Dutta's *Hathyar* and Vidhu Vinod Chopra's *Parinda* were stylish, violent, dark – and a huge leap forward. No campy crime lords, no lurid sets, no comic relief. For the first time, here were films that gave you a sense of the underworld and the people who operate within it, either willingly or because they're compelled to.

A bearded man dressed in white answers the phone. 'Anna,' he says. Then, '*Kiska aadmi hai? Accha. Mere aane talak zinda rakho use* (Whose guy is it? All right. Keep him alive till I reach).' There's a deathly shriek, a cut and a dull thud. We see a face in profile, silhouetted, eyes staring upwards, lifeless. There's a man standing over him with a hammer, another wiping blood off his knife.

What if *Parinda* was Anna's story? A Hindi film about the rise of a south Indian gangster in Mumbai – Satya before *Satya*. But Anna isn't the centre of this film. Instead, it's about two brothers, Kishen (Jackie Shroff), who works as a hitman for Anna, and Karan (Anil Kapoor), who's just returned from college abroad. He immediately makes plans to reunite with his childhood friend, police officer Prakash (Anupam Kher), and Prakash's sister, Paro (Madhuri Dixit), whom he's in love with. But Prakash has been making life difficult for Anna, and the reunion turns tragic when he's shot several times by Anna's men and dies in Karan's arms. The young man vows revenge; a frantic Kishen tries to talk Anna out of killing his brother. As plots go, it's a doozy, borrowing from *On the Waterfront*, pivoting on events that took place when Karan, Kishen and Paro were still children. This links it to both *Nayakan* and Bachchan classics like *Zanjeer*, *Deewar* and *Muqaddar Ka Sikandar*, in which (often tragic) childhood memory works as a catch-all explanation for future courses of (often violent) action. 'In the revenge narrative, the past is the site of traumatic memory to be settled in the future,' Ranjani Mazumdar writes in *Bombay Cinema*. *Satya*, notably, breaks with this tradition by centering its story on a man whose past is never alluded to or revealed.

Parinda managed to look richer and darker than any crime film since the days of Navketan. When one desperate henchman shoots himself in Anna's factory, the whirring machinery slices the light into jagged patterns typical of noir cinema. Binod Pradhan's photography echoes the paranoid American cinema of the '70s – some of the scenes are dark enough to have been lit by Gordon Willis, cinematographer on the *Godfather* films. When Karan and Paro make love on a boat drifting out to sea, their bodies are bathed in a ghostly dark-blue light that's not unlike Willis' lighting of Deep Throat in *All the President's Men* (1976). Renu Saluja's expert editing adds another layer of technical finesse. The ambush of the brothers at the Gateway of India is a masterful set piece, unfolding at first in quick fragments, then stretching into slo-mo as Kishen is shot, and ending with a majestic god's-eye view from the top of the structure.

Anna meets a gruesome end, burnt alive in his home, just as he'd set on fire his wife and child. But the violence of Karan and Paro's killing a few scenes earlier on the boat was even more shocking. Stars had, of course, been dispatched in films before, but this was a particularly quick and brutal way to go – bodies riddled with bullets like the end of *Bonnie and Clyde* (1967). *Satya*'s deaths were less baroque, but the suddenness, the messiness was the same.

While Chopra has largely abandoned directing to concentrate on producing Rajkumar Hirani's wildly successful movies, *Parinda*'s reputation has only grown over the years. This is not the case with *Hathyar*. The film, which tracks the gradual immersion into organised crime of a young man named Avi (Sanjay Dutt), is largely forgotten today, and for the few who want to watch it, it's almost impossible to find a decent print. This is a pity, for Dutta's film, though less polished and streamlined than *Parinda*, has more to say about the cyclical nature of violence. 'In cinematic terms, *Hathyar* is a forerunner to Ram Gopal Varma's *Satya* and other sleek, realistic city-crime films that would herald the multiplex era,' wrote critic and author Jai Arjun Singh. Indeed, it is easier to draw a line from *Hathyar* to *Satya* than it is from *Parinda*. Like *Satya*, *Hathyar* is set at the street-level, with characters struggling to make ends meet, whereas Karan and Paro and Anna live in well-furnished upper middle-class homes. Avi takes the local train; Karan and Kishen drive around in cars. There's a musical sequence that revolves around the cooking of dinner in *Parinda*. In *Hathyar*, Avi ends up killing someone over food.

Even in the atrocious print I watched, that sequence is wrenching. Realising that his mother has gone to sleep hungry so he can eat, a distraught Avi bursts out of the house. He wanders over to a roadside stall, watches a man eat *pav bhaji* – coincidentally, the same thing Dutt's character in *Vaastav* is cooking when he takes his first unwilling step towards a life of crime. Something in him snaps. He follows the stranger into the subway with a friend and attempts to mug him. The man, a plainclothes cop, pulls out a knife. In the scramble of bodies, Avi ends up fatally stabbing him. He's forced to go to the local don, Khushal Khan (Dharmendra), for help, which paves the way for his entry into serious crime. One bad decision escalates until Avi becomes a hired killer. It's the same in *Satya*. A migrant slashes a nobody across the face, gets thrown in jail, has a fight there, makes a friend, and boom, he's in a gang.

Hathyar makes it clear that violence has been passed down the generations in Avi's family – they move to Bombay at the start of the film because of a village feud. The Hong Kong industry was particularly adept at films like this, gang narratives colliding with family stories and codes of honour. There's a pulpy finesse to the violence in *Arjun* and *Hathyar* and *Siva* that brings to mind the films of Ringo Lam and John Woo – talented, unpretentious directors making commercial films on tight budgets. It might be a coincidence, but the ending of *Hathyar*, with Avi trapped by the police, dying in a dramatic shootout, bears a strong resemblance to the climax of Lam's *City on Fire* (1987), where Chow Yun-fat and Danny Lee meet a similar end. A couple of years later, Sanjay Gupta remade Woo's 'heroic bloodshed' classic *A Better Tomorrow* (1986) as *Aatish* (1994), reworking its story of a Triad member and his cop younger brother. If this sounds familiar, there's a reason. In 1979, *Deewar* was loosely remade in Hong Kong as *The Brothers*. The film was a success, and very likely gave *A Better Tomorrow* its warring-brothers plot.

OUT OF THE BLUE, INTO THE BLACK

A new decade brought a series of slick, violent films about larger-than-life anti-heroes. Mukul Anand's *Agneepath* (1990), a reworking of Brian De Palma's 1983 *Scarface,* was to *Parinda* what *Vaastav* was to *Satya*: a flashy gangster film made for a mass audience, blunt and effective. Though the film ends up ironing out the psychosexual kinks of Tony Montana and softening Amitabh Bachchan's gravel-voiced mafia don somewhat, Anand has a considerable gift for visual snap and crackle. His Leone-like close-ups and elaborate action sequences must have registered with Varma – the Telugu director was just starting to use these tricks himself (as seen in the previous chapter, Bhau's murder in *Satya* has much in common with the assassination attempt on the beach here). Ghai's *Khal Nayak* (1993), starring Sanjay Dutt as a killer-for-hire and Madhuri Dixit as the woman sent to entrap him, was in a similar vein. *Ram Jaane* (1995) was a lurid remake of *Angels with Dirty Faces* (1938), with Shah Rukh Khan in the James Cagney part. But another film released around that time allowed its gangsters some psychological depth.

In Shashilal K. Nair's *Angaar* (1992), Jackie Shroff plays slum-dweller Jaggu, who takes on the criminals and leaders trying to raze the *chawl* he lives in and build high-rises there. The film lays out in some detail the politician–builder–mafia nexus that had taken over Mumbai real estate (which we see echoed six years later in *Satya*). There were whispers even then of Nair's links to the mafia. Perhaps this had some bearing on the uncommonly nuanced treatment of the gangster figures, especially the godfather-like Jahangir (Kader Khan) – loosely based on Karim Lala – and his son Majid (Nana Patekar). Jahangir has a quiet forcefulness, like Dilip Kumar's reluctant don from *Vidhaata*. And Majid is a wonderfully shaded character – a terrible human being but also wounded and thoughtful, capable of mass murder but also full of concern for his wife and special-needs son. The film anticipates *Satya* in the matter-of-factness of its violence, and the way this is juxtaposed with humour. In the opening minutes, a man is being beaten bloody by Farid (Mazhar Khan), Jahangir's other son. Jahangir lightly admonishes him, and soon, the two are joking about Farid putting on weight.

There's an eerie footnote to *Angaar*. It builds up to a sequence in which bombs planted by Jaggu as payback for the destruction of the *chawl* level Majid's empty skyscrapers. The film released in September 1992. Six months later, actual bombs planted by gangsters went off in Bombay, ripping through offices and markets; only these ones weren't empty.

The moral universe was still that of the '70s, with the hero's descent into crime blamed on society. *Gardish* (1993) ends with Jackie Shroff crying that he didn't want to be a criminal, but that his friends and family, the legal system and society made him one. Priyadarshan's film does have some remarkable sequences, though. The murder by the sea is startling in its directness – a benign-looking man in a kurta walking up to a politician in a Gandhi *topi* being led along by a young boy, greeting him calmly and shooting him in the head (he ends up buried under a pile of oranges – *The Godfather* is never far away). And there's a great set piece where Shroff is chased through a traffic jam by armed goons. The camera moves from the thick of the action to a high-angle view – something Varma does several times for dramatic effect in *Satya* – as Shroff jumps from the roof of one black-and-yellow taxi to another. As with the murder under the umbrellas in *Arjun*, the pursuit down the temple steps in *Parinda* and the shooting of Guru Narayan with the train passing underneath in *Satya*, *Gardish*'s chase is beautifully integrated with the city.

The collision of genre filmmaking and everyday Bombay life informs the best gangster set pieces, like the kidnapping in broad daylight that opens *Is Raat Ki Subah Nahin* (1996). In Sudhir Mishra's neo-noir, a philandering adman finds himself on the run from a gangster having a very bad night. The film had the most limited release imaginable, and isn't spoken of by anyone today except a handful of critics yammering on about it being a cult film (a couple of them are me). Its obscurity is unfortunate, for the film is both a forerunner of *Satya* and a different sort of crime film altogether. A combination of moody noir, gangster film and social satire, it was hardly noticed at the time, though one can see its belated influence on nocturnal narratives such as Reema Kagti's *Talaash* (2012) and Anurag Kashyap's *Raman Raghav 2.0* (2016). An explosive scene early on has gangster Ramanbhai (Ashish Vidyarthi) confronting Vilas (Saurabh Shukla), a former associate who now wants him dead. The two of them yell like estranged siblings, reminding each other of sacrifices made in the past. This pained outburst of backstory is startlingly close to the scene in *Satya* where Bheeku Mhatre spews out his history with Guru Narayan before killing him. It's easy to imagine Shukla recalling this scene while writing *Satya* a year later. (Ramanbhai also says '*Maar maar maar maar*' (shoot me) just like Bheeku does in his prison fight with Satya.)

Mishra's film carried forward an idea from *Parinda*: distinct personalities for all the criminals. Instead of a gang boss and a bunch of faceless henchmen, you got the quiet one, the hothead, the guy with the stone in his shoe, the overenthusiastic youngster (there's also the grieving stranger who helps out Vilas, one of the most mysterious characters to grace the genre). *Is Raat* also allowed for representations of members of the mob as everyday people. There's a great comic scene with Ramanbhai at home, trying to keep his cool as he unsuccessfully attempts to reach someone on the phone while his father criticises him, his sister tries to get him to give her husband a job and a priest conducts prayers loudly in another room.

The mundanity was key. Hindi cinema had never allowed its gangsters to be regulars guys – they were either streets goons or psychopaths or suave businessmen. Here, they were ordinary, but also complex and affecting – more so than the shallow high-society crowd they brush up against.

The movement from country to town (even if it's one scene at the start), seen in films from *Shree 420* to *Deewar* to *Agneepath*, was no longer the dominant trajectory. 'We are trapped inside the city; the extended initiation in violence makes the character an expert user of the city, whose slums and lanes are choreographed into a performance of shock and survival,' Moinak Biswas wrote about *Maqbool* (2003) – but you could argue this was already the case by the mid '90s. Deprived of the essential fallback of the village, the Bombay gangster found himself with nowhere to escape to, no memories of a more innocent time and place.

We're almost at *Satya* now, but there's one significant forerunner left. It's a gangster film, but no one thinks of it as one because it takes place in the countryside. Shekhar Kapur's *Bandit Queen* is based on the life of Phoolan Devi, a famous dacoit who later became a member of Parliament. It premiered at the Cannes Film Festival in May 1994. Before the film could release in India, though, it had to pass the censors. The Central Board of Film Certification asked for cuts in profanity, references to caste and scenes of sexual violence, which Kapur and producer Bobby Bedi refused to make. Over the next year, they went through every stage of India's opaque censorship process, finally challenging the decision in the Supreme Court. They won, and the film released in January 1996, a year and a half after its first showing.

This might be a good time to assure readers I haven't skipped over an entire genre. The dacoit, or *daaku*, is a hugely important figure in Indian cinema, more widely used and recognisable up until the '80s than the urban criminal. In Mehboob's classic *Mother India*, Nargis' matriarch ends up having to shoot her own son, a bandit, played by Sunil Dutt. *Ganga Jumna* (1961), with Dilip Kumar as a farmer compelled to become a dacoit, was another big hit; its cop brother versus *daaku* brother plot was a precursor to *Deewar*. And Hindi cinema's most famous villain, Gabbar Singh, played by Amjad Khan in *Sholay* (1975), was a *daaku* with a price on his head. I haven't dealt with the dacoit figure in this book because it's not just a different ballpark, it's a different ballgame. The dacoit film has its own codes, history, cultural markers. It's like trying to view the Western and the Hollywood gangster film as one big genre, differentiated only by setting.

Film academic Lalitha Gopalan has written in her book *Cinema of Interruptions* about how *Hathyar* straddles the Western and gangster genres, moving from the former to the latter as the action moves from village to city. Theorist and critic M.K. Raghavendra too notes a thematic consistency between Dutta's rural action films, *Ghulami* (1985), *Yateem* (1988) and *Batwara* (1989), and the largely Bombay-set *Hathyar*, writing: 'In Indian cinema a *daku* film that moves to the city becomes a gangster film.' Given the vastly different environments they operate in, this seems an overstatement; for instance, caste dynamics play a huge role in *daaku* films, but are absent in gangster films. Still, it's a fascinating idea. One can see this movement from dacoit to gangster in Raj Kapoor's *Awara*. K.N. Singh starts off as the *daaku* Jagga, who takes revenge on the magistrate who put him in jail by kidnapping his wife, who, unbeknownst to her husband, is pregnant. When he releases her, the lawman refuses to believe their soon-to-be-born son is his. Jagga is initially shown in standard dacoit attire: dhoti, kurta, shawl. His men ride horses. Like all self-respecting bandits, he has a moustache. He says that his father before him was a *daaku*, and his father before him. But when we meet Jagga years later in Mumbai, he's the head of a street gang. He's traded the kurta for trousers and shirt. He's clean-shaven, though still menacing; and he carries a knife. The judge's boy, Raj (Raj Kapoor), whom he's trained to be a thief, does a stick-'em-up routine as a joke with him. Jagga is a character in a gangster film now, even if the others aren't. You can see the same transition years later in *Parvarish* (1977), with Amjad Khan starting the film as a dacoit with a turban and a rifle, and surfacing later as a suit-wearing mob boss.

Even as I excuse myself from the *daaku* film, I have to talk about *Bandit Queen*, which loomed large in the mind of Ram Gopal Varma in 1997. Though he knew he wasn't going to be able to attempt anything like it in commercial cinema, Varma was canny enough to realise that its gains might be appropriated. Kapur's film was far outside the mainstream, but the year-long battle with the censors had brought it into the limelight, and helped shift the goalposts of what could be shown on Indian movie screens. Varma borrowed its vivid realism, making his Mumbai rough and immediate, just as Kapur's Chambal valley had been art-film gritty. 'I want to portray stark reality', he said in late 1997, 'as Shekhar Kapur did in *Bandit Queen*.'

The film lit a fire under young cinephiles at the time. One such fan was director Dibakar Banerjee, who described in an interview how *Bandit Queen* seemed to capture the violence and upheaval of the times – the rise of Hindu nationalism; the protests surrounding the implementation of caste-based reservations; and the Bombay riots of 1992–93. Another was Anurag Kashyap. '*Bandit Queen* was still banned when Sriram (Raghavan) sourced a VHS copy of it for one night,' he said. 'We watched it on a small television set in a packed room, with some people standing.' Its influence is still strong. Abhishek Chaubey's brilliant revisionist *daaku* film, *Sonchiriya* (2019), had Manoj Bajpayee as dacoit Maan Singh (he'd played a Maan Singh in Kapur's film as well) and, in a smaller role,

Sampa Mandal as Phuliya, the name by which Phoolan Devi was known in those parts.

Bandit Queen inspired *Satya* to speak freely and foully. Kapur, never shy of claiming credit, has said that his censorship battles cleared the ground for *Satya* and for Kashyap's invective-filled films. The cussing in *Satya* isn't as heavy-duty as *Bandit Queen*, but is actually a bigger breakthrough given that Varma was operating in a commercial space (and not the lenient art film world), and that he manoeuvred his expletives past the censors without them apparently realising it. But the most visible link between the two films is the many *Bandit Queen* crew members who later worked on *Satya*: action director Allan Amin, actors Manoj Bajpayee, Saurabh Shukla, Aditya Srivastava, Govind Namdev. Kannan Iyer, an assistant on Kapur's film, helped with casting on *Satya*. Even cinematographer Mazhar Kamran might have been sought out on the basis of a Kapur referral.

That a dacoit film was one of the biggest influences on *Satya*, an urban crime film, isn't so strange. As we'll see in the next chapter, Varma's film found inspiration in even unlikelier places. I'll pick up the thread of post-*Satya* gangster cinema later. For the moment, it's time to take to the streets.

4

Bombay on Film

'When I first came to Bombay from Hyderabad to shoot Rangeela, *I couldn't get over the experience of a train ride through Dharavi. To me it looked like one single roof and I couldn't believe that people actually lived there. I saw two-year-olds crawling just about three feet away from the railway track where trains were rushing to and fro. I was fascinated by the busy, business-like atmosphere of Mumbai.'*

– Ram Gopal Varma, *Guns & Thighs*

There is the filmic city. And there is the city film. Once it went by Bombay, or Bambai; now it's Mumbai. The filmic city may resemble the actual one, but it's really a gigantic movie set. Certain roads, buildings, vantage points appear in film after film, become markers of a certain idea of progress, or modernity, or glamour. Gyan Prakash wrote about growing up in Bihar and getting his impressions of Bombay from Hindi cinema: 'Songs and films introduced me to fabulous bits and pieces of the city, although I knew little of Bombay's actual topography. I understood the city only as a configuration of powerful symbols. Marine Drive, Chowpatty and Juhu Beach lodged in my mind as emotive images. The shots of the gigantic Victoria Terminus – crowded with travellers, coolies, taxi drivers, beggars, touts, and con men – called to mind the city's immense size and population.' A little later, he adds, 'Hindi cinema stood for Bombay, even if the city appeared only fleetingly on-screen.' This line hints at the divide between the filmic city and the real thing – the place where people take buses and trains, but without romanticising them; where people dream of living in a Bombay like the one they've seen in the movies. You don't see this city often onscreen. Directors will tell you it's because shooting there is impossible, but the truth is it's easier to keep selling the dream.

There's not much separating the real city and the cinematic one, especially if you're bent on not noticing the difference. In Hrishikesh Mukherjee's *Guddi* (1971), Jaya Bachchan's movie-obsessed schoolgirl is visiting Bombay. There's a brief glimpse of the real city in the traffic around Victoria Terminus, though the station is such a typical marker of Bombay that it belongs more to the cinematic realm than the physical one. Mukherjee proceeds to frame the ride home as a series of painted movie billboards glimpsed by Guddi from the car window. We hear fragments of movie dialogue. 'Dedo Pyar Lelo Pyar', a song from a film starring Guddi's celebrity crush, Dharmendra, plays on the soundtrack. There's a whole metropolis out there, but Guddi only has eyes for cinematic Bombay.

The opening credits of Ram Gopal Varma's *Rangeela* conflates the two realms as well. Each crew member's name is accompanied by a still image of a movie star – Madhubala, Dev Anand, Meena Kumari. The soundtrack, instead of a musical score, is street noise:

autos groaning, buses honking, dogs barking. It's a stunningly effective way to begin a film that's set both in middle-class Bombay and the world of movie-making. In *Rangeela*, the city's a film set and everyone's always performing, as if some cosmic director had forgotten to call 'cut'.

When Varma was making *Rangeela*, he barely knew the city. After the film released, he moved to Mumbai and began to examine it with the curious eye of an outsider. Compare *Rangeela* to *Satya*, released three years later, and you can tell the difference – one in love with the idea of Mumbai, the other seeing the city for what it is. *Satya* is what you get when you boil Mumbai down: a combustible mixture of loud, fast, emotive, enterprising and desperate. It's not a pretty metropolis, whatever residents may tell you, and Varma knows this. 'What makes *Satya* particularly interesting is its aesthetic strategy, which establishes Bombay as a giant garbage dump,' Ranjani Mazumdar writes in *Bombay Cinema*. This might seem harsh, but only if you haven't lived there. It's why the scene with Satya and Vidya chatting on the roof is so liberating – for once, the framing is expansive and there's nothing but blue sky in the background. Immediately after, the film returns us to a dark room, as if we don't deserve open spaces any more than the characters do.

To look at *Satya* is to look not only at earlier gangster films but also at *27 Down* (1974) and *Salaam Bombay* (1988), which have nothing to do with organised crime. Some of the films I discuss in this chapter will seem very distant from the world of *Satya*. Dilip Dhawan's minor-league thug in *Albert Pinto Ko Gussa Kyoon Aata Hai* (1980) isn't anywhere as dangerous as Bheeku Mhtare, but they have the same wild look in their eyes, the same swagger. Shammi Kapoor singing 'Govinda Aala Re Aala' in *Bluff Master* (1963) is as far removed in tone and tenor as possible from the killing of Bhau.

Yet, it's the same feverish energy, the same dense assembly of bodies, just a different purpose and outcome.

'AND CITY OF BOMBAY'

Like the other Navketan films of the 1950s, Chetan Anand's *Taxi Driver* (1954) is at best an intermittent noir. Switching from hardboiled posturing to softboiled love story, it shows the influence of American B-movies but doesn't have their toughness or cynicism. Its interest in crime is limited to the knife-wielding goons Mangal (Dev Anand) saves Mala (Kalpana Kartik) from and then fends off at regular intervals, and the lively, rough atmosphere of the dive bar, with card games and Sylvie the smitten dancer (Sheila Ramani). Yet, there is one respect in which this film, a big hit, can be seen as an early link in a long chain leading up to *Satya*.

The opening credits of *Taxi Driver* could trip up the keenest collector of Hindi film trivia. Just when you're congratulating yourself for knowing who Bhagwan Sinha is, along come Shujju and Patanjal. There's Vernon Corke, making his only film appearance – a happy by-product of being the Anands' landlord at a time in their careers when the quantum of rent probably mattered a great deal (that's Vernon on guitar, along with his sister-in-law and son, in the musical number 'Dil Se Mila Ke Dil Pyar'). And there's Hameed Sayani, a name not many will know today, though '50s audiences would have recognised the radio announcer, magician and elder brother of Ameen Sayani, host of Radio Ceylon's massively popular *Binaca Geetmala*.

The most unusual credit is the last cast member: 'And city of Bombay'. It is, however, well-deserved. Chetan Anand went out of his way to incorporate the city in *Taxi Driver*. Perhaps he had one eye on the American B-movies that had increasingly begun to use real locations by the latter half of the '40s. But this was also an economic decision. After two failures, Anand didn't have the funds for studio shooting. So he and Dev hit the streets, attaching a lightweight Éclair camera, imported from France, to the bonnet of a Hillman Minx*. In his autobiography, *Romancing with Life*, Dev recalled: 'We would all leave early in the morning, slog the whole day long, canning the maximum footage possible minus the soundtrack, leaving the dubbing of dialogues to be done at the post production stage, and come back home late in the evenings.'

It may have been born of necessity, but the film's commitment to location shooting lends it a freewheeling look denied to its studio-bound brethren. Bombay audiences at the time must have enjoyed seeing their everyday city on film. Sylvie gets into a taxi at Berry's restaurant in Churchgate and, as the opening credits are ending, steps out of Mangal's cab with a date at the Taj Mahal Hotel in Colaba. Later in the film, we're shown Kala Ghoda, with glimpses of the David Sassoon Library and Watson's Hotel, where, in 1896, the first motion-picture screenings in India took place. There's Eros Cinema, showing Disney's *Peter Pan* (1953). The documentary quality is underlined by reactions at the corners of the frame, which suggest that not everyone was a paid extra, or even pre-warned that a shoot was going to take place. Two men dressed in whites and caps, possibly US Navy, turn and stare as Kalpana Kartik, dressed as a boy, sprints past them. A man in a turban emerges from a building and shyly waves at the camera – a moment that's obviously staged and completely charming.

---

* Before the black-and-yellow Premier Padmini (also known as Fiat 1100 Delight) established itself as the quintessential Bombay taxi, the British-made Hillman Minx was a popular choice. Dev Anand's first car was a Minx.

Taxi Driver predates the fly-by-the-seat approach adopted by the filmmakers of the French New Wave a few years later. Anand's feature isn't as innovative or playful as the films that Varda and Godard and Truffaut would make, but it does share with them a certain freshness and an eye for urban poetry. Raoul Coutard shot Godard's game-changing debut, *Breathless* (1960), with an Éclair Cameflex, lightweight and good for hand-held shots – the same camera Anand had used. Anand not only beat the New Wave directors in putting the Éclair to use, but also Orson Welles, who used it for *Touch of Evil* in 1958 (the unbroken three-and-a-half-minute travelling shot that kicks off the film is one the most famous opening sequences of all time).

Ranjani Mazumdar writes of a similarity between sequences in *Taxi Driver* and *Satya*: Mala (in drag) being chased by street kids who think she's a boy, and Guru Narayan chased by Satya and Bheeku; though the only real similarity I see is a sprint up railway platform stairs (decades later, there's another desperate dash up a Bombay railway platform in *Is Raat Ki Subah Nahin*, and a comic one in the Manoj Bajpayee series *The Family Man*). In a broader sense, the thread that connects these two is that they're both films of the Bombay streets. They are primarily shot on location. They engage with the infrastructure of the city – roads and buses and housing.

You can map the changing topography of Bombay through its films. In *Taxi Driver*, the statue of the Prince of Wales, later King Edward VII, on his horse, which gave the neighbourhood its name (*kala ghoda* is Hindi for 'black horse'), can be seen for a few seconds as Dev Anand drives with Johnny Walker onto Mahatma Gandhi Road. Four years later, in *Chalti Ka Naam Gaadi* (1958), a comedy starring Madhubala and siblings Ashok, Kishore and Anoop Kumar, you get a better look at the statue, across the road from the David Sassoon Library and the Army & Navy Building. You can also see it for a shaky second in another Kishore Kumar-starrer, *Mr X in Bombay* (1964), in a sequence with quite possibly the worst trick effects ever committed to film (*Mr X* saves its actual location shooting for the 'Mere Mehboob Qayamat Hogi' number, with Kumar wandering morosely around the Gateway of India and Apollo Bunder). A year later, the installation was gone, a wave of nationalistic sentiment relegating it and other British-era statues to Byculla. In 2017, the *ghoda* returned, but without its colonial baggage. A new statue of a riderless black horse was introduced where the old one used to be. The original stands, frozen in mid-canter, in the Byculla Zoo.

The movies weren't finished with the horse, though. In Muzaffar Ali's *Gaman* (1978), this conversation takes place between a cabbie and his friend as they drive through Kala Ghoda:

'There was a statue of a big black horse here. He belonged to the king. He was like lightning. Like Rana Pratap's Chetak.'

'Why was it removed?'

'Why do you think? The horse was English.'

TALKING BAMBAIYYA

If *Taxi Driver* was a new way of seeing, *Aar-Paar* (1954) was a new way of speaking. Guru Dutt's film was an early example of the colourful polyglot style familiar to viewers across India as Mumbai street slang. 'It's my belief that with *Aar-Paar*, we started the trend of modern writing in Hindi film,' screenwriter Abrar Alvi says in Nasreen Munni Kabir's documentary *In Search of Guru Dutt* (1989). 'You see in today's films, there's a lot of Bambaiyya inflection, different dialects. That wasn't the case back then. Films used to have very theatrical language.'

'In a city of migrants, where new migrants meet old ones, language tends to acquire a life of its own,' writes Mazumdar. Alvi, who'd go on to write Dutt's *Pyaasa* and *Kaagaz Ke Phool* (1959), looked to Bombay's different communities, migrant and resident, for inspiration in *Aar-Paar*. The hero, Kalu, played by Dutt, is from southern Madhya Pradesh, and is given some unusual linguistic tics, like referring to himself in the third person. His employer, a burly garage owner, has a thick Punjabi twang. Johnny Walker speaks typical fractured Parsee Hindi. A young Jagdeep, as Kalu's sidekick, is a predecessor of the chatty *taporis* Aamir Khan would later play. '(Alvi) used absolute spoken language of his time,' Kashyap told me, adding that he tried to bring a similar 'spoken-ness' to *Satya*.

In the '70s, Bombayspeak became as strong a marker of the city as anything else. Mehmood's bus conductor uses phrases and constructions typical to the middle and working classes – '*tumko kidhar jaane ka?*' (where do you want to go?), '*aap se paisa kaun maangta hai?*' (who's asking you for money?) – in the road trip comedy *Bombay to Goa* (1972). This was Amitabh Bachchan's first significant solo starring role. Five years later, by which time he'd become the biggest star in Hindi cinema, another film of his had audiences across India trying to talk like a *tapori*. *Amar Akbar Anthony* mixed melodrama with screwball, Kader Khan writing Bachchan's dialogue as funny hardboiled patter, Bombay in every syllable. Khan repeated the trick the next year in *Muqaddar Ka Siqandar* (1978), though this time it wasn't Bachchan who said '*apan*' and '*akkha*', but the film's villain, played by a seething Amjad Khan.

Even the non-commercial titles of the time were forging a more authentic Bombay speech. In Muzaffar Ali's *Gaman* (1978), our first impression of the city as an intimidating place for a small-town visitor is established through language. Ghulam (Farooq Shaikh) gets off the train that's brought him from his village and boards a bus with his luggage and bedding. The bus pulls away, and we hear overlapping snatches of brusque dialogue as it moves through the city streets:

'*magachmari nahi karne ka*' (don't mess with my head), '*seedha* police station *gaadi leke jayenga*' (I'll take this vehicle straight to the police station), '*saatve aasman pe chadela*' (he's in seventh heaven). Saeed Akhtar Mirza, too, would update the *Aar-Paar* argot for his brash street philosophers in *Albert Pinto Ko Gussa Kyoon Aata Hai* and *Salim Langde Pe Mat Ro* (1989).

Varma's *Rangeela* pushed this sort of colourful chatter to its extreme. Here's an exchange between Munna, seller of movie tickets in 'black', and his tout friend:

'*Kaisa chal raha hai dhanda?*' (How's business?)

'Solid *bole toh, paisa laane ka,* taxi *mein jaane ka, kya?*' (Solid, making money, cruising in taxis?)

This was a culmination of what Alvi was trying to achieve with *Aar-Paar* all those years ago – a hustling of language, rhythmic, built for both speed and effect. 'People come here from all over India with their languages like Gujarati, Marathi, Bengali,' *Rangeela* writer Sanjay Chhel told Mazumdar. 'All these languages merge to form a unique language of survival in the city, to stubbornly fight for existence in the city. This language is understood by all. This is a language of the street, with its own texture. It may not be grammatical, but this Bambaiyya language is hard-hitting and satirical.'

There's a difference in the Bambaiyya Hindi spoken in *Rangeela* and *Satya*. *Rangeela* is a musical – a kind of fairy tale – and the language is appropriately *filmi*. *Satya* is rougher, more direct. It would be surprising to hear someone in *Rangeela* say 'game *baja rahe the*' (did a number on someone). In *Satya*, it's used in two contexts: to murder and to have sex. That *Rangeela* sounded authentic wasn't surprising – it had a cast full of Mumbaikars, and two writers (Chhel and Neeraj Vora) who were familiar with the city. It's a testament to the keen ears of Kashyap and Shukla, both of whom are from Uttar Pradesh, and the adaptable performers who spoke their lines, that *Satya*, a film bursting with north Indians and directed by a Hyderabadi, was convincing in its Mumbai speech rhythms.

Chander showing Satya his new quarters is a masterclass in Mumbaispeak. On the way, in the autorickshaw, the jolly gangster explains how he went from 'Chander *motu*' (fatso) to 'Chander *bhai*' ('brother' in Hindi, but also Mumbai slang for a made man). He addresses Satya as '*bhidu*' (dude) and the driver as '*khajue*' (who knows, really? Possibly the plural of *khajoor* (date), slang for a daft person). More Mumbai talk on the way in: '*apna-ich mohalla*' (our hood), '*bindaas rehne ka*' (stay cool), '*ekdum mast*' (totally chill), '*lafda*' (trouble), '*thoda rush maangta hai*' (you want a bit of a rush), '*kalti*' (scram). Some gangster lingo: '*game baja daala*' (bump someone off), '*ghoda*' (revolver). Pager becomes '*chidiya*' (bird), mobile phone is '*kauwa*' (crow). Chander throws open the door and says, without a hint of irony, '*Ekdum jhakaas*' (just superb), as if he was showing Satya his room at the Taj Hotel and not a boxy one-room in a *chawl*. The capper: '*Ek TV, ek fridge ...*' – he looks around – '*... aur ek bhagwaan bhi diya*' (He's given you a TV, a fridge ... and a god). Kashyap wrote the scene; Barnali Ray Shukla says Snehal Dabi ad-libbed '*bhagwaan bhi diya*'. In a great bit of consistency, Chander uses the same 'TV, fridge' construction later on in his Ram-Shyam joke before the shootout at the under-construction building – also a scene written by Kashyap.

THE CITY ON FOOT

Fourteen years after *Taxi Driver*, it was Chetan Anand again who found a new way to look at Bombay. Then, he'd changed the method, grabbing a light camera and heading out of the studio. In *Aakhri Khat* (1966), he changed the point of view, transforming the city by showing it through the eyes of a toddler let loose on its streets.

Aakhri Khat is one of the most unusual Hindi films ever – part romantic melodrama, part vérité experiment. Govind (Rajesh Khanna in his first starring role) falls in love with village girl Lajjo (Indrani Mukherjee) in the hills of Kullu. He leaves to study art in Bombay, and she finds out she's pregnant with their child. With infant Buntu (Bunty Behl, then 15 months old) in tow, she heads to the city in search of her lover. Hungry, broke and suffering from what appears to be a heart ailment, she considers leaving the child on Govind's doorstep along with an *aakhri khat* (last letter), but can't go through with it. She leaves the letter and heads off with the child. But she dies soon, leaving Govind the impossible task of finding his infant son whom he's never laid eyes on in a crowded metropolis.

It sounds weepy beyond belief, but Anand's approach is anything but conventional. The audacious opening credits set the tone. The film starts with a car pulling up to a railway junction, mournful plucks of the sitar giving way to rock 'n' roll piano and sax as the signal lifts and it speeds away. By the time the director credit appears, almost seven minutes have elapsed, Lajjo and Buntu have been introduced, day has turned to night and Khayyam's already eclectic score has been interrupted by church music, temple chants and azaans. There's even a quick flashback. If all this had happened in a European or American film, it would've been hailed as an impossibly brilliant subversion of the very idea of opening credits.*

---

* This sort of energetic opening was seen in several films in the late '60s, an experimental time in Hindi cinema. The crowded streets of Agra clatter by in the first scenes of *Sara Akash* (Basu Chatterjee, 1969) as if viewed from a speeding tonga. In *Bhuvan Shome* (Mrinal Sen, 1970), the credits unfold over the image of a railway track as seen from the front of a moving train, accompanied by a furious *taan* on the soundtrack. S.N.S. Sastry's captivating short *I Am 20* (1967), made for

Anand parcels out Lajjo's story in short flashbacks that continue well into *Aakhri Khat*, even after she's dead. By the time the viewer is aware of why she's in Bombay and what happened between her and Govind, Buntu is already negotiating the city on his own. This cut-up style of storytelling was novel enough for Hindi cinema at the time, but more radical still is how Anand imagines a child's-eye view of a city. The scenes with Buntu wandering the streets, straying onto railway tracks, crying for his mother, grabbing food and balloons and sparklers, are unlike anything else in Hindi cinema (in a mildly shocking scene, he lies down on the tracks and a train passes above him). Cameraperson Jal Mistry does a terrific job of following the child as he waddles around, stumbles and looks for instruction, though the cinematographer probably heaved a sigh of relief in the scenes where he was asked to shoot more conventionally (the elegant 'Rut Jawan Jawan', picturised on singer Bhupinder Singh, is a whole different world).

This isn't a Bombay of dreams; it isn't even the exciting, low-down Bombay of *Taxi Driver*. There isn't a familiar building or tourist spot shown in the entire film. These may not be mean streets, but they're unsparing, and everyone's looking out only for themselves (though several people stop to talk to Buntu, no one bothers to find out where his parents are). Fifty years after its release, *Aakhri Khat* still feels audacious. Anand probably regarded it as an art film aimed at a festival-going audience. It wasn't popular then, and it's hardly remembered today, but it brought the immediacy of handheld documentary-like photography to bear on Bombay. And it was a step towards the sort of city shooting that would be explored more

Films Division, the newsreel wing of the government, also has a frenetic beginning, intercutting faces of young men and women with scenery seemingly captured from a moving train.

fully in the '80s and lead to the gritty Mumbai aesthetic that *Satya*
would draw on.

In the '70s, the drive to document the city faded from commercial
cinema. Mumbai was often the setting, but you didn't see the streets
much anymore – just cultural shorthand like police uniforms,
accents, beaches. Apart from fleeting glimpses of Mumbai landmarks
– the Mahalaxmi *dhobi ghat* in *Don* (1978), the docks in *Deewar*
(1975) – the city was largely absent in the films of Manmohan Desai,
Ramesh Sippy, Yash Chopra and Prakash Mehra. The most famous
showdown of the decade, Amitabh Bachchan and Shashi Kapoor
meeting under the bridge in *Deewar*, was shot in a studio, on a set
created by art director Desh Mukherjee. Bachchan may have been
a hero of the masses, but directors couldn't place him among those
masses. Yet, while it was close to impossible to shoot with huge stars
in public places, an Amol Palekar sighting was less likely to cause a
riot. And so the real Bombay started showing up in middle-of-the-
road and art films.

Basu Chatterjee is usually bracketed with Hrishikesh Mukherjee
as a master of Middle Cinema, a uniquely Indian genre that gets
its name from the middle-class milieu of its films, and from being
situated at the midpoint of art cinema and the straightforwardly
commercial. There are many similarities in the approach and subject
matter of these two filmmakers, though Chatterjee, to my mind,
had the better eye. In several of his '70s films, he photographed
Bombay beautifully. *Chhoti Si Baat* (1976) immortalised the city's
once-ubiquitous bright-red BEST buses. The 'Rim Jhim Gire Saawan'
sequence in *Manzil* (1979), with Bachchan and Moushumi Chatterjee
wandering around Churchgate, soaked and happy, was a vision of
Bombay rains unequalled in any film. *Piya Ka Ghar* (1972) had local
trains, a walk-and-talk on Marine Drive – and a spot-on Bombay
real estate joke. A priest, trying to sell Jaya Bachchan's family on

marriage to a prospective groom, mentions that the boy's apartment is in a building called Rajmahal – 'king's palace'. The next shot is of the building – dilapidated, dourly functional, like most affordable housing in the city.

Chatterjee isn't the first, or 15th, name that comes to mind when *Rangeela* is mentioned. Yet, remove the songs and the MTV gloss from Varma's 1995 film and what you're left with is a story of middle-class citizens trying to move up in life – something Chatterjee repeatedly explored in his work. One of the most surprising stories in *Guns & Thighs* is Varma saying he saw *Chitchor*, Chatterjee's delightful 1976 romantic comedy, seven times in the theatre. 'The simplicity of narration that I learnt from it', he writes, 'was pretty much what shaped my vision of *Rangeela*.'

Even in *Satya*, there's a passage that has the feel of a Chatterjee film. The montage that accompanies the dolorous 'Badalon Se', with Chakravarthy and Urmila wandering near Girgaum Chowpatty, isn't far removed from Chatterjee's famous getting-to-know-you sequences in *Rajnigandha* (1974) and *Baton Baton Mein* (1979). The playback artist, Bhupinder, had sung 'Do Deewane Shehar Mein' in *Gharonda* (1977), a film written by Gulzar, another Middle Cinema practitioner. It's a rare romantic song unfolding in working-class surroundings; Zarina Wahab and Amol Palekar walk around a building site as labourers carry bricks and lay cement. 'Badalon Se', similarly, places Satya and Vidya in a fishing village, eating at a roadside stall the same way a daily wager would, before returning them to the temple, the bazaar and the crowded streets.

In his dyspeptic essay film *Los Angeles Plays Itself* (2003), Thom Andersen reflects on the differences between cinematic L.A. and the actual city in which he lives. Towards the end, the voiceover offers a small ray of hope. 'But there is another city … and another cinema. A city of walkers, a cinema of walking … Who knows the city? Only those who walk, only those who ride the bus.' The idea that a city belongs first and foremost to those who walk its streets and use public transport is a powerful one. You can see it in the quintessential Bombay films – in the cabs taken and driven in *Aar-Paar* and *Taxi Driver* and *Gaman*, the innocent jaywalking of Buntu in *Aakhri Khat*, the many bus journeys and leisurely strolls in Chatterjee's films. Yet, central as black-and-yellow taxis and red buses have been to its image, the city runs on another transport network. In 1974, a remarkable film paid tribute to Bombay and its trains.

Awtar Krishna Kaul's *27 Down*, with its freeze frames and ellipses, is closer to a European New Wave film than an Indian parallel cinema title. Sanjay (M.K. Raina) wants to study art but comes under pressure from his domineering father to get a job. He becomes a railway ticket-checker, but drifts through life unsatisfied. Kaul's film was shot almost entirely on location. Though it mostly takes place in crowded rail bogeys and cramped flats, it looks like a grungy dream, photographed in high-contrast black-and-white by A.K. Bir. One particularly memorable high-angle shot shows the arrival of a train at Chhatrapati Shivaji Terminus. Even before it slows to a halt, passengers jump off – a Bombay custom that's second nature to residents and terrifying to newcomers. It takes all of 10 seconds for the empty platform to become a thick swarm of bustling bodies. All those worker ants, and somewhere in this mass of humanity, a man without a plan.

CITY OF DECAY

In 1976, the other *Taxi Driver* released, the one by the fast-talking kid from Little Italy. Martin Scorsese's film showed a New York crawling with junkies and hustlers, pimps and prostitutes – an all-encompassing 'filth' in the head of Travis Bickle, the Vietnam vet who decides to clean it up. The spirit, if not the influence, of *Taxi Driver* was palpable in a Hindi film released two years later. Saeed Akhtar Mirza's *Arvind Desai Ki Ajeeb Dastaan* (1978) is about a directionless young man in Bombay who, like Travis, is revolted by the ugliness of his big-city surroundings. Unlike Travis, he's too much of a slacker to do anything about it, but his complaints, often voiced in a moving vehicle with a jazz score in the background, have similar qualities of self-hatred and sexual frustration.

There are other parallels with *Taxi Driver*. Arvind visits a sex worker, experiences bouts of loneliness, ends up pointing a revolver at his head. But it's really the look of *Arvind Desai*, and the prevailing mood of decay and corruption, which mirrors Scorsese's film. Mirza's Bombay isn't picturesque; it's grimy, muddy, lashed by rain. The rot encompasses all of society. Over lunch in a dimly lit restaurant, Arvind (Dilip Dhawan) points out a 'demolition contractor' to Alice, his secretary and girlfriend. 'He'll clear anything in half an hour.' He waves to somebody else. 'Friends. They're in advertising. They sell everything.' He won't even spare himself. 'We're such clean people, aren't we? Can't stand a mess or stench. Remove it, or put colour or perfume on it. Beautify this shit.'

Though *Arvind Desai* released in 1978, it can be grouped with such '80s films as *Ardh Satya*, *Jaane Bhi Do Yaaro* and *Parinda*, works united in their depiction of a city on edge. Other directors were heading in that direction too. The couple in *Gharonda* puts money down on a flat only to be swindled by the broker, which forces them to follow through on a heartless scheme (decades later, the same thing happens to the ill-fated immigrant couple in Hansal Mehta's *CityLights*, 2014). Even the mild Basu Chatterjee ended the decade on a worried note. In *Manzil*, Amitabh Bachchan's Ajay is so desperate to appear wealthy that he borrows a suit and car from a better-off friend to keep up appearances. He starts a business selling scientific precision instruments but is betrayed by his supplier and taken to court.

The malcontent was spreading. In Mani Kaul's *Arrival* (1980), a wordless documentary short, the city drags itself through a long, gruelling day. The same year, Naseeruddin Shah ranted his way through *Albert Pinto Ko Gussa Kyoon Aata Hai*. Car mechanic, skeptic and dispenser of useless wisdom, Albert is unhappy with his lot and eager to move up in life, which he thinks will happen by keeping his head down and not making waves. His reckoning comes when his father joins his fellow factory workers on strike.* Albert is a fascinating study in working-class angst, but when I watched the film recently, I found myself transfixed by Dominic (Dilip Dhawan), Albert's younger brother and a charismatic street thug. At one point, their sister, played by Smita Patil, tells Dominic he needn't return the 20 rupees she's lent him. His reply is astonishing. 'Are you embarrassed that I'm your brother? Wherever the money comes from, what does it matter? Wherever you look, people change their appearance to steal ... I steal forthrightly. Everyone's stuck with their own problems, I alone am free.'

The opening credits of Mirza's *Mohan Joshi Hazir Ho* (1984) are documentary-like, pieced together from what must have been a mass of second-unit footage (*Satya's* opening credits are similarly constructed, b-roll images and discarded scenes cobbled together with a voiceover). A comic number, 'Amchi Bambai', plays, but the mood is bleak. It belongs to the tradition of songs about how difficult it is to live in Bombay, a subgenre which stretches from Johnny Walker singing '*Ae dil hai mushkil jeena yahan*' (O heart of mine, it's

---

* Mirza, as always, had his finger on the pulse of the city. The Great Bombay Textile Strike of 1982 saw around 2,50,000 participants and changed the city in profound ways.

difficult to live here) in *C.I.D.* to 'Bambai Bambai Bam' (*Disha*, 1990), in which a group of migrant workers curse their miserable city lives. In *Gaman*, Ghulam, a villager from UP, moves to Bombay in search of work. He becomes a taxi driver, but his mind is back home. Letters go back and forth between him and his wife. She urges him to bring them to Bombay, but he can barely keep himself afloat. He can't even afford the journey back home – the city is purgatory. '*Iss sheher mein har shaks pareshan sa kyun hai?*' (Why does everyone in this town look troubled?), Suresh Wadkar sings as we see Ghulam lost in his thoughts in traffic – perhaps the saddest Bombay song of all.

Since the city's mills, taxis and factories ran largely on labour from other states, migration has been a long-standing theme of the Bombay film. One of the best-known musical numbers in Indian cinema, 'Mera Joota Hai Japani' from *Shree 420*, is a song of migration, with Raj Kapoor travelling from Allahabad to Bombay in search of work. Years later, there's a moving scene towards the end of *Albert Pinto* where Naseeruddin Shah asks a striking mill worker his name. He answers; Mirza cuts to another who says his name and state of origin, then another. They address the camera as non-actors would. They're from all over India: Uttar Pradesh, Rajasthan, Kerala, Tamil Nadu, Madhya Pradesh, Goa, Bihar. It's a snapshot of the migrant origins of the city's workforce from a filmmaker who understood Bombay like no other.

Depicting the reality of Bombay didn't always mean showing the real thing. Rabindra Dharmaraj's *Chakra* (1981) is set in a *chawl*, and looks like it's been shot in one. In reality, Bansi Chandragupta, Satyajit Ray's art director, designed a convincing-looking slum set since it proved too difficult to shoot in the actual tenement. Dharmaraj wove in shots of Smita Patil walking unrecognised through Dharavi into the footage shot on set. Decades later, Zoya Akhtar shot a good deal of *Gully Boy* (2019) in Dharavi, constructing smaller structures within the slum rather than recreating it elsewhere.

While Varma was still in college, the Bombay of *Satya* was being assembled on screen. This was a working-class world, unadorned and unlovely – a city of sex workers and pimps, lawmen and criminals, activists and daily wagers. The films – action thrillers, dramas, even comedies – seemed to be cut from the same cloth. Vinod and Sudhir from *Jaane Bhi Do Yaaro* are nothing like Anant, *Ardh Satya*'s troubled cop, but they're all ultimately tragic figures, their idealism ground down by a rigged system. The miserable *chawl*-dwellers of *Chakra*, living three or four to a room, are only a few steps removed from the intertwined lives in Sai Paranjpye's light-hearted *Katha* (1983). Maybe Chaipau from *Salaam Bombay* grows up to be Tom Alter's gentle junkie from *Salim Langde Pe Mat Ro*; more likely he becomes street hustler Salim.

1989 AND CHANGE

There are years which, when unfolding, seem like any other, and only in retrospect reveal themselves as the start of something new. Hindi cinema in 1989 appeared to be trundling along as usual. The big earners that year were *Maine Pyar Kiya*, *Ram Lakhan*, *Tridev*, *Chandni* – all very much within the ambit of popular taste. Sridevi appeared in 13 films that year, Madhuri Dixit in 11. Anil Kapoor and Sanjay Dutt had taken over, though no one had told Bachchan this. The Khans were still being assembled – Salman had a big hit with his first lead role in *Maine Pyar Kiya*; Shah Rukh was seen for a few minutes in the cult comedy *In Which Annie Gives It Those Ones*; Aamir, who'd made a splash as the lead in *Qayamat Se Qayamat Tak* the year before, starred in *Love Love Love*.

On the less glamorous end of the spectrum, dark clouds were looming. Over the course of that year, a handful of gritty, grimy, violent films would release: *Hathyar*, *Parinda*, Aditya Bhattacharya's *Raakh*, *Salim Langde Pe Mat Ro*. And though it came out the year before, Mira Nair's *Salaam Bombay* is an honorary 1989 film; it came to prominence that year with its Oscar nomination for Best Foreign Language Film. The Bombay of these films was a shock. It was like a veil had been lifted off one of the most photographed film cities in the world, and a dirty, frantic, paranoid world revealed. At a superficial level, these films weren't alike. They operated in, or combined, disparate genres: neo-noir, gangster film, social drama, cinéma vérité. *Parinda* and *Hathyar* were mainstream films with big stars; *Salaam Bombay* was mostly non-actors. *Salim Langde* came out of the parallel cinema tradition; *Raakh* came seemingly out of nowhere (and went back just as quickly). What binds them is that each observed Bombay from the ground up, and they all converged in one place: the street. The composite picture was of a desperate, unforgiving city.

We've examined them as gangster films in the previous chapter, but what do *Hathyar* and *Parinda* reveal when looked at as city films? The local trains that rattle through scenes in *Hathyar* are a reminder that no matter what kind of criminal enterprise is unfolding in the foreground, normal life continues on the edges of the frame. Varma employs a similar strategy in *Satya*, the most dramatic example being the train that passes underneath just after Bheeku and Satya shoot Guru Narayan on the bridge. *Parinda* proudly includes a list of locations in the end credits; it saves the three studios (Natraj, Filmcity, Filmistan) for last. Chopra's film subverts the normal function of tourist landmarks by using the Gateway of India as the site of an assassination attempt on Kishen and Karan. That scene became even more chilling when the Taj Hotel, across the road from the Gateway, came under siege in 2008 during the 26/11 attacks. Earlier in the film, there's a shot of the Gateway and the Taj from a boat at sea – possibly the same view the terrorists had that day.

If *Parinda* and *Hathyar* made the everyday city feel unsafe, *Raakh* turned it into a paranoid nightscape. After his friend is raped by a local gangster, mild-mannered rich kid Amir (Aamir Khan) sets out to kill the perpetrators with the help of a corrupt cop (Pankaj Kapur) who, he later finds out, witnessed the assault but did nothing to prevent it. Unfolding in an unnamed city that's visibly Bombay, the blasted landscape matches the harshness of the storyline. Most scenes unfold at night and are shot by cinematographer Santosh Sivan in the blackest of neo-noir palettes. Academic and author Laliltha Gopalan identifies one of the locations – an abandoned shoe factory on Reay Road – which she connects to the fraught history of mill workers in the city. 'How can one not read the leftover scaffolding as a mausoleum for factory work', she writes, 'after an era of strikes and lockouts, after arson and extortion gained purchase, and after the ordered hits and accidental murders that plagued factory life in Bombay?'

Almost a decade after *Albert Pinto Ko Gussa Kyoon Aata Hai*, Saeed Mirza directed *Salim Langde Pe Mat Ro*, another film about working-class lives in the city. Salim (Pavan Malhotra) is a low-level street operator, a dropout, unemployed and footloose. He and his friends collect *hafta* (protection money) from local storeowners and steal merchandise off trucks for crime bosses and traders higher up in the chain. Salim's a carefree sort and not too bright, given to occasional explosive rants in the manner of Jimmy Porter in John Osborne's *Look Back in Anger* (though millions of Indians associate 'angry young man' with Amitabh Bachchan, the phrase was first used by critics to describe '50s playwrights and novelists like Osborne and Kingsley Amis).

At its heart, *Salim Langde*, shot in the Muslim-dominated Dongri and Bhendi Bazaar neighbourhoods, is an indictment of the disenfranchisement and ghettoisation of Muslims in Bombay and, by extension, India. Salim doesn't lack an education because he's lazy; his parents could only afford to send one child to school, and picked his brother. He may lack direction, but the film suggests this is because he can't see any worthwhile future, and has therefore transformed his life into a boisterous, performative present. By the inclusion of once-familiar tropes – the courtesan, the reformer, the Sufi philosopher – Mirza updates the Muslim Social, a genre pretty much extinct by then. There are several references to the Bhiwandi riots of 1984, in which over 200 people died. Mirza calling attention to the political roots of communal disharmony becomes all the more poignant when you consider that the worst rioting Bombay would ever see – fomented, like Bhiwandi, by the provocations of the Shiv Sena – was just a couple of years away.

Mirza can be didactic trying to drive home various messages in *Salim Langde*. Still, in their engagement with the world around them, with real events and the problems of ordinary citizens, this film and *Albert Pinto* are a clue to the kind of film *Satya* isn't. Varma doesn't have the reformative streak that nearly all independent filmmakers of the '70s and '80s did. No one complains about corruption or politics in *Satya*, they just live with it or try to game the system. The anger against the city has gone. It is what it is.

Mira Nair's *Salaam Bombay* premiered at Cannes in June 1988, winning the Camera d'Or for best first film. It released in India later that year, but came to wider notice in early 1989, when it was nominated for a Best Foreign Language Oscar. The film centres on a young migrant, known to all as Chaipau, who has to fend for himself on the streets of Bombay. He gets a job delivering tea in the red-light district of Kamathipura. A sex worker takes care of him, but his luck never holds for long. All the children in the film are played by non-actors, Nair coaxing unselfconscious performances from her cast. *Salaam Bombay* was shot on location, often guerrilla-style, which is mostly what happened on *Satya* as well. The two films have much else in common – migrant protagonists; directors who were outsiders to Bombay; cinematographers with a background in cinéma vérité and documentary; and the desire to locate their stories in an authentic world. Varma says there was no influence of *Salaam Bombay* on *Satya* – he was more taken by *Bandit Queen*, another Indian film that made a splash on the global arthouse circuit. But influence isn't always a straight line. None of the films of 1989 may have directly led to *Satya*. But they did create a new filmic Bombay, one which *Satya* could find itself in.

Gritty realism would have to wait its turn. Mainstream cinema was undergoing major changes at the start of the 1990s, but in a different direction – towards youth, love and prosperity. *Qayamat Se Qayamat Tak*, a star-crossed-young-lovers film starring Aamir Khan and Juhi Chawla, was a huge hit in 1988. *Maine Pyar Kiya*, starring Salman Khan, released a year later. *Raju Ban Gaya Gentleman*, with Shah Rukh Khan, and *Jo Jeeta Wohi Sikandar*, with Aamir, came out in 1992. By 1994, the three Khans were Hindi cinema's reigning stars, and the romantic drama was the dominant genre, consolidated by the wild success that year of *Hum Aapke Hain Koun*, for a while the highest-grossing Indian film ever. Four more years of undying love and family values and polite cinema would follow before *Satya* went off like a bomb.

India would tear itself apart at the end of 1992, when Hindu nationalists, spurred on by right-wing politicians, tore down a mosque in Ayodhya, in the northern state of Uttar Pradesh, which they claimed had been made on the same site where there had once stood a Ram temple. Religious riots broke out across the country. Some of the worst rioting was in Bombay, where the Shiv Sena government fanned existing tensions through its mouthpiece, *Saamana*. The mobs had access to voter rolls, which meant Muslim houses and shops could be easily targeted. Official estimates put the dead at 900, a majority of whom were Muslim, in addition to countless others driven from their homes and their livelihoods destroyed. The city had barely started putting itself back together when 13 bombs went off at various locations on 12 March 1993. This was revenge for the riots, allegedly at the behest of Dawood Ibrahim, by then operating from Dubai.

We saw in the previous chapter how *Angaar* (1992) eerily foreshadowed the blasts with its climactic scene. Two other films that year seemed to anticipate a city on the brink. One was *Zulm Ki Hukumat*, which starts with communal riots instigated by one mafia boss and prevented by another. The other was Sudhir Mishra's *Dharavi*. Rajkaran (Om Puri) is a migrant taxi driver living in Dharavi, whose hard and unsatisfying life is eased by Madhuri Dixit (as herself) appearing in his dreams. The film's grimy visual palette is contrasted with the Madhuri interludes, shot in glossy pastel shades. Here again is the cinematic city and the real one, but without the false promise of overlap.

There's a stunning set piece. The cloth-dyeing factory that Rajkaran has sunk his savings into is being torn down, vats of bright dyes overturned by goons, splattering the screen with colour, everything unfolding in slow motion. In the foreground, men in skullcaps offer namaz. It's a dream of destruction, and the destruction of a dream. By the time *Dharavi* released in India, in April 1993, another orgy of destruction had played out on smaller screens across the country: the dismantling of the Babri Masjid.

In Mani Ratnam's *Nayakan*, Velu Naicker's Bombay journey begins at Chhatrapati Shivaji Terminus. Ratnam again uses the station as a starting point in *Bombay* (1995), as Shaila (Manisha Koirala), a Tamil Muslim, arrives in the city to join her Hindu husband, Shekhar (Arvind Swamy). The filmic city makes two other cameos – after the couple are married, they walk along Marine Drive, and the Gateway of India turns up in the 'Halla Gulla' musical number. But what appears to be the actual city is only a simulacrum. *Bombay*, a Tamil-language film, was shot over a thousand kilometres away in Chennai. Like Ernst Lubitsch, who famously preferred Paris, Paramount to Paris, France, Ratnam might have preferred Bombay, Chennai to Bombay, Maharashtra – with good reason. Shiv Sena would never have allowed a film about the riots to be shot there (Ratnam is rumoured to have later made cuts mandated by Bal Thackeray). The film is vivid and upsetting, though if the symbolism of two half-Hindu, half-Muslim kids lost in the riots is too on-the-nose for you, follow it with Kashyap's morally murkier *Black Friday*, which shows the aftermath of the 1993 serial blasts.

Six months after *Bombay* made the city look unsafe, *Rangeela* reassured audiences that this was still a place for dreamers. Though a musical fantasy, Ram Gopal Varma's film was rooted in the city, delighting in its streets and backchat and movie culture. A year later, *Is Raat Ki Subah Nahin* conjured an after-hours Mumbai, summoning the memory of K.A. Abbas' evocatively titled *Bambai Raat Ki Bahon Mein* (1968) – 'Bombay in the Arms of Night'. Then it was 1998. Vikram Bhatt's *Ghulam* released in June – *On the Waterfront* transplanted to the Mumbai streets, with Aamir Khan in the Brando role singing '*Kya bolti tu?*' (What do you say?) to Rani Mukerji. Spare a thought for the critics who described it as 'gritty' and 'hard-hitting', and were sent scrambling for a thesaurus when *Satya* released a month later.

5

Getting the Team Together

'Right from my teens, I used to look up to bullies in class. I used to have a fascination for street goons in Hyderabad. Anyone who could beat someone up, I used to look at them kind of as heroes.'

– Ram Gopal Varma

Varma kept wild company during his civil engineering days in Vijaywada. 'I pretty much used to move around in gangs back then,' he told me. He wasn't a big physical threat, but he proved to be a shrewd tactician. He once dismantled a rival gang by winning over or isolating its members. 'Anything that becomes an organisation, where a group of people get together and try to outwit or beat up the other gang – some kind of politics will start. That psychological aspect used to fascinate me.' The fascination only grew, from the street gangs in his first film, *Siva*, to the organised crime of *Satya* and *Company*, and the criminal–political set-ups of *Sarkar* (2005) and *Rakta Charitra* (2010).

In between being in a gang and making a film about one, Varma opened a video-rental library back home in Hyderabad. There's a parallel here to be made with Quentin Tarantino, another director who used the video store he worked in as a means to devour every kind of cinema under the sun. But if the store had an influence on Varma's film education, he's never been forthcoming about it, painting it in his autobiography as a pure business venture. At any rate, it was a success, bringing in 20,000 rupees a month where his previous job had earned him only 800. It also helped him realise his flair for storytelling. 'I used to narrate the stories of the films to my customers depending on their tastes,' he wrote. 'In due course of time, they became so addicted to my story sessions, many said my narration was better than the films.'

Varma was film-crazy from the start. His father was a sound engineer in Annapurna Studios in Hyderabad, but it was his uncle who'd take him to the movies after school. 'English, Hindi, Telugu films, Westerns – anything which was there, we used to watch,' he said. 'I think that's where the obsession started.'

I asked Varma when he first became aware of the presence of a director. *Ankur* (1974) was his surprising reply, a film by Shyam Benegal, a director as diametrically opposed to Varma as you could imagine. 'In the end, a little boy throws a stone in anger and a glass breaks. My uncle told me, that's a director's touch. That's the first time I can consciously remember hearing the word "director."' He began noticing film technique in the works of Alfred Hitchcock and Steven Spielberg, and in his all-time favourite, Ramesh Sippy's *daaku* Western, *Sholay*. He read books on the making of films, on special effects, pored through issues of *American Cinematographer*. He had wide-ranging tastes – he loved Ridley Scott's *Alien* (1979) and also Richard Attenborough's *Gandhi* (1982). And, like most young men at the time, he was blown away by Amitabh Bachchan. His first memory of the actor was in *Bombay to Goa* (1972). He'd gone to see Aruna Irani, but was struck by the lanky man who continued to chew gum after being hit. 'The bunch of us – hooligans, college *dada*s – looked at each other and said, "Who the fuck is he?"'

By the time Varma was in college, he was watching eight films a week. Before opening the video store, he tried, unsuccessfully, to break into the Telugu industry as a director. After the rental business took off, he tried again. He used the same tactics he'd employed in his college gang, telling the producer one thing, the director something else, and finding favour with stars who could call the shots. After some complicated manoeuvring, he found himself – with no prior writing, directing or even assisting experience – in charge of a feature production with Nagarjuna, then only a couple of films old, as the star.

For his Telugu-language debut, *Siva**, Varma threw various flavours of rebel cinema into a big pot and stirred. He took the plot from *The Way of the Dragon* (released in the US as *Return of the Dragon*), in which Bruce Lee's out-of-towner martial artist defends a restaurant in Rome under siege from gangsters. Varma changed the setting to a college, with Siva (Nagarjuna) taking on thuggish student union president JD (Chakravarthy) and, later, crime boss Bhavani (Raghuvaran). Both films end with a rooftop fight – Lee and Chuck Norris in the 1972 film, Bhavani and Siva in *Siva*. 'Atmosphere' came from *Ardh Satya* – 'especially the villains', he told me (one can, indeed, draw a line from Sadashiv Amrapurkar's thoughtful, smiling Rama Shetty to Raghuvaran's relatively considered portrayal of mid-

---

*   The film was remade in Hindi as *Shiva* a year later. There were a few changes in the cast – Raj Zutshi as Shiva's friend, Amrish Puri and Paresh Rawal as antagonists – but it mostly matched the original, scene for scene. The descriptions of scenes here are as per the Hindi version.

level mafia). And *Arjun* ('A guy who's employed, pushed to a corner, himself joins crime, but probably with a good cause') influenced the kind of street-fighter protagonist Nagarjuna would play. Rawail's film was a touchstone in other ways. Made four years before *Siva*, it tells a similar story of disenfranchised youth taking to violence as a means of providing justice, but also, one suspects, because it gives them purpose and a little respect. *Arjun* is intermittently impressive as an action film – Varma rips off the chase sequence with Sunny Deol on a bicycle – but *Siva* is on a different level. The screen explodes whenever there's a set piece of any kind – a fight, a chase, a dance.

A mix of crude storytelling and technical finesse, *Siva* is visibly the work of a talented filmmaker just starting out. The writing, at least in the Hindi version, rarely manages to break away from cliché. All the characters are archetypes: stoic hero, damsel-in-distress heroine, smarmy politician, progressively psychotic villain (not to take anything away from Raghuvaran's excellent scenery-chewing). The film is all surface – but what a surface it is. Varma is evidently excited by the visual possibilities of the medium – there are long, unbroken takes, trippy superimpositions, a fourth-wall-breaking dance number. He also had the knowhow and the hustle to get hold of a Steadicam, and become the first Indian director to make use of its fluid shot-taking.*

---

* Varma wrote in *Guns & Thighs*: 'I read about the Steadicam in *American Cinematographer*, and while talking of it admiringly to a camera assistant in the studio, was shocked to learn of the existence of a Steadicam in Chennai for four years that nobody was using. I wanted to use it but my cameraman was reluctant, saying that one couldn't centre it or balance it. I told him if we were using it in a chase scene as a point of view, it wouldn't matter.'

One scene in particular typifies the restless energy Varma brought to his debut. We see, in long shot, Asha (Amala) standing by the road with her friends. As the camera pulls back, we realise that we're watching them from under a car that belongs to Bhavani's goons. The camera pans up, and we now see her through the car window. The door closes and there's a cut. Then we're travelling along with the car, the camera at tyre level. It screeches to a halt in front of Asha. The men jump out, drag her inside, drive off. Varma seemed pleased when I asked him about the shot. He said that he always uses the camera to 'add an additional layer' instead of just recording what's happening in front of it. 'It brings in a lot of dynamism. You could just pick her up and throw her in the car, but the fact that you remember the shot means something unique is happening there.'

There was no reason Varma had to make a standard scene like this so intricate. He did it, one assumes, because he could. This is true for all the action set pieces in *Siva*, which come in a variety of styles and moods. J.D. and Siva's fight in the street is chaotic and messy. Siva sprinting through the narrow lanes inspired similar frenetic runs in other Varma productions (*Satya*, *Company*), and in films by other directors (*Black Friday*, *Slumdog Millionaire*). The night-time chase involving Siva's friend is close to noir, with giant shadows looming across the walls. Even the final scene, the one Varma filched from Bruce Lee, is unique for the way he kills the background score – not a done thing in Hindi films of any era – and keeps only grunts and thuds on the soundtrack.

—

A man in a black shirt, badly wounded, breaks through the door and staggers into the room. There's a woman there; he's pleading with her, but she's frozen. As he moves to come closer, she flinches, shakes her head. Then, someone shoots him from behind. He falls at her feet.

Yes, you might say, this is the ending to *Satya*. And you wouldn't be wrong – but what if I told you the scene continues? The man gets a few dying words in. The woman cradles his head in her arms. This is a Varma film, but from 1992. The woman is Urmila Matondkar, but the actor isn't Chakravarthy. The film is *Antham*.

The reason *Satya* and *Antham* (or its Hindi version, *Drohi*) have similar endings, and subplots in which a woman falls for a mysterious loner she doesn't know is a criminal, is because they draw from the same James Hadley Chase novel. In our conversation, and in other interviews, Varma identified the source as Chase's *My Laugh Comes Last*. But when I read the book, I couldn't find anything resembling this storyline. So began a comical few days in which I, having never read a Chase novel in my life, found myself sifting through his ninety-odd titles to try and discern the plot which led to *Antham* and *Satya*. Chakravarthy suggested it might have been *Like a Hole in the Head*, but that didn't seem to fit either. The closest parallel I could find was *Strictly for Cash*, in which a boxer gets mixed up with gangsters, falls in love with a girl, tells her he's an insurance agent, but can't shake off his criminal past.

I'll digress a bit here, because Chase is an influential figure for Indian pulp literature and cinema. An Englishman, born René Lodge Brabazon Raymond, he started writing thrillers in 1939 and continued till 1984. His thrillers never caught on in America, which is probably why he isn't regarded as essential pulp the way Dashiell Hammett or Raymond Chandler are. But he was popular in Europe (his work was published under the influential Série noire imprint in France), Africa and Asia – particularly in India, where his direct prose and racy plots were appreciated by thrill-seeking readers. His paperbacks, often sporting lurid covers, were a familiar sight at railway stations, roadside stalls and run-down bookstores for decades. Because his writing was fun and dangerous and easy to understand, he was the first English-language author for many Indians. This was true of Varma himself. 'The first book I ever read was James Hadley Chase's *No Orchids for Miss Blandish*,' he told *Khaleej Times*. 'Who needed studies when I could read of interesting women like Miss Blandish?'

Chase's books are the source for many Hindi crime films, though he's rarely credited. *Tiger by the Tail* inspired *Kashmakash* (1973), *Akalmand* (1984) and *88 Antop Hill* (2004). *Shalimar* (1978), with Dharmendra, Zeenat Aman and Rex Harrison, is based on *The Vulture Is a Patient Bird*; *Ek Nari Do Roop* (1973) on *The Wary Transgressor*; *Aar Ya Paar* (1997) on *The Sucker Punch*. *Come Easy, Go Easy* became *Aakhri Dao* (1975), written by Salim–Javed. Vijay Anand adapted *Just Another Sucker* as *Bullet* (1976). Sriram Raghavan capped a half-century of Chase influence by dedicating the noir caper *Johnny Gaddaar* (2007) to him and Vijay Anand. In one scene, a character is reading a battered copy of *The Whiff of Money*.

At least one Indian gangster was a Chase fan too. In *Dongri to Dubai: Six Decades of the Mumbai Mafia*, S. Hussain Zaidi wrote of Manya Surve: 'Before almost every heist, robbery, or murder, he would spend hours working out the details of the job, using ideas and material from the (Chase) books.'

Antham continued Varma's experiments with slick action after *Siva*. Shekhar (Nagarjuna), an orphan, is brought up by a mob boss (Danny Denzongpa), and eventually works for him as a contract killer. He falls in love with ornithology student Bhavna (Urmila Matondkar), though he keeps his identity a secret. *Satya* also has a protagonist who's an orphan who hides that he's a killer from his lover. Yet, unlike the 1998 film, *Antham* has nothing particularly interesting going on between its stunning setpieces (cinematographer Teja shot several films for Varma before becoming a successful director himself). *Satya* is as much a writer's and actor's film as a director's. No one would say the same of *Siva* or *Antham*.

Lately, a vague and sometimes condescending label called 'genre filmmaker' has become common in critical circles. It's normally used for directors who work in popular forms such as science-fiction or horror but aren't seen as prestige filmmakers (John Carpenter is regarded as a genre director, David Cronenberg isn't). Varma would probably fit this definition, given his lack of preciousness and his willingness to try his hand at almost any kind of film. After reinvigorating the action film with *Siva*, he could have continued working on similar material. Instead, his next two releases, *Kshana Kshanam* (1991) and *Raat* (1992), were a genre *khichdi* and a horror film. The former was a mashup of road movie, action and slapstick – loosely remade by Varma in Hindi as *Daud* (1997). It starred Sridevi (playing a character named Satya) and Venkatesh as strangers on the run from the cops and Paresh Rawal's gangster. The opening sequence, a bank robbery, is a neo-noir dream, but when we first see Sridevi, the scene glows with the bright white of screwball comedy. And on we go, playing hopscotch with genres – Rawal bathed in horror-film red, a motorbike chase out of a Hong Kong action film. Then there's the 'Jaamu Ratiri' musical number, the tenderest moment in Varma's filmography. In the forest at night, Venkatesh sings the scared Sridevi a lullaby, she relaxes and joins in, then puts her head on his shoulder and goes to sleep.*

Raat, released after *Kshana Kshanam* and before *Antham*, was Varma's first great sustained film. He's still throwing everything he

---

* Given how besotted Varma was with Sridevi at the time, it's a miracle he could keep it together enough to direct her. As he later admitted, 'I wrote *Kshana Kshanam* with the one and only purpose of impressing Sridevi. *Kshana Kshanam* was my love letter to her. Throughout the making of *Kshana Kshanam*, I just couldn't take my eyes off her.'

can at the screen – aerial shots, intricate camera moves, soundtrack manipulations – but for the first time, it's under control, coherent. At the time it was rare to see Indian horror done by someone with actual directing chops (no apologies to the gloriously trashy Ramsays, who need no apologising for). The film begins with an unbroken 90-second Steadicam shot that recalls the stalker-ish openings of John Carpenter's *Halloween* (1978) and Brian De Palma's *Blow Out* (1981). The camera prowls through a deserted village, eventually locating its quarry – a young woman, dressed in a baggy orange shirt and slacks, walking the streets alone. The soundtrack escalates from ambient noise and low moans to a pounding riff as the scene becomes a full-blown chase. It's a stunning start, and proof that Varma's technical ability wasn't limited to action cinema. The opening credits start with the names of the Steadicam operators and sound designers instead of Revathi, the star of the film, which might have been Varma's way of indicating, for this film at least, that whatever's happening behind the camera is more important.

William Friedkin's horror classic, *The Exorcist* (1973), made a big impression on Varma when he saw it back in college, scaring him so much he had to watch three more films afterwards to calm himself. *Raat* has shades of *The Exorcist* (it eventually becomes clear that Mini, the protagonist, is possessed by a vengeful supernatural force), though it also splices in ideas from *Psycho* (a woman in a swivelling chair with her back to the audience) and *A Nightmare on Elm Street* (the school dream). *Raat* is also the best-acted of Varma's pre-*Rangeela* films, with Revathi's frantic lead turn supported by Rohini Hattangadi and Akash Khurana as her parents, and Om Puri as a *tantrik* with slicked-back hair performing a similar function to Father Merrin in Friedkin's film. I may be imagining things, but when Puri gives a quiet speech to Mini's mother about *roshni* (light) and *andhera* (darkness), it plays like a small tribute to the restaurant scene in *Ardh Satya* where Puri reads aloud a poem with the phrase '*nirnay ki roshni*' (the light of decision).

Varma had four films out in 1993. He directed *Gaayam* and *Govinda Govinda*, produced Siva Nageswara Rao's *Money* and co-wrote *Thiruda Thiruda* with Mani Ratnam (who helped him with the story of *Gaayam*). In all, he'd directed seven films in the four years since he'd started out. There were signs that he was plateauing. *Gaayam* was another exploration of gang warfare, based on the real-life rivalry of the Devineni and Vangaveeti factions in Vijaywada, but without the high style of *Antham* and *Siva*. And *Govinda Govinda*, starring Sridevi and Nagarjuna, was a tacky-looking mishmash of supernatural thriller, action comedy and road movie. It was time for a change. Bollywood was calling.

He'd begun a project with Sanjay Dutt called 'Nayak', Hindi for hero – an amusing title given that the actor was coming off the hugely successful *Khal Nayak*, or villain. But they'd barely started when the actor was sent to jail for the second time, in 1994, for possession of illegal firearms. 'Nayak' was shelved; years later, it formed the basis for *Sarkar*. Varma picked up another project he'd been developing – his first out-and-out musical, *Rangeela*.

1995 was the year *Dilwale Dulhania Le Jayenge* broke box-office records. It was also the year of *Rangeela*. Anyone who was young then and a fan of Hindi movies will remember the wave of excitement that carried us from the airing of the first song to the film's release. Music countdown shows were ubiquitous then on TV – variety programmes interspersed with the latest hits. It was on one of these that we first heard the thunderclaps that open 'Rangeela Re'. Many would have recognised the sound as A.R. Rahman's – there was a clarity to his production that eluded other composers of the era. Few would have known the girl in the colourful short skirt high-kicking her way down the street (and startling a dog en route). A few weeks later, the whole country knew who Urmila Matondkar was.

In its own unassuming way, *Rangeela* was as much an industry-altering film as *Satya* would be three years later. It was the first Hindi film with an original (as opposed to dubbed) Rahman soundtrack, a thrilling prospect for fans like me who'd followed his trailblazing progress in Tamil cinema, from *Roja* (1992) to *Thiurda Thiruda* to *Bombay*. 'Rangeela Re' was radical in the way it paired Asha Bhosle's voice with thundering percussion but little orchestration. 'Yaaron Sun Lo Zara' did a similar thing with Udit Narayan's voice, and Rahman daringly left in only the faintest of basslines (Prince's 'When Doves Cry' might have given him the idea). But 'Tanha Tanha' was lush like a rainforest, and the slinky forward drive of 'Maangta Hai Kya' had a Broadway quality.

Rangeela was also a watershed moment for how the songs were realised on film (though only by the standards of Hindi cinema – Tamil film was already doing brilliant, surreal dance sequences in the early '90s). Ahmed Khan's choreography had an exuberance and a naturalism complimented by the street backdrops of 'Rangeela Re' and 'Yaaro Sun Lo Zara'. Few would deny that, over time, Varma's camera has acquired a leering gaze. But this was not in evidence in *Rangeela*. The sensual charge in the musical sequences was freeing rather than limiting. No matter what Urmila wears or how openly she expresses her desire ('Hai Rama' has an almost feral intensity), the film is always in her corner, cheering her on.* It's a rare Hindi film from that era in which an actress could dress as she pleased and not be shamed for it.

---

*   Whether this lack of objectification is because of Varma's best efforts or in spite of them is another matter. The passages in *Guns & Thighs* describing Matondkar are cringe-worthy ('One of my primary motives in making *Rangeela* was to capture Urmila's beauty eternally on camera and to make it a benchmark for sex symbols ... Urmila's swaying hips are the content, and the particular way I want to see them swaying will constitute my frame').

I mentioned in the previous chapter that Varma credited *Chitchor* with showing him how to tell a simple story with feeling. In Basu Chatterjee's film, Zarina Wahab falls for Vinod (Amol Palekar), but is promised by her family to the well-settled Sunil (Vijayendra Ghatge). When the flamboyant engineer enters the picture, Vinod withdraws, only to be called back by Sunil. This mirrors the actions of movie star Raj (Jackie Shroff) in *Rangeela*, who eventually reunites Mili with Munna, the *tapori* played by Aamir Khan, who has given up hope of being with her. *Rangeela* also has shades of another Chatterjee film, *Rajnigandha* (1974), in which Vidya Sinha is caught between jokey Amol Palekar and the more intense Dinesh Thakur. Remove the surface sheen and *Rangeela* – with its warm, life-like family scenes, its winks at the all-encompassing reach of cinema and gentle psychological battles (both Munna and Raj love Mili, but neither imposes their feelings on her) – isn't that far removed from the Middle Cinema of Chatterjee and Hrishikesh Mukherjee (who made a film called *Mili* in 1975).

Then again, it's hardly possible to separate *Rangeela* from its surface sheen – all the sights and sounds of a newly liberalised nation looking for some fun. Matondkar's entry in skirt, boots and hat. Khan, entirely unselfconscious in a half-open yellow shirt, black vest, yellow pants and dark glasses with red frames. The stunning opening credits – naturalism on the soundtrack, escapism on the screen. '*Tu pair dekh raha hai,* picture *dekh raha hai*?' The post-liberalisation confidence that reverberates through '*maangta hai kya*' – what do you want?*

---

*   The Hindi word '*maangna*' – 'to ask', but used in the sense of 'demand' or 'crave' – turned up again in 1998 when Pepsi introduced the immensely popular jingle '*Yeh dil maange* more' (This heart wants more).

Rangeela's commercial success made Matondkar a star and signalled the slow demise of the Jatin–Lalit/Nadeem–Shravan era of film soundtracks. It also showed that Varma could thrive in Hindi cinema as he had in Telugu. Now, he was keen to make an action film with a Bollywood star. Sanjay Dutt had been released after a year and a half in jail. Varma, who'd tried to 'Nayak' with him before the imprisonment, immediately signed him. Work began on *Daud* (1997), a reworking of *Kshana Kshanam*, with Dutt and Matondkar in the lead. Simultaneously, there was another project taking shape in Varma's mind. He'd left Hyderabad by then and was working in Mumbai. After the 1993 blasts, the underworld became more visible – a system unto itself, complicated and often malfunctioning, like the local train network or the municipal corporation. 'At that time, it was rampant,' Varma said. 'It was a part of life, part of the city.' He remembers 1995–96 as a time of 'heavy-duty underworld activity', with gang-related stories appearing in the papers almost on a daily basis.

For a filmmaker already fascinated by criminal behaviour, this was an exciting time to be in Mumbai. It was Chicago, 1929 all over again. And Hindi cinema was about to get its *Public Enemy*.

—

Varma first heard of D-Company, Dawood Ibrahim's criminal network, years before moving to Mumbai. 'It was told to me by a sales boy in this cassette wholesale shop in Grant Road,' he told Film Companion. 'I used to run a video library in Hyderabad. I used to come here to buy cassettes. This was around '86–87, and during the couple of times I visited, he took me to Caesar Palace Hotel in Bandra, which was owned by Mahesh and Arvind Dholakia, big underworld figures at the time. He told me this place belongs to guys who are against Dawood Ibrahim's D-Company … I could see the atmosphere and the people hanging out there. I was fascinated by the whole thing – and some years later, both the brothers were killed due to some underworld feud with Chhota Rajan.'

From the time he moved to Mumbai, Varma, almost subconsciously, began collecting stories about the underworld. A particularly helpful one was told to him by a friend who lived in a high-rise in Oshiwara in north Mumbai. Now and then, he'd pass this one man on the way to the elevator and exchange a few neighbourly words. One day, he found out that the police had come to the building and arrested the man, who, it transpired, was a gangster. 'That is Bombay – you could be having a neighbour for 20 years, but you don't know his name,' Varma told me. 'That gave me the plotline for Satya and Vidya.' (This is a story retold by Varma on many occasions. In *Guns & Thighs*, he describes the man not as a gangster but as someone 'absconding in a murder case'.)

In the mid '90s, if you lived in Mumbai, it wasn't unusual to know someone who knew someone who maybe knew someone in a gang. The chances of that were even higher if you were in the entertainment business. An important source of insider gossip for Varma was Dutt, who'd always had a line open to the mob, and had picked up even more stories during his two stints in jail. One can imagine the incarcerated *bhai*s, generals and foot soldiers alike, lining up to tell the tough-guy Bollywood star their best anecdotes. Suketu Mehta, who spoke to Dutt about his time in prison, wrote in *Maximum City*: 'Gunmen from all the gangs mixed freely in the jail. Sanjay met a number of shooters, studied how the recruiting was done, starting from the children's barracks, where the sharp boys were picked up, their bail arranged, their families taken care of. After he was released, he shared this knowledge with directors of gangster movies, who made films based on the characters he'd met.' At least one story told to Dutt in jail made it into Varma's film: the killing of Jagga by Satya.

Then there was Ajit Dewani. As someone privy to the inner workings of the underworld, he became another source of information for Varma (he's thanked in the opening credits of *Satya*). Dewani met a grisly end, gunned down in 2001 by one of Abu Salem's sharpshooters. The papers ran a rumour that Manisha Koirala, the enigmatic star of *Bombay* and *Dil Se*, for whom Dewani worked as a secretary, had taken out a *supari* (hit) on him, but this was rubbished by the investigating team.

Finally, there was the story strand Varma had long wanted to do something with, the one from the James Hadley Chase book – a criminal who keeps his identity secret from his lover. He'd tried to make something of this in *Antham*, but that wasn't a success. Varma knew it would be a terrific hook for a gangster film. Already, even before he'd begun, he could see how it would end – a wounded man falling at the feet of his sweetheart, who's just found out he's a killer.

BAGGING BHEEKU

Varma's first hire on *Satya* was Manoj Bajpayee. At the time, the actor was known (if at all) for his supporting role in *Bandit Queen*. He'd started out in Delhi theatre, only moving to Bombay on Shekhar Kapur's insistence in 1993. He had to struggle for parts early on – his being in *Bandit Queen* meant little to most Bollywood directors and producers, and he didn't have the look of a leading man (I still remember his groan when he spoke about laying eyes on Nirmal Pandey for the first time and realising the second lead he'd hoped to get in Kapur's film would go the way of this 'Jesus-looking fellow'). Even Varma, a huge admirer of *Bandit Queen*, wasn't exactly beating the bushes for the near-silent *daaku* whose name no one knew.

Bajpayee had a steady gig on the popular TV soap *Swabhimaan*, but he really wanted to break into Hindi film. One day, he got a call from Kannan Iyer. They'd gotten to know each other on *Bandit Queen*; Iyer was Kapur's assistant then. Now, he was co-writing *Daud* for Varma. Would Bajpayee be interested in auditioning for the part of Paresh Rawal's henchman? The actor wasn't thrilled, but Iyer advised him to meet Varma anyway. 'Ramu is a very temperamental guy,' he said. 'If he likes you, he'll give you a very big role in his next film.'

When Bajpayee turned up, he found three other actors there to read for the part. He was the last to audition. When he finally got in the room with Varma, they began talking about his previous work. Bajpayee mentioned *Bandit Queen*. Varma was puzzled. 'Which role?' he asked. Maan Singh, Bajpayee replied. The director jumped up. 'I've been trying to locate you since I saw the film. Where were you?'

Varma told him not to bother about the bit part in *Daud*. 'There's this gangster film I'm planning – you'll be perfect for the central character.' Bajpayee, though, wasn't about to let 35,000 rupees walk out of the door. He politely told Varma that he would love to do the gangster film, but would he please cast him in *Daud* as well? And so *Satya* began, with a director on the way up, and an actor hungry to break out.

Had he not been making *Daud*, it's possible Varma would have rushed into production on *Satya* with whoever was at hand. Serendipitously, there was time and willingness on Varma's part (not always a given) to assemble a crack team. *Bandit Queen* was the benchmark. Though Shekhar Kapur was a friend and business partner,* the thought of bettering his film had Varma fired up. 'I want those kinds of actors, I want those kinds of department heads,' he told Bajpayee. 'You supply me with the talent, let me choose from them.'

---

* In 1995, Varma, Kapur and Mani Ratnam started a production company called India Talkies with the intention of making a film each under the banner. Only one film ended up getting made: Ratnam's *Dil Se*.

Anurag Kashyap
Photo credit: Gerard Hooper

Gerard Hooper on location
Photo credit: Gerard Hooper, Sree Vas

Manoj Bajpayee unwinding with a cup of tea between scenes
Photo credit: Gerard Hooper

Gerard Hooper in the gully down which one of the gunmen who kill the producer flees in the film
Photo credit: Gerard Hooper, Sree Vas

(From left) Saurabh Shukla, Gerard Hooper and Anurag Kashyap

Photo credit: Gerard Hooper, Sree Vas

Mazhar Kamran
Photo credit: Gerard Hooper

(From left) Assistant director Adithi Rao, executive producer P. Som Shekar and
production controller Chinna
Photo credit: Gerard Hooper

Ram Gopal Varma and (right) Sabir Masani
Photo credit: Gerard Hooper

Ram Gopal Varma and (right) Sabir Masani
Photo credit: Gerard Hooper

(From left) Anurag Kashyap, Mazhar Kamran and Ram Gopal Varma set up the iconic 'Mumbai ka king kaun?' shot

Photo credit: Mazhar Kamran

Cast and crew on the last day of shooting

Photo credit: Mazhar Kamran

Bheeku (Manoj Bajpayee) and (right) Satya (Chakravarthy) chasing Guru Narayan

Photo credit: Mazhar Kamran

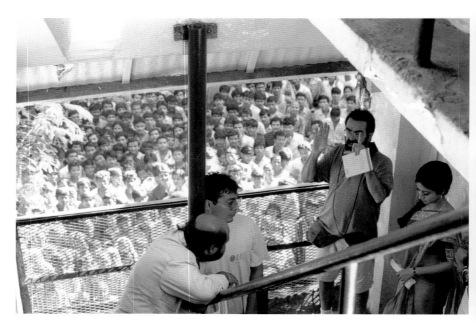

Gerard Hooper explains a set-up to Saurabh Shukla (leaning on the railing), Anurag Kashyap and Urmila Matondkar

Photo credit: Gerard Hooper, Sree Vas

P. Som Shekar and (right) Ram Gopal Varma

Photo credit: Gerard Hooper

Setting up the shot where Satya is
beaten on the terrace by Jagga's men
Photo credit: Gerard Hooper, Sree Vas

Urmila Matondkar with the slate on Gerard Hooper's last day of shooting

Photo credit: Gerard Hooper

Urmila Matondkar on the landing of the chawl building where Vidya and Satya live

Photo credit: Gerard Hooper

First, they needed a writer. They offered the job to one of the best-known playwrights in the country. They ended up with a kid who'd never written a feature film before, and another who didn't want to write at all.

THE WRITERS

Ram Gopal Varma had a writing credit on all his films before *Satya*. For his Telugu films, he wrote the screenplay or dialogue or both; when the films were dubbed in Hindi, the dialogue was written by someone else. On *Rangeela*, his first non-remake Hindi film, he wrote the screenplay. But his grasp on Hindi was shaky in those early years, and it was writers Neeraj Vora (who plays the sleazy music producer in *Satya*) and Sanjay Chhel who supplied the lines, including Aamir Khan's breathless *tapori* monologues. Varma used Chhel again on *Daud*, another musical fantasy. Some instinct must have told him he needed a different kind of voice for the gangster film taking shape in his mind, though Varma would likely deny any sign of such obvious planning. At any rate, he decided, for the first time in his career, to farm out the writing of a film he planned to direct.

One of the many production houses dotting the Mumbai suburb of Andheri in the '90s was Media Classic. It was a minor player, mostly turning out Gujarati and Marathi serials. Through chance more than anything else, it became the meeting place for a group of young film buffs trying to break into the industry. Shivam Nair, who'd later direct *Ahista Ahista* (2006) and *Naam Shabana* (2017), was an executive producer there. He was joined by Sriram Raghavan, who, with the serial killer noir *Raman Raghav* (1991), was already showing signs of becoming an artful, cine-literate director. There was Pankaj Advani, who'd make the cult classic *Urf Professor* (2001) and the rowdy comedy *Sankat City* (2009). There was also an excitable writer in his early twenties from Gorakhpur, Anurag Kashyap.

Other people would drop in – writer Sridhar Raghavan, Sriram's brother; future writer–director Abbas Tyrewala; writer–actor Shiv Subramaniam, the only one with a noteworthy screen credit (as co-writer of *Parinda*). Media Classic had an edit bay, and the group would often spend their evenings huddled around a small monitor, drinking endless cups of tea and watching battered VHS tapes. Sriram Raghavan remembers a bunch of them watching *Goodfellas* there for the first time – a 'pirated *ka* pirated *ka* copy' – and being blown away.

In an interview to film journalist Ajay Brahmatmaj, Kashyap recalled his Media Classic time nostalgically. He had recently moved from Delhi, and was part of the Mumbai theatre circuit (and dodging calls from Govind Nihalani) when he met Nair. Someone had brought a tape of *Taxi Driver* that day, a film Kashyap had never seen, and one which he developed, as he put it, a strange fascination for. He probably had an inkling that Sridhar, Sriram and Shivam were his kind of people. He asked the Media Classic regulars if he could write for them.

As it happened, Manoj Bajpayee used to swing by the office as well, to gossip and see if there was any good work floating around. Kashyap ran into him one day. In college in Delhi, he'd seen Bajpayee act in a play called *Netua*, which made a big impression on him. A couple of years later, he watched *Bandit Queen* and was surprised to see the same theatre-circuit guy as one of Vikram Mallah's gang. The two got talking. Bajpayee had loved *Raman Raghav*, so when Kashyap told him he was writing another instalment in that series, he made a mental note. Later, he visited Kashyap's apartment and was impressed by the number of books strewn about. By this time, two writers had been considered for *Satya* and rejected. Bajpayee took a leap of faith. Listen, he told Kashyap, why don't you come meet Ramu?

Kashyap had been trying, unsuccessfully, to break out of Media Classic. He'd written another in the serial killer series – *Nagarajan*, to be directed by Kamal Swaroop (it never got made) – and rewritten, in an overnight blitz, the script for Shivam Nair's *Auto Narayan*. He was also working on daily soaps, like Bajpayee, Hansal Mehta, Imtiaz Ali and so many others who made a living in TV while angling for film projects. Kashyap remembers meeting Varma for the first time on the sets of *Daud*. 'He took me on a long drive. He said, I want to make this film. I want to put Howard Roark in the underworld. What do you think?' Varma asked the young man if he was working on anything, and warned him he couldn't pay much. Kashyap told him it didn't matter.

Varma's lack of Hindi at the time might have contributed, in a roundabout way, to their not being able to snag Vijay Tendulkar as a writer. Tendulkar was one of the foremost Indian playwrights of the modern era; his *Ghashiram Kotwal* and *Sakharam Binder* are among the most performed works in Marathi theatre. He'd also written several important films, including *Nishant* (1975) and *Ardh Satya*. Both films influenced Varma, especially *Ardh Satya*, which he credited with opening his eyes to a new kind of cinematic realism. It's not surprising Varma would consider Tendulkar to pen *his* gritty Mumbai film.

It's difficult to imagine the two of them working together – the playwright almost twice the director's age, probably used to more deference than Varma had a habit of showing. Still, Tendulkar was offered *Satya*. There was only one meeting, and it didn't go well. Varma told me Tendulkar was 'tied up with other things' and disgruntled with mainstream cinema. Kashyap remembers it going differently. In his telling, Tendulkar wasn't feeling well when they met him, but that was only part of the problem. 'I don't think he understood Ramu – the language communication was missing. Ramu did not speak Hindi at all; he spoke Telugu and English, and Vijay Tendulkar was more Marathi and Hindi. I was communicating everything. Ramu said Howard Roark, Ayn Rand, trying to explain the whole philosophy, and I was in the middle translating.' If Kashyap isn't exaggerating, it's hard to blame Tendulkar for declining the offer.

By this time, *Daud* had released and flopped. It was a strange creation – a boisterous road movie with a parodic bent. Dutt is a small-time crook on the run with Matondkar's dancer. There's a neutron bomb in a box, Paresh Rawal as a demented mafia don, Manoj Bajpayee glowering in the background and music by A.R. Rahman. 'I always liked films like *Romancing the Stone*, spoofy entertaining action films,' Varma told me. 'This was probably at the back of my head with *Daud*.' He admitted casting Dutt, a straightforward action hero, was probably a mistake (Shah Rukh Khan told him this as well). Amitabh Bachchan – tickled, perhaps, by the nod to *Sholay* in the motorbike-with-sidecar – told Varma the film was ahead of its time.

———

Perhaps because he broke into the film industry entirely on his own, Varma has always been ready to bet on newcomers. Yet, entrusting the writing of his first Hindi gangster film – one he evidently wanted to get right – to Kashyap, a newcomer in his early twenties, was asking a little too much. And so the search for screenwriters continued. Kashyap remembers Sudhir Mishra being approached, and the writer–director showing some interest. It's tempting to think the maker of *Is Raat Ki Subah Nahin*, an exemplary gangster noir, was asked to script this film, but Varma has never corroborated this. In Kashyap's telling, Mishra declined, and the possibility of his writing *Satya* – assuming it was there at all – remains a tantalising what-if.

(Mishra told me it's possible he was asked to write or at least discuss *Satya*, but that he has no specific recollection of it.)

Is Raat Ki Subah Nahin had a small army of writers. The story came from Mishra's younger brother, Sudhanshu. The screenplay was credited to Mishra, Nikhil Advani (who'd direct the 2003 hit *Kal Ho Na Ho*) and Shiv Subramaniam, better known as a supporting actor, though he also has three stellar writing credits: *Is Raat*, *Parinda* and Mishra's *Hazaaron Khwaishein Aisi* (2003). The dialogue was by Imtiaz Hussain, another *Parinda* alumnus. And there was another person rumoured to have contributed to the dialogue – Saurabh Shukla, who played gangster Vilas Pandey in the film.

Like Bajpayee, Shukla came out of Delhi theatre, working with the Sakshi group, and later joining the National School of Drama (NSD) Repertory Company. He was still at NSD when he landed the part of Kailash, Phoolan Devi's cousin, in *Bandit Queen*. Like his fellow cast member Manoj Bajpayee, he then moved to Bombay after prodding from Shekhar Kapur. He found work in TV, playing opposite director Vijay Anand in the detective series *Tehkikaat* (Kapur directed an episode). *Is Raat Ki Subah Nahin* was his second film. Both he and Mishra maintain he didn't contribute to the film's writing – at least not officially. 'I was a bounce board,' Shukla told me. 'I suggested a lot of things. I was an active participant. But I won't call it a writer.'

When I asked him about *Is Raat Ki Subah Nahin*, Varma was complimentary but brief, saying it was a realistic film for its time, and that he liked it in parts. Yet, both Kashyap and Shukla suggested the film was very much on Varma's mind. 'I don't know if Ramu accepts it or not', Shukla said, 'but at that point of time, he very clearly told a lot of us – to Sudhir also I'm sure – that he was really inspired by *Is Raat*, and *Satya* had a lot to draw from that film.' Mishra remembers Varma calling to congratulate him after watching it, and saying he felt encouraged that films like this were now possible. 'I think he meant ensemble films', Mishra said, 'in which there's no hero, just a bunch of interesting actors.' Kashyap goes further, saying *Is Raat* was the direct inspiration for Varma to make his gangster film, and that *Satya* wouldn't exist if Mishra's film didn't. He felt Varma's reservations stemmed from his irritation with Nirmal Pandey's protagonist in *Is Raat*. 'Why is he slouching?' he complained to Kashyap. 'Is he doing theatre?'

Kashyap told me that when Varma spoke to Mishra, he asked the *Is Raat* director why certain scenes unfolded the way they did. 'Ramu has this peculiar habit,' he said, grinning mischievously. 'He'll start interrogating people. He sees every single film the way he would have made it."*

We may never know how deeply Varma was influenced by *Is Raat Ki Subah Nahin* (nor is it terribly important). What we do know is that he liked Shukla in the film. Vilas is a memorable character in a film full of them – an Indian iteration of Warshow's gangster-as-tragic-hero. Shukla's performance has pathos and genuine hurt, presenting a more human *bhai* than Hindi film viewers were accustomed to. As a bonus, he'd been in *Bandit Queen*. Bajpayee, who knew Shukla from his theatre days, and had roomed with him in Mumbai, vouched for him. Kashyap threw in a good word as well. Shukla got the call to come and see Varma. They met at Varma's Four Bungalows apartment sometime in early 1997.

There was only one problem: Shukla didn't want to write. Heading to his first meeting with Varma, he suspected he wasn't being called

---

* There is some truth to this. Varma himself said in a 2008 interview to the *New Indian Express*, 'Today, I can't watch a film anymore, because I don't watch a film to be entertained. I see a film to judge it. I am constantly looking at camera angles, sound, this, that – which is not the way audiences look at the film.'

to act. 'I was prepared to say no', Shukla told me, 'because I wasn't interested in writing a film – it's tiresome and I am *fitrat se* not a writer.'

Varma said he always wanted Shukla as an actor *and* a writer. He told him he was making a gangster film, that he had a few characters in mind – Bheeku, Satya – and he wanted him to play the mobster with brains, Kallu Mama. 'He started with the offer of acting, so I couldn't say no,' Shukla chuckled. 'Then after that, he said I also want you to write. So I said, fine, I'll write it.' Varma, Bajpayee and Kashyap must have heaved a sigh of relief – they could move ahead. The four people who'd do the most to shape *Satya* were now together.

MEN WITH THE MOVIE CAMERAS

When *Slumdog Millionaire* became an unexpected hit in 2009, it was the first time many in the West had seen a realistic-looking Mumbai on the big screen. But it wasn't the first time a top foreign cinematographer had trained a camera on the city. A half-century before *Slumdog*, Roberto Rossellini made *India: Matri Bhumi* (1959), a collection of documentary scenes that begins on the streets of Bombay. Behind the camera was the great Aldo Tonti, who'd shot *Ossessione* (1943), *Europe '51* (1952) and *Nights of Cabiria* (1957) – all classic Italian films. Ten years later, Frenchman Étienne Becker shot Louis Malle's seven-part documentary, *Phantom India* (1969). The series ran into trouble with the Indian government for focussing, in their view, too much on poverty and not enough on development. The BBC, which aired the film, was forced to shut down its India operation from 1970 to 1972 after it refused to censor Malle's work. Whether or not you feel it's 'poverty porn' – a charge that never gets levelled at Indian films, no matter how miserablist – there's no denying the sharp eye of Becker. His images, shot on 16 mm, lend an immediacy to everything from a young, uncredited Hema Malini dancing on stage in Madras to Bombay street kids. The image of a child staring back at the camera in *Phantom India* finds an echo in Mira Nair's *Salaam Bombay*. The film ends with a shot of Chaipau, a child of the streets, looking dead ahead. American cinematographer Sandi Sissel, whose background was in documentary, shot Bombay like it had never been before, at least in fiction film. Coming at the end of the '80s, it opened up possibilities for directors looking to capture an unvarnished Bombay, explored in films like *Raakh* and *Dharavi*, and later in *Satya*.

Varma knew he wanted a different sort of look for his gangster film. He asked Kannan Iyer if he could think of someone without any preconceived notion of Indian film aesthetics – a foreign cinematographer, perhaps. Today, there are half a dozen cinematographers from other countries working in India. In the late '90s, though, importing a cameraperson from another country was a radical idea. Iyer had studied film at Temple University, Philadelphia. He suddenly remembered a cinematographer named Gerard Hooper who was teaching at Temple then. He'd known him through a college buddy, and had liked what he'd seen of his work. Iyer mentioned him to Varma. Hooper was asked to send his reel over. 'The remarkable thing about RGV is that he doesn't dither,' Iyer told me. 'He's very decisive. Something must have clicked in his head. He said, I'm going with him.'

Gerard Hooper was the unlikeliest crew member on *Satya*. A cinematographer by training, he'd shot and directed programmes for the *Discovery* channel, environmental documentaries, commercials, some non-fiction work for companies, an experimental feature and a short fiction film. Around the time Varma got in touch, he'd just started teaching at Drexel University, Philadelphia (he's still on the faculty there). *Satya* would be the first feature film he photographed for someone else. His exposure to Indian cinema was, like so many American film professionals, limited to the work of Satyajit Ray. He'd never seen a Hindi film before he got an offer to work on one. And he'd never been to India.

Hooper asked the university for three months off. He received no script before coming over – there was no script to give. All he had was a general idea – Mumbai, gangster film, not your regular song-and-dance. He somehow sourced a VHS tape of *Shiva* and watched it before leaving. He found it rough around the edges, but with a certain force and feeling.

It's apt that a film about an outsider was shot by an outsider. 'Ramu thought of using someone who will look at Bombay with fascination, a different eye altogether,' Bajpayee said. And Hooper really was fascinated by Mumbai. His flight landed at 1.30 in the night; by the time he reached the hotel, he was half in love with the city. Over the next few days, he wandered the streets with his still camera and accompanied Sabir Masani on his location scouting. And he watched *Sholay*, which, thankfully, he liked – it's difficult to imagine how he and his director, who saw the film 27 times in the same theatre, would have gotten along otherwise.

Nothing about Varma suggests he's the sort to make contingency plans. I can't picture him calmly working out that Hooper would have to return to his job at Drexel in less time than it normally takes to shoot a Hindi film, and that it would be useful to have someone who could fill his place when he did. Of course, if he did plan it out, it would also be like Varma to deny it. At any rate, another name was sought – a cinematographer, Indian this time, close enough to the start of his career that he wouldn't mind working as part of another cameraperson's team. Again, it was Iyer who tossed out the suggestion: Mazhar Kamran.

Kamran had studied at the Film and Television Institute of India, specialising in cinematography. His area of interest was documentary; he'd started out making non-fiction shorts on commission and for the popular TV serial *Surabhi*. In 1992, he shot a 30-minute fiction short, *Chakori*, directed by Sumitra Bhave and Sunil Sukhthankar. Here again the story circles back to *Bandit Queen*. In the opening minutes of *Chakori*, we see a young village girl patting cowdung into a cake. A boy drives past on a bicycle, splashing some of the dung on her. There's a close-up of her face as she looks up and yells at him. When I met Kamran in his office at the Indian Design Centre, IIT Bombay, he suggested I watch this scene and see whether it reminded me of anything. And, of course, it did: the scene early in *Bandit Queen* where young Phoolan is walking home with a pot on her head. A group of boys shatter this with a slingshot, drenching her, which leads to a profane outburst from the girl.

Bandit Queen premiered two years after *Chakori*. Both treat village life realistically without prettifying or romanticising it, so Kamran's suggestion that Shekhar Kapur might have been influenced by the short film isn't farfetched (Kapur, he says, 'really loved this film'). It's also possible Kapur might have mentioned *Chakori* to Varma as an example of realistic camerawork by a young DP. Or maybe Iyer, knowing Varma's fondness for *Bandit Queen*, suggested that the director look at something with a similar aesthetic. 'Somewhere, I feel that connection happened,' Kamran said. 'Why was my name being suggested at all? I was not asking for work. I was not in Bombay.'

Kamran wasn't asked to work on *Satya* initially. Instead, he was in talks to shoot another film, with Iyer directing and Varma as producer. When the project fell through, he figured he'd go back to documentaries. But then *Satya*'s executive producer, P. Som Shekar, called him in Delhi: Ramu's shooting a new film, he's hired this American cinematographer – would you like to be his Indian counterpart? Kamran wasn't keen; he didn't want to be an assistant cameraperson. But his friends advised him to give it a shot. Kamran admired Varma, so he eventually agreed and left for Mumbai. When the two of them met, they spoke about the film – though only a little, Kamran said. Hooper echoed this, but said Varma had a strong feel for the kind of film he was envisioning. 'He wanted to make a realistic film about contemporary crime in Mumbai. I think from the start it was clear we were going to shoot on location.'

THE REST OF THE GANG

By the time the cameramen had been hired, the rest of the team had largely fallen in place. Hindi film casting in the '90s wasn't the (relatively) professional business it is now. Much of the responsibility for sourcing actors and crew members fell on Iyer and Kashyap, with Bajpayee and a few others pitching in. Kashyap pulled Makarand Deshpande from the Mumbai theatre scene. Deshpande started doing plays at the famous Prithvi Theatre in 1986, and founded his own troupe, Ansh, in 1993. Along with acting and directing for the stage, he appeared in supporting parts in films; one of his earliest roles was as Pavan Malhotra's hot-headed friend in *Salim Langde Pe Mat Ro*. Deshpande proved a stellar addition, not only bringing a distinctive stoner vibe to his portrayal of advocate Mule but also chipping in with improvisations and script ideas.

Varma roped in several key players. Chakravarthy, who'd acted in five of Varma's Telugu productions and assisted on most of them, was cast as Satya. There was no audition – Varma simply told the actor, who was holidaying in the US, to get on a flight back. Chakri hastily returned and went to meet the director in his new foreign-bought clothes. Nothing came of the meeting, and he went back disappointed. Not long after, Varma turned up at his home. Chakri had fallen sick, and was dishevelled and grumpy. Amazingly, this worked in his favour, with Varma seeing the gangster he wanted in the unshaven man sitting before him, which he hadn't in the well-dressed one earlier. There and then, he handed Chakravarthy his first starring role in a Hindi film.

Allan Amin was recommended to Varma – he can't remember by whom – when word went out he was looking for a stunt coordinator who could handle realistic action. They met, Varma was impressed and Allan was hired (he too had worked on *Bandit Queen*). The director's brief to him was simple: no '*filmi*' action. In *Rangeela* producer Jhamu Sugandh's office, Varma came across a producer named Raju Mavani. He liked his menacing air and cast him as Bheeku's rival, Guru Narayan.

Film critic and writer–director Khalid Mohamed was asked to recommend someone who knew Mumbai's streets and the people who ran them – the kind of local ringer every production needs. Mohamed put them in touch with a young man named Sabir Masani, then working as a film journalist and a production controller with producer Yash Johar. Masani not only knew central Mumbai like the back of his hand but was also familiar with the gangster life. His friends, people he grew up with, had been in gangs; some had even been shot and killed. Masani ended up finding many of the locations used in the film. He also became the production's de facto cultural guide and interpreter of slang, and was rewarded with the small part of Yeda, the silent killer in Bheeku's gang.

Mahima Chaudhry, fresh off her debut in *Pardes* (1997), was pencilled in to play Vidya. It's not clear what happened next – there were reports that Chaudhry turned down the role, but Varma said she was only considered, not signed, and he went with Matondkar because he needed a more experienced performer. At any rate, the actor and director were reunited for the sixth time after *Antham*,

Gaayam, Rangeela, Anaganaga Oka Roju (1997) and *Daud*. Whether Matondkar was right for the part is debatable – I've always found her Vidya a little too naïve and virtuous. On the other hand, her presence brought with it some industry attention to a film that needed it. The only other (relatively) big name was Paresh Rawal, the actor who'd played a villain in Varma's last film, *Daud*, and in three of his earlier ones, *Siva*, *Kshana Kshanam* and *Govinda Govinda*. Rawal was known at the time for playing criminals of various stripes. Here he was cast against type, as a tough but upright police commissioner.

Apurva Asrani, only 19, was working for a company that cut film promos. One of the films he was assigned was *Daud*. Varma was impressed by the trailer, and invited Asrani to his studio. Later, dropping him home, he asked if he'd like to edit a film. Asrani told him he'd never done one before, and that he didn't use a Steenbeck, the traditional flatbed editing machine. Avid, the first digital editing system, was just starting to be used in Hindi film then to cut songs and promos. Varma ended up using two editors on the film: Asrani, who worked on Avid, and Bhanodaya, who'd edited his *Daud* and *Anaganaga Oka Roju*, and could operate the Steenbeck.

For the small but showy role of Bheeku's wife, Bajpayee thought of a friend of his, Shefali Shah. But there was a problem. A couple of years earlier, she had signed on for Varma's *Rangeela*. That part didn't pan out as expected and she walked off the production – a gusty move for an actor with some TV work and no films behind her. Varma wasn't enthusiastic when her name was brought up, but Bajpayee insisted she was right for the part. He eventually got the go-ahead to speak to her. After a story narration by Kashyap, she agreed to work on the film.

As the time for the shoot drew nearer, word had spread about Varma's new film. Up-and-coming actors scrambled to get their headshots to him through someone they knew on the production.

Sushant Singh was then just another theatre actor trying to make it in the film industry. He'd worked with Ibrahim Alkazi's theatre company in Delhi before moving to Mumbai. In 1997, he was living in an apartment in Four Bungalows. He'd just shot for *Dr Babasaheb Ambedkar* (2000), his first screen role. One day, Kashyap, who knew his flatmate, came over. Singh cornered him, said he was an actor, that he'd done theatre in Delhi. Was there a part in *Satya* he could read for? Kashyap told him the major casting was over, but he'd see what he could do. Weeks went by. Scouting for work, Singh bumped into a friend, Barnali Ray Shukla, an assistant director on *Satya*. She asked him, 'Weren't you supposed to send Anurag your photographs?'

Singh had stills from a stage production of Tennessee Williams' *A Streetcar Named Desire,* in which he'd played Stanley Kowalski, sporting a crew cut. He passed these on to Shukla. A few days later, he got two calls. One was from Mansoor Khan's office about a substantial role in *Josh* (2000), with Shah Rukh Khan and Aishwarya Rai. The other was from Varma's office. Varma had cast someone else as Pakiya, the local goon whose face Satya slashes, but then he saw Singh and liked his snarl and short hair. After a wardrobe test, he told Kashyap to hire him. It couldn't have seemed like an important decision at the time, but it would have a profound impact on how the film turned out.

Kashyap warned Singh it was a miniscule part. He didn't care. Like most young actors at the time, he just wanted to impress Varma. 'I decided to treat *Satya* like an audition,' he told me. 'He'll see a couple of scenes, get to know I'm an actor, then he'll give me a bigger role.' Amazingly, it worked out just like that. *Satya* was still in edit when Singh was cast as the third lead in Varma's next film, *Kaun* (1999).

Finally, there was Bharatbhai. One of India's biggest diamond merchants, Bharat Shah channelled his fortune into movies, financing everything from *Border* to *Aunty No. 1* (1998). Despite the unlikelihood of commercial success, Shah decided to fund *Satya* (along with nine other films that year). One of the people I spoke to for this book told me a story about how Shah came to be the film's financier instead of the more artistically discerning Jhamu Sugandh, producer of Varma's last two films. It involves Sugandh, Varma, Shah, Mani Ratnam, and Shah Rukh Khan and his Bandra mansion, 'Mannat'. There is no earthly way to verify it, so I'll just let you try and tie these players together with a suitably outlandish theory.

6

Making the Film

'No one knew what the hell was happening, including me.'

– Ram Gopal Varma

There's a term used by film industry folk called the 'one-line'. It's what directors and screenwriters offer when someone asks them to describe the film they're making in a few words. *Satya*'s one-line, as told to Anurag Kashyap by Ram Gopal Varma, was 'Let's put Howard Roark in the underworld.'

One of the many disparate influences bouncing around in Varma's mind – along with Sridevi, Bruce Lee, Amitabh Bachchan, *Mackenna's Gold*, assorted porn stars – is Ayn Rand's *The Fountainhead*. The director has long been a fan of the 1943 novel about the uncompromising (and insufferable) architect Roark. Rand is referenced four times in Varma's memoirs, and his enthusiasm for the author was common knowledge among his associates. It may even have influenced a key hiring. Kashyap has written about how he was a communist in college until he read Ayn Rand. One of the things Manoj Bajpayee – by then already working with Varma – noticed when he first visited Kashyap's apartment was that he had Rand on his bookshelf.

How exactly Varma envisioned the hero of *The Fountainhead* in a gangster film is unclear. When I asked him what he'd intended, he said it only existed as a vague idea, and spoke of his lack of clarity in the beginning. Traces of Roark may have survived in the wilful Satya, but there's a fundamental difference between the two characters. Roark is Rand's ideal of an Exceptional Man, whereas Satya is ordinary from the moment the camera finds him among the crowds at CST. If Kashyap didn't mention the one-line whenever he was asked about the film, the Randian origins of *Satya* would probably never have come up.

By the time Saurabh Shukla was hired, Roark was history. But *Satya* was still an amorphous idea – the underworld, a gangster, the girl he loves and some guy named Bheeku. 'When he narrated it to me for the first time, it clearly felt like *Shiva*,' Shukla said. He remembers trying to sell Varma on *Goodfellas*. '*The Godfather* – it's a great film, but I never get scared,' Shukla told him. 'I know these people exist, but they are not crossing my path. Whereas *Goodfellas* scares the hell out of me, because the gangster is right next door.'

Varma told the two writers to come up with a structure. In Shukla's recollection, 'Anurag and I went back. Talked. Drank. Partied. Didn't write. Two days later, we had another meeting. By then, we'd started reacting on ideas. I put a few questions in front of Ramu – character arc, what if we do this, what about that? After 15 minutes, he stopped me and said, don't give me this intellectual shit. Tell me, what's the story you have? It put things into perspective – that we were faffing and not really working.'

The writers hunkered down and came up with an elaborate sequence to open the film. A man on a plane, ordinary-looking, but with a slightly desperate quality to him. Drops of blood drip from his coat. He's revealed to be a gangster. There's a shootout. Varma heard them out. When they were done, he told them he was off to supervise some dubbing and they'd meet the next day (the sequence never made it into *Satya*, though it's the sort of thing that would have worked nicely in *Company*). As Varma was leaving, he told Shukla, who hadn't yet been officially hired, to ride with him. In the car, the director asked him how much money he was looking for. 'I wanted to buy a house,' Shukla told me. 'Houses at that time were seven lakhs or something. I didn't have the courage to ask for seven lakhs, so I said, Ramu, I want three lakhs, which was a pretty big sum for someone like me to ask for. He said, okay, but don't discuss it with the others.'

TAKING SHAPE

In the early stages of pre-production, few people were as useful to Varma as Ajit Dewani, a man with a toehold in the film industry and in the underworld. Much of what the director heard from him about the everyday workings of the mafia made it into the film in some form. One day, Dewani started telling Varma of a particularly crazy gangster he knew, saying, 'This man has probably not studied, not gone to school. You can see that wild behaviour in his eyes, in the way he laughs, the way he sits in the chair.' Varma, always on the lookout for rebels with an edge, began envisioning a character along similar lines. He can't remember why, but he named him Bheeku. Kashyap said Bheeku was the boy who used to bring Varma tea.

Though he's thanked in the opening credits, Dewani doesn't receive any official billing. Yet, he was integral to both the authenticity of the production and the access it got to the world it was portraying.

'He knew most of the gangsters,' Kashyap said. 'He had the inside stories.' Masani told me that most of the locations in the suburbs – Bandra, Andheri, Juhu – were suggested by Dewani.

One of Dewani's stories about the tempestuous gangster provided Varma with the 'soul of Bheeku's character'. The man's brother had been killed by the police. At his funeral, instead of mourning, he started berating him, cursing violently. This inspired the scene in the film after the jovial Chander is killed by the police in a staged 'encounter'. Satya, Kallu Mama and Bheeku are framed tightly, sitting around a table in a dimly lit room. They've had time to digest the news, but Bheeku won't stop talking about Chander. '*Mar gaya saala. Kya zaroorat thi udhar jaane ki? Mana kiya tha uss haraami ko*' (He's dead. Why did he have to go there? I told the bastard not to). Kallu Mama tries to cut him off, but Bheeku continues to rant about Chander's lack of seriousness, his eagerness to prove his gangster credentials, his mother's efforts to get him married. When he talks about Chander's constant silly humour, there's a quick shot of the big man laughing at his own Ram-Shyam joke.

Initially, Bajpayee was slated for the titular role, back when Bheeku didn't really exist and Satya, an outsider who gets sucked into the Mumbai mafia, was the one established character. But Dewani's magnetic, emotional gangster was coming to life in Varma's head. One day, he called the actor and said, Manoj, it will be better if you do this other role instead. Bajpayee was disheartened. He'd been looking forward to his first lead part. Now it felt as though his big break was slipping away. '*Anurag, kya ho raha hai, main kya kar raha hoon?*' (Anurag, what is happening, what am I doing?), he asked Kashyap. The writer tried to calm him down. 'Satya can be played by anybody,' he told him. 'For Bheeku, we need an actor.'

The funny thing is, Satya is the kind of brooding, intense criminal Bajpayee had played in *Bandit Queen* and *Daud*. It's to Varma's credit he realised the actor had other gears. Also, he'd decided that Satya, an immigrant and a new entrant to Mumbai crime, would be more authentic if the actor playing him was an outsider. That's part of what made him think of Chakravarthy. The Telugu actor was a stranger to Bollywood; on top of that, he wouldn't speak Hindi like the others, which would underscore his character's migrant roots. Also – and though it sounds strange, casting decisions often turn on details like this – Varma thought Chakravarthy had the right eyes for the part. 'There's an element of cold bloodedness in him', he told me, 'and also a lost guy who comes to Bombay to make a living.'

In the initial version of the screenplay Chakravarthy read, Satya was the outgoing one and Bheeku the brooder. The actor had recently played the lead in Varma's Telugu horror film *Deyyam* (1996), in which, he told me, his character was 'exactly like Bheeku Mhatre'. He went to Varma and said, let me do something different. In Chakravarthy's recollection, by the time they were ready to shoot, Satya and Bheeku had swapped personalities.

Satya's otherness is never discussed or made part of the narrative like, say, the otherness of Velu Naicker in *Nayakan*. We never get to know where Satya is from, but judging from his lightly accented Hindi, he belongs to one of southern states. It was important to Varma that the character be from another town. 'I wanted to see it through the eyes of a stranger. Most of my films have this recurring theme. I think I've picked it up from Bruce Lee – in all his films, he comes from somewhere else.'

It's easy to forget that *Satya* is a film about one migrant, made by another. A year after the film's release, Varma said in an interview, 'A lot of people ask me how I know this city when I am a south Indian. I think the truth is actually reverse. When you are an outsider, you tend to see much more objectively than a person who has lived here all his life.' The unit had people from Andhra Pradesh (Varma,

Chakravarthy, Bhanodaya), Uttar Pradesh (Anurag Kashyap, Saurabh Shukla, Aditya Srivastava, Sushant Singh), Bihar (Manoj Bajpayee) and Madhya Pradesh (Govind Namdev). They were, of course, migrants by choice, not circumstance, leaving their homes to make a name for themselves in the one place where Hindi films are made. It's the sort of miracle you can't will into being – all these people who grew up thousands of miles from the city coming together to make one of the great Mumbai films.

Satya's success turned out to be a subtle ideological victory too. At the time, the Shiv Sena was the ruling party (in a coalition with the BJP) in the state of Maharashtra, of which Mumbai is the capital. The party had a history of targeting immigrants of all stripes, especially the ones from Uttar Pradesh and Bihar, disdainfully called '*bhaiyyas*'. But the Sena loved this film, unconcerned or unaware that it was made by people mostly from UP and Bihar and Andhra Pradesh. The party leadership made it tax-free, twice. Bajpayee was invited to have tea with Bal Thackeray.

How many Sena supporters cheered for Bheeku, not realising the actor playing him was from Bihar? And how many knew it and cheered anyway? Novelist Amitava Kumar, who grew up in Bihar not far from where Bajpayee went to school, wrote about his deep connection to the film and its lead actor: 'While watching *Satya*, therefore, I was watching Bheeku Mhatre as a Bhojpuri-speaking man who had taught himself to pass as a native in the Marathi-dominated metropolis. It was a magnificent performance, of course, but for me, more than an actor's prowess, what the film revealed was a talented individual's ability to rise above, and escape, his origins. And even that was not all. What was real about Bheeku Mhatre, his earthiness and his authenticity, was the subtle result of a persistence in Bajpayee's performance: the result of the enormous toil that had gone into the making of what he now was. That presence of opposites – and nothing else – made his every gesture a livewire act.'

—

With Kashyap throwing him clues about how his character was shaping up in the writing, Bajpayee began his own process of creation. The first step was adding a little menace. In person, the actor is thin, mild-voiced, not too tall. Chakravarthy, though not an imposing physical presence either, at least had a killer glare and a beard. Bajpayee told me: 'When Chakri was cast, I looked at his beard and told myself, I'm also going to have one, otherwise he'll look much more dangerous. I should look as heavy as him.'

Because there weren't always designers for bit players in those days, newer actors would depend on the costume *dada*. Bajpayee decided to take matters into his own hands. 'Since I'm working on the character', he told Varma, 'I'd like to get my own clothes.' He had a look in mind. A local hood in the town where he grew up used to wear floral prints, so Bajpayee went out looking for cheap shirts with flowers on them. In a small store in Hill Road market, a shopkeeper showed him some options – made from a light fabric, they seemed to flow. 'I wanted to show that this character is very colourful, that he has too many moves. For his darker mood, I wanted dark jeans, dark *baniyan* (undershirt).' Bajpayee bought some 20 shirts. He said they only cost him 15,000 rupees.

Other actors figured out their own wardrobe as well. Shah said she 'added the colours, the style and the look as my contribution to my role'. The only actor who definitely had clothes made for her (even if they were simple saris) was Matondkar. This explains the rather incongruous presence of Manish Malhotra, high priest of Bollywood fashion and costumer to the stars in *Kuch Kuch Hota Hai* earlier that year, in *Satya*'s decidedly unglamorous opening credits. But Malhotra had designed for Matondkar in *Rangeela* to such culture-altering effect that both actor and director were happier having him around, even if there wasn't much scope for glamour.

Having settled on a look, Bajpayee started putting together the rest of Bheeku. 'He's real – but he's always one notch higher,' he decided. Rehearsing alone one day, he tried out a wild laugh, and it sounded right. Years later, he wondered if the childlike uncontrollability of Bheeku's giggle coupled with the man's brutality had made him seem even more dangerous.

Bajpayee had been in Mumbai five years, but still spoke Hindi like a north Indian. Bheeku would have to have a Maharashtrian, or at least a Bambaiyya, accent. Casting around for distinctive voices, he started picking up the cadences of the *bai* who worked at his place, who was from Kolhapur in south Maharashtra. 'I made the backstory in my mind that Bheeku's father was from Kolhapur, and knew Bhau. His father died when he was young, and Bhau looked after his family.' This bit of unspoken history surfaces in the scene where Bheeku goes to see Bhau at his home. Upon entering the room, Bheeku touches Bhau's feet before sitting down. 'Why did you do that?' Varma asked after calling cut. Bajpayee explained that Bheeku still felt indebted to Bhau. Varma was impressed, and the scene was shot with a close-up of hand touching feet.

Kashyap and Shukla were bundled off to Hyderabad, where Varma had a farmhouse (in a blog post written years later, Kashyap remembers his partner reaching Mumbai airport late: 'He had the tickets … we missed the flight … we took the next one'). Varma gave the writers a brief about the characters and the beats he wanted them to incorporate, and left them there. 'He didn't check in,' Shukla said. 'We both were locked in there. We were provided ample beer and food and time to write. In 15 days, we came up with a first draft.' There is a famous precedent that may not have occurred to the three: Orson

Welles marooning Herman J. Mankiewicz on a ranch in the desert, miles from Los Angeles, so he would stop gambling and drinking and write *Citizen Kane* (1941).

It was an unlikely but fruitful collaboration. Kashyap had drive and a great ear, Shukla could casually pull ideas out of the air. 'Saurabh wouldn't write,' Kashyap chuckled. 'I volunteered to do the penning. Saurabh is a great ideas guy, but super lazy.' It's advisable to take most Kashyap pronouncements with a pinch of salt, but I believe him here – he repeated 'Saurabh is super lazy' four times during our conversation. Shukla might have been a more easy-going individual than Kashyap (as most people tend to be), but he could rise to the occasion brilliantly. We already know how he came up with the Bheeku and Pyaari fight on the spot. On another occasion, Varma called him to narrate a scene he'd been asked to write. Kashyap, who was present, noticed Shukla was speaking rather slowly, though otherwise it seemed to be going great. As Shukla grew increasingly rapt, Varma quietly beckoned to Kashyap and indicated the paper his partner was reading from. It was blank.

I asked Shukla how he and Kashyap and Varma, having grown up far from Mumbai, went about capturing its speech patterns. 'Common sense,' he said. 'The three of us knew as much Bambaiyya Hindi as we heard in films. The authenticity of the language was brought by the actors who were from here. We also met some people – not many – for research, and we heard how they talked.'

One of the smaller pleasures of *Satya* is the melding and clashing of accents and tones. There's Shukla's no-nonsense rasp; Snehal Dabi's *tapori* patter; Chakravarthy's look-before-you-step negotiation of the Hindi language. Bajpayee's lilting voice contrasting with Shefali Shah's middle-class Maharashtrian accent adds an extra bit of frisson to their combustive pairing. ('Bheeku doesn't sound like a Maharashtrian, Pyaari does,' Kashyap told me. 'But when they use Bambaiyya, people don't question it because it's a mix of all immigrant languages.') Some of the people I met pointed to this or that actor who didn't speak accurate Bambaiyya. This may be true, but the idea of imposing standards of excellence on a mongrel tongue seems to miss the point. *Satya* would be a less exciting film if everyone spoke like Chander.

My favourite line in the film comes when *Satya* is seen talking to Vidya by his gang buddies. 'Item *bahut bhaari hai*' (That's a hot number), growls Yeda – something Sabir Masani improvised. Chander has the clincher: '*Poora Mumbai lafde mein* blast *ho gaya, aur Satya ekdum* fast *ho gaya*' (Mumbai's been levelled in a bomb blast, and Satya's wasting no time). This proclamation, though in keeping with Chander's penchant for silly jokes, doesn't make any sense. The reference could be to the serial bombings of 1993, but this has nothing to do with Satya's behaviour – it's just an excuse to rhyme 'blast' with 'fast'. Yet, this line cracks me up every time. This isn't the first time a Mumbai tragedy is referenced in a comic scene in a Varma film. In *Rangeela*, Aamir Khan's ticket tout loudly protests his innocence as a cop frisks him, asking why he's being persecuted while the instigators of *danga-fasaad* (a possible reference to the communal riots of 1992–93) go scot-free.

Language is also used to hint at the class divide. There's little difference between Vidya's station in life and Pyaari and Bheeku's. But, as we see when they're out for dinner, Vidya has something the couple don't: an English education, which counts for a lot in India. She's the only one who can pronounce 'Jurassic Park' (Bheeku calls it '*chhipkali wali pikchar*' – that film with the lizard). When she says 'You both love each other so much,' Pyaari asks what 'so much' means. The film doesn't make too much of this, but it adds a little wrinkle of social commentary – just as Bheeku's checked shirt, buttoned right to the top, does. As Bajpayee told me, 'This is his way of looking like a gentleman.' There is again a precedent in *Rangeela*, when Aamir Khan, dressed like a Mumbai taxi in a yellow shirt, yellow trousers and shades, takes Matondkar on a lunch date and exhausts his meagre supply of English in a bid to show that he can be fancy too.

Satya's language also kicked open a door that was long-closed. For years, cussing in Hindi films rarely went beyond '*kameenay*' (rascal) or '*haraami*' (bastard). *Satya,* by my estimate, has four '*chutiyas*' (roughly, 'cunt'), one '*behen ke lund*' (sister's dick) and a muttered '*madar …*' (mother …) – a significant upgrade. *Bandit Queen*, released three years earlier, had more explosive language – the first image is of a young girl looking at the camera and saying, '*Main hoon Phoolan Devi, bhenchod*' (I'm Phoolan Devi, sister-fuckers). But that was an art film, whereas Varma was playing in the same ballpark as Aditya Chopra. He wanted to get past India's notoriously interfering censors, release his film and make some money. But he also knew tough language was appropriate for the setting, and it would cause a stir. Years later, he told the *New Indian Express*, 'Even with a movie like *Satya*, I'm not sure that its commercial success has anything to do with what the critics liked it for. There were people who said they loved it because it was the first time they heard the word *chutiya* in the theatre.'

Shukla said the idea was to include just enough cussing to make it sound natural. '*Thoda idhar udhar halka* (a touch here and there) … to give the feeling that this person exists. A gangster is not going to talk in poetic terms, for god's sake.' And he was right – to hear a character say *chutiya* in a quasi-mainstream Hindi film was something unprecedented. The street toughs of *Parinda* and *Is Raat Ki Subah Nahin* and *Ghulam* never came close to that.

—

Before Sabir Masani played Yeda, he was the unit's (uncredited) location scout, brought in as a guide to gangland Mumbai. 'Where should we start looking?' Ramu asked when they first met. 'Your assistants will show you places in Andheri and Borivali', Masani replied, 'but you want to go where organised crime actually started in Mumbai – the mill area, Bombay Central, Madanpura, Nagpada, Tardeo.' Varma told him to head out with a photographer and bring back recce images. (In the film, Bheeku's area is said to be around Mohammad Ali Road, Nepean Sea Road and Grant Road – south-central Mumbai. Guru Narayan's areas are to the north-east of Bheeku's – Wadala, Antop Hill, Bhandup.)

Locations were sourced all across the city. A cowshed in Goregaon West became the site for the pivotal face-slashing scene. The abandoned building complex where the Ram-Shyam joke is told and the shootout takes place was near Link Road in Versova. Kallu Mama's den was in Bandra, near Mehboob Studio. The torture sequence was also shot in a bungalow in Bandra. The Girgaum Chowpatty area was used twice – Chakravarthy and Urmila walk there during the romantic number 'Badalon Se', and, late in the film, it's the site for the huge Ganesh immersion (the killing of Bhau, though it appears to take place here, was filmed across town at Juhu Chowpatty). A restaurant near Juhu beach was recruited for the double-date scene. Neeraj Vora suggested Bhaidas Auditorium, a popular theatre venue in Vile Parle, for the movie hall where the stampede happens. In places where local gangs held sway and a go-between was needed, Ajit Dewani, with all his contacts, came in handy.

At the time, dance bars were still legal in Mumbai. These were establishments where women danced to Bollywood numbers and patrons showered them with money – like strip bars, except here the clothes stayed on. Varma decided Satya would work in one such dive, so he went with a few crew members to Topaz on Grant Road for a recce party. The visitors drank, enjoyed themselves and eventually got up to leave, at which point they caused a stir. It was standard practice in these bars to rain currency notes on the dancers – only Varma never carried any cash. He loved Topaz, but it was too popular to get the management to shut it down for shooting. So the team settled on Charwak bar in Borivali East instead. In the first bar scene, the song playing is 'Mujhe Pyaar Hua Allah Miyan', from the Matondkar, Sridevi and Anil Kapoor-starrer, *Judaai* (1997) – a little meta-reference.

On another occasion, things got tense. Varma asked Masani to show him the kind of *chawl* where Satya and Vidya's quarters might be. Masani took him to Tardeo, a rough neighbourhood then. There was a gangster living there by the name of Rao whom the police were hunting, which meant the area was on edge. Leaving Varma in the car with instructions not to wander off, Masani went to find someone with enough clout to get them permission to shoot. When he returned, he found the director surrounded by a small mob. It turned out Varma had exited the car and started taking photographs, which made the locals suspicious. '*Arre*, this is Ramu,' Masani told them, thanking his stars he wasn't showing around some obscure art film director. 'He made *Rangeela*.' Luckily, it worked. In the car, Varma muttered, 'Whatever happens, we're not shooting here.' Ultimately, Masani, with some help from Dewani, managed to find a suitable replacement in Agripada, not far from Dagdi Chawl, home of don Arun Gawli.

When *Satya* released, it was rumoured that Bheeku was based on Gawli, given both dons were Maharashtrian, ran Hindu gangs (most crime bosses were Muslim) and operated out of central Mumbai. But the comparison can only be taken so far. Bheeku has neither the smarts nor the career trajectory of Gawli. No one I spoke to mentioned Gawli as a direct inspiration for Bheeku, though Varma's fascination for the don was brought up. I think it's ultimately to the film's advantage that it doesn't hew too closely to any real-life example. Varma and the writers struck a fortuitous balance between allusion (to Gawli, to Bal Thackeray) and invention, allowing the viewer to join the dots or simply enjoy the narrative on its own terms.

—

Two films released within two years of each other on the cusp of the millennium changed the way Hindi cinema looked. One was Farhan Akhtar's *Dil Chahta Hai* (2001), a film whose muted shades and superior design sense introduced a new kind of tasteful upper-class Bollywood look. The other was *Satya*, which didn't invent this sort of gritty realism so much as bring it into the mainstream. What's surprising is how little planning went into creating its supremely influential visual aesthetic. Certainly, Varma chose wisely (or let Kannan Iyer choose wisely for him). He knew he wanted a realistic film, and hired a cinematographer and a backup with roots in documentary. But beyond that, there doesn't seem to have been a lot of head-scratching about how the film would look.

'*Satya* wasn't intensely discussed,' said Hooper. 'It's not like we did this kind of extensive pre-visualisation. We talked in more general terms.' Some things were clear, though. It was decided well before production began that shooting would be done, as far as possible, on location. This suited Hooper fine. 'I was interested in trying to make reality look like itself, in terms of the way it was lit and framed,' he said. 'I think there was a conscious effort on both our parts to make it look real, to use soft light, to use light that looks motivated, so you can imagine being in those surroundings.' During Hooper's time on the film, he estimates they shot for maybe two days in the studio;

everything else was on location. Kamran said Varma gave him and Hooper a one-line brief: it should look real and not lit up.

Varma knew he wanted *Satya* to look different from his earlier stylised action films. '*Shiva* is very designed – every shot, every composition, every cut,' he told me. '*Satya* is more or less a people's film. The camera is pretty much letting the actors do what they're supposed to do, and is not intruding into their space.' Kashyap said Hooper kept the camera at an objective distance from the actors – an observation that rings truer if you compare *Satya* with later Varma films like *Company* and *Sarkar*, where the camera is constantly invading the actors' personal space.

This insistence on realism didn't mean Varma wanted his gangster film to resemble a documentary. Despite its everyday locations and practical lighting, *Satya* looked like a fiction feature. If the word 'documentary' popped up in several reviews, it's only because this seemed much closer to reality than the mainstream Hindi cinema of that time. It's the difference between straight-ahead reality and realism as an aesthetic; compared to *Satya*, something like Dibakar Banerjee's *Love, Sex Aur Dhokha* (2010) really does have the look of non-fiction film. Kamran told me flatly: 'For most people, realism means you just point the camera and shoot. It's not that. Realism is a style.'

Did Varma have the down-and-dirty look of *Satya* in his head from the start? His early films were overtly 'designed' – crazy angles, attention-calling shots. *Satya* was the tonal opposite. It must have helped that Varma kept himself and his cinematographer free of the anxiety of influence. An Indian DoP entrusted with Varma's first gangster film might have tried to imitate the visual palette of *Parinda* or *Nayakan*. But Hooper didn't know these films; he'd barely seen any Indian cinema at all. And Varma never asked his cinematographer to use an existing film, Indian or foreign, as a reference point.

Several people I spoke to mentioned Hooper as being instrumental in creating *Satya*'s visual aesthetic. Varma was a little defensive when I asked about their collaboration, saying people didn't understand that the cinematic image was a cumulative effect of ambience, the look of the actors and the location. 'I wouldn't like to think there is any great camerawork in *Satya*,' he said. Kashyap told me the look of the film was 'all Gerry'. He cited Varma's tendency to get right up close to the actors; the slight distance the camera maintains in *Satya* came from Hooper, he said. 'Gerry had a very objective point of view. He moved away from the character, unlike Ramu.' Hooper was also responsible for the city shooting – all those images of animals, children, sea, sky, buildings, crowds that anchored the narrative to its setting.

Because Kamran and Hooper came from documentary film, they were used to shooting quickly and efficiently. This came in handy when they had to film scenes on the run, guerrilla-style. Doing away with the excessive lighting typical of Bollywood films was key. 'Ramu would joke that usually he couldn't see his actors because there'd be so many lights on them,' Hooper said. The American used lower exposures and fewer and softer lights, placing them further away from the actors than was the custom. Kamran, as lighting cameraman, was not only on board but enthusiastic. When I spoke to him, he recalled his FTII days, when he'd experiment on the streets of Pune, testing what happened when you shot without light, or with just a tubelight or a bulb.

One potential barrier was that of language. Hooper spoke no Hindi, and not all of the camera team was comfortable with English. Even the deep pockets of Bharat Shah couldn't afford the production turning into a scene from Jean-Luc Godard's *Contempt* (1963), with every instruction translated for the benefit of a multilingual crew. Thankfully, this never came to pass. Hooper said he and Kamran communicated just fine, and that 'when you're working on the same function together, there's a common unspoken grammar'. Also, by all accounts, Hooper was well-liked by the crew, and his enthusiasm for the city was genuine.

Things continued to come together in this slapdash manner. Then it was August, and the start of shooting was upon them. No one could have known two essential pieces of the puzzle would only fall into place after production started.

A SCREAM AND A MURDER

Everyone I spoke to agreed that the earliest scenes shot were the ones in the *tabela* (cowshed) where Satya rents a place to stay. However, only one person – assistant director Barnali Ray Shukla – could give me a start date: 11 August 1997. We met on a balmy October afternoon at Love & Latte, a coffee shop in Lokhandwala favoured by film industry folk. I asked how she was so sure when her husband, Saurabh Shukla, could barely zero in on the right month when we had spoken. I was half-hoping she'd say she maintained a meticulous diary during the film's production which she'd be delighted to hand over to me. 'It was my first film,' she said, simply. 'One remembers these things.'

The *tabela* scenes follow immediately after the opening credits. The shed's owner (Manoj Pahwa) shows Satya, who's presumably come there directly from the train station, around the premises and tells him it'll cost 20 rupees a night if he wants board. 'This is how I used to stay when I came here, pay per night,' Kashyap murmured when we watched the scene in his apartment.

After a scene at the dance bar, where Satya finds work, comes the moment at the *tabela* everyone remembers. It's the first link (or the first we know of, as Satya's past is never revealed) in the chain that tethers this character to a life of crime. We already know Satya's not one to back down – in the scene at the bar, when Jagga, the local strongman, throws a drink in his face, he gives him a look that suggests he's weighing violent options. Back in the *tabela*, a hood by the name of Pakiya (Sushant Singh) approaches Satya with an associate. They want money. 'Orchestra *karane ka hai*' (We will hire a band), Pakiya says. They're Jagga's men, the *tabela* owner warns. Chowta's score does a Morricone-like 'hoh!' Satya doesn't say anything, and just stares at Pakiya as he'd stared at Jagga. Pakiya pulls out his *ustra*, the ubiquitous Indian shaving blade – included at Allan Amin's suggestion. '*Geela ho gaya?*' (Pissed yourself?), he smirks. As he turns for a second, Satya, with frightening speed, grabs the blade and slashes the man's face. Pakiya screams, clutches his bleeding cheek in horror and falls to his knees. His friend drops the collection box. Satya throws the razor and walks off. The *tabela* owner yells for water.

This wasn't how things were supposed to go. Varma had planned to end the scene when Pakiya was slashed. But because of the intensity of Singh's scream, he forgot to call cut. Singh's theatre instincts kicked in. 'That was the training,' he told me. 'You improvise until someone says stop.' One option was to retaliate, but Shukla, explaining the scene earlier, had told him Pakiya wasn't a real gangster, more of a *tapori* who probably hadn't seen a real blade in his life. So Singh decided to fall to the ground instead and yell the kind of vague threats that people who are only pretending to be tough do. Pahwa, also from Delhi theatre, was alert to the situation, and added his own comic shouts.

Varma finally called an end to the scene. He came up to Sushant and shook his hand. 'He said, excellent, excellent, excellent,' Singh recalled. 'Barnali and everybody were looking at me like, boss, *abhi teri nikal padi* (you're on your way).'

Varma credits the scream and its aftermath with revealing to him the tone of the film. Until then, he had not been big on improvising, apart from a few scenes with the Neeraj Vora character in *Rangeela*. Now, he realised he could use a looser style of working to achieve something approaching naturalism. 'While capturing a scene, most directors have a tendency to pre-decide how it should start and how it should end,' he wrote in *Guns & Thighs*. 'All the realistic performances happened because I stopped restricting actors to a script. I just wanted them to improvise whatever they felt like. Actors were instructed not to follow written lines but just say whatever they felt like.'

Out of nowhere, Varma had found the metre of the film. Almost immediately after, fate would conspire to show him the skeleton.

—

On 12 August 1997, at around 10 in the morning, Gulshan Kumar, founder of T-Series, India's biggest record label, entered Jeeteshwar Mahadev Mandir, a Shiv temple in Lokhandwala. He was a devout man – the T-series empire was founded on religious music as much as on film songs – and this was how he normally began his day. He left half an hour later and headed for his car. Suddenly, two strangers walked up to him. One of them pointed a gun at him and fired. The bullet hit him, but Kumar managed to stagger away. The shooters followed, firing 16 bullets into Kumar before fleeing the scene in a taxi – a fittingly Mumbai getaway. Kumar was rushed to the nearby Cooper hospital, where he was pronounced dead on arrival.

Years later, one Abdul Rauf Merchant confessed to the killing, which he said was ordered by mobster Abu Salem. Salem and his boss, D-Company head Dawood Ibrahim, had been trying to extort a monthly sum of a few lakhs from Kumar. The T-series founder initially paid up, but then refused (composer Runu Sagar attempts to do the same in *Satya*). The murder sent seismic waves through the Hindi film industry, which by then was used to extortion by Mumbai dons but not the bloody fallout of resisting them. Hits had been taken out on Bollywood directors Rajiv Rai and Subhash Ghai in the past, but in both cases the killers were unsuccessful. Saurabh Shukla summed up the general feeling in the industry then: 'That was the time I felt personally how close we were to the underworld.'

How disconcerting must it have been to learn of the killing of one of the most powerful figures in Bollywood while beginning work on a film about the Mumbai underworld? *Satya* wasn't a huge production, but Varma was a hot director then, Matondkar was a star and word had gotten around that a realistic gangster film was underway. Did crew members ever wonder if they'd inadvertently stumbled into the crosshairs of the mob? Or did it make the production more exciting, like Ben Hecht and William Wellman must have felt when reviews of their gangster films shared newsprint with the bloody exploits of their subjects?

Nearly every person who worked on *Satya* mentioned the Gulshan Kumar murder to me. If Barnali Ray's start date of 11 August is accurate, then the killing happened on the second day of production. Other accounts place the shooting on the first, second, third or fourth day, some in the morning, others in the evening. Everyone agrees the murder was early on in the shooting schedule, while they were filming the *tabela* scenes. Varma told me he heard the news in the morning, on set, and cancelled the shoot for the day. Apurva Asrani remembers the director getting that call and looking shell-shocked.

To complicate matters (for me, if no one else), Varma had two versions of events. When I transcribed our conversation, I found he'd placed himself on set, and, at a different point in the interview, in producer Jhamu Sugandh's office, at the moment of being informed of Kumar's death. The Sugandh version appears in *Guns & Thighs* and in several of Varma's interviews. In it, as Sugandh is telling Varma about Kumar's last moments, his thoughts stray to how the shooter's day must have unfolded. 'If Gulshan Kumar woke up at 7 o'clock, then at what time would the killer have woken up?' he writes in his memoir. 'Did he tell his mom to wake him up because he had a shooting to carry out? Did he have his breakfast before committing the crime or after? ... Then it suddenly struck me that you always hear about gangsters only when they either kill or die. But what do they do in between? That was the thought which eventually resulted in *Satya*.'

If you take the account at face value – if Kumar's death was indeed 'the thought which eventually resulted in *Satya*' – it would mean that the actual journey began after production was already underway; that one of the most influential Hindi films of the last 25 years found its raison d'être only after shooting had begun. I prefer the version where Varma gets the news on set, and Kumar's death is a catalyst, not the origin, for *Satya*. Then again, this might be my way of imposing order on what seems to have been an atmosphere of intensely fruitful chaos.

Whatever the circumstances of his finding out, the bloody end of Gulshan Kumar sparked something in Varma. He told me he threw out most of the existing script and started afresh. 'After the death, we stopped shooting for a very long time. The bulk of the film formed in my mind in this interim period.' They began meeting people who had details of, or could offer insight into, Kumar's killing. What led to the murder, what kind of people were involved, why someone would become a shooter, why a contract to kill someone is given – every new bit of information now had a purpose. Kashyap's version of events was similar – he remembered Varma saying 'We need to make a different film', and junking whatever they'd written. Every day, journalists were writing about the underworld. Varma and his writers started scanning the papers for material. They met reporters and cops, including, Kashyap said, Dhanushkodi Sivanandan, who'd been Mumbai's additional commissioner of police (the Mohanlal character in *Company* is supposedly based on him).

Had Gulshan Kumar not been murdered at a juncture when plans could be upended, *Satya* would probably have turned out a very different film. And if *Satya* hadn't been made, there might not have been *Company* or *Sarkar* or the dozen or so gangster films Varma would go on to produce or direct. Kashyap wasn't exaggerating much when he said, 'Ramu's filmography changed after that incident.'

SHOOTING

No one I spoke to could agree on how long production stopped (if it stopped at all, which several players insist it did not) while Varma figured out how the twin epiphanies of Gulshan Kumar dying and Sushant Singh screaming would affect his film. When it resumed, shooting proceeded, according to Kamran, in roughly chronological order, which is to say, the order in which the scenes appear in the film.

More drama was to follow. On the afternoon of 16 September, several floors of Poonam Chambers, an office building in the south-central Mumbai district of Worli, came crashing down. Fifteen people died, several were injured and a few dozen firemen were lucky to escape with their lives when the remaining floors collapsed while they were taking a breather. Hours after the incident, the site was overrun with rescue teams and government officials, including the police commissioner and the chief minister. In the chaos, no one noticed the skeleton crew shooting under false pretences.

It had barely been a month of shooting on *Satya*. The crew was in Bandra when Varma told Sabir Masani, 'A building has collapsed. Go shoot it. Take the Steadicam guy.' Masani wondered privately if

Varma was losing his marbles, but he set out for Worli. When they reached, the area had been cordoned off and was swarming with police. Masani approached a cop and improvised: 'We're from the BBC and we're making a documentary on the police and how they work under arduous conditions.' Miraculously, they were let into the compound.

The shots of a collapsed building in the film's opening montage is the wreckage of Poonam Chambers. Asrani, who assembled that sequence, admitted it was useful to have some footage of 'real physical destruction'. 'The bomb blasts had happened a few years ago,' he said. 'This was as close as you could get to that.' It was a rare documentary film impulse in Varma – get the footage, we'll see where it fits later. Khalid Mohamed recalled this excursion in an article he wrote years later in the aftermath of the Mumbai train bombings: 'When the footage was shot … (Varma) didn't have the foggiest idea about where, when and how he would use it in one of his films.' Something similar had happened during the making of another quintessential Bombay film a decade and a half earlier. Kundan Shah was still waiting for his *Jaane Bhi Do Yaaro* script to be approved by NFDC when the Byculla bridge collapsed. He immediately sent someone to shoot the rubble before it was cleared, figuring he'd be able to use it somewhere.

Scoping a disaster site for a few good shots in a commercial film is a moral grey zone. At the very least, you have to pick your tragedies. The 26/11 terrorist attacks of 2008 left over 170 dead and the city in a state of shock. In the aftermath of the siege, Chief Minister Vilasrao Deshmukh visited the Taj Hotel, which saw some of the worst killing. With him was a small group that included his son, actor Riteish Deshmukh, and Ram Gopal Varma. News channels caught wind of this, and Deshmukh was roundly criticised for bringing along 'tourists'. Varma insisted he hadn't gone there to recce a film. Three years later, *The Attacks of 26/11*, starring Nana Patekar and directed by Varma, opened in theatres.

—

Rain is an inescapable part of life in Mumbai. The monsoon makes several appearances in *Satya* – 'Geela Geela Paani', of course, but also during the killing of the movie producer. You could swear the actors were sent out in a downpour, but it was actually a rain machine drenching Rajesh Joshi and Sanjay Mishra as their characters receive instructions over the phone. The matter-of-factness with which they go about the hit, driving their scooter right up alongside the target's Maruti Esteem and firing close to a dozen bullets into his kurta-clad torso, is the first indication that *Satya* isn't interested in stretching out its violence, and will instead give it to the viewer straight. The getaway is anything but smooth. Their scooter skids in the mud and overturns, trapping Vitthal (Mishra) under it; among his muffled cries is a fairly high-octane cuss-word – a warning that the film is looking to dish out its language straight as well. Bappu (Joshi) tries to help him, then takes off, his run through the *chawl* echoing in a dozen future films, from *Black Friday* to *Slumdog Millionaire*. Hooper remembered starting the *Satya* shoot with this scene. 'I loved being up on the crane, shooting with the manufactured rain coming down. It was a hell of a lot of fun – coming down on the crane and catching him, doing the shots up the alley.'

Before I'd spoken with anyone, I was sure *Satya*'s writers must have drawn from the Gulshan Kumar killing for the producer assassination sequence. There was enough in common – the white kurta of the target, his being a Bollywood power-broker, the public nature of the crime and unglamorous getaway vehicle (scooter in the film, taxi in the actual incident). But if Hooper's recollection is accurate, the scene was written before the murder took place, and shot before, or on the very day. Still, there would hardly have been a viewer at the time whose mind didn't jump to Gulshan Kumar while watching it.

To set the story in motion, the writers had to figure out how to get Bheeku and Satya together. A practical solution was found: they're criminals, so they'll meet in jail. Satya attacks the pimp, Jagga, who uses his connections with the police to get him tossed in prison. Bheeku, meanwhile, is arrested on suspicion of having ordered the killing of the producer (which he did). When Satya gets into a scuffle with one of the inmates, Bheeku moves to separate the two. Satya resists and gets punched in the stomach by Bheeku. There's a furious fist fight which ends with Bheeku pulling a chisel, then letting go when it's clear he's won. Satya grabs the chisel which Bheeku has carelessly placed on the window sill and holds it to his throat, saying '*Mauka sabhi ko milta hai*' (Everyone gets their turn).

This fight hasn't aged as well as some of the other action sequences in the film. 'No sorted gangster would leave the blade,' Kashyap grumbled when I showed him the scene. The punches sound like wood being chopped, which was still a sight more realistic than most hand-to-hand combat in Hindi cinema then. Choreographed by stunt director Allan Amin, the sequence is made memorable by Satya's lightning dart at the chisel (Chakravarthy is most adept at revealing Satya's personality through physicality and movement) and Bajpayee's performance throughout – his opening taunt of '*maar maar maar maar maar maar*' (hit me); the musical lilt in his '*kya re*' after punching Satya; the panic on his face when his opponent grabs the chisel; and his firm '*Bheeku bola na*' (Bheeku said so) when he decides the stranger is someone to be befriended. The actor also improvised the '*kam umar mein shaadi*' line – Bheeku attributing his own lack of speed to having married early.

Instances like this – actors coming up with lines and bits on the spur of the moment – were common on the sets of *Satya*. This was a novel approach for a Hindi film then (and now). With a different set of performers, it might have backfired. Luckily, the majority of *Satya*'s cast had honed their craft on the stage, where improvisation is a necessary part of an actor's toolkit. Bajpayee, Kashyap, Shukla, Aditya Srivastava and Govind Namdev all started in Delhi theatre. Shefali Shah acted in plays in college. Makarand Deshpande had his own theatre troupe in Mumbai. Even the bit roles went to theatre guys: Sushant Singh, Manoj Pahwa, Sanjay Mishra – performers who wouldn't freeze if the person they were sharing a scene with tried something new (for instance, Pahwa's unscripted '*Paani lao!*' (Bring water!) after Singh's face-slashing).

Everyone's favourite ad lib came from Bajpayee, during the interrogation that follows the first shootout. After the captive gives up the name of Guru Narayan, Yeda says, 'If we let this guy go, he'll just blab everything.' Kallu Mama thinks for a second, then grabs his gun and shoots the man, making everyone jump. All this was scripted, but then Bheeku, who's standing just to Kallu's side, winces and growls, '*Bolne ka na pehle*' (Give me some warning).

It was crucial that these actors were capable of taking a last-minute instruction and running with it, because this was a film essentially written on the fly. Kashyap is probably exaggerating only a little when he says that, after the scene at the *tabela*, the writing process became a series of 'one-liners' conceived by Varma and fleshed out by Shukla and himself. 'Ramu would say, today we'll shoot this scene … this happens, that happens, so and so is killed. We'd go there and write the scene based on the actors available.' One can picture Shukla and Kashyap frantically scribbling last-minute zingers, handing these to the actors minutes before the shot and saying, forget what we told you earlier, just say this. How exhilarating it must have been if you were an actor used to situations like this, how utterly unnerving if you weren't.

Once Kashyap and Shukla came up with a scene, the actors – Bajpayee and Deshpande in particular – would throw in their suggestions. Inspiration came from other sources too. Sometimes, Amin had something to add, or one of the cinematographers, or an assistant. Whenever someone came up with an idea, Kashyap would write it down. Varma remained open right until the moment he'd say, okay, this is what we'll do.

From time to time, Varma (and Kashyap and Shukla) would reach for the classics. Vitthal, the shooter who gets trapped under the scooter after killing the producer, is being interrogated by Khandilkar in jail. Telling him to give up the name of his handler, the cop rests his nightstick on Vitthal's injured leg, making him wince. Varma told me he got the idea from *The Guns of Navarone* (1961), the Gregory Peck WWII film beloved by dads in India, which has a scene where a sadistic German officer similarly nudges an injured prisoner's leg.

Satya's shooting of Jagga, his blood induction into the gang, recalls another famous first kill – the Sollozzo hit by Michael Corleone in *The Godfather*. Before he heads in, Bheeku gives Satya a gun and brushes away his concerns about never having fired one before, saying, 'In our profession, you keep it two inches away from the head. After that, boom, *khallaas* (all over).' This is similar to what Michael's brother Sonny tells him in Coppola's film: 'You've gotta get up close like this and – bada-bing – you blow their brains all over your nice Ivy League suit.' The killing, too, has shades of the Sollozzo murder – a restaurant, shooter standing over the victim, bullet point-blank to the head.

Varma added a wonderful finishing touch. Back in the car, Bheeku embraces Satya and laughs uncontrollably. We look at them through the windshield; as it starts to rain, their figures become a blur. The distorted effect, coupled with Chowta's plangent score, makes it seem as if the universe is weeping for Satya. This was a rare artistic flourish. From the start, the idea was to shoot simply and cleanly. Hooper couldn't recall a single instance where he had to suggest a camera move or a lighting decision felt fake or unwarranted. 'The simple style allowed for very good performances', he said, 'and maybe it became clear early on that the performances were meaningful enough to carry the film. It didn't need that kind of bravado, either from the camera or the directorial point of view.'

Later in the film, *The Godfather* turns up again. The camera descends on a sleeping figure in bed in a dark room. Light filters in through the window, we can see the street below. A car pulls up, stops in direct view of the window. Almost immediately, the phone by the bedside rings. The sleeper, groggy, sits up, turns on a lamp, picks up the receiver. 'Runu Sagar,' says a voice – probably Yeda. 'A girl came to audition yesterday. You'll get her to sing.' Sagar tells the caller not to talk rubbish and hangs up. A second later, a shot rings out. Sagar squeals and jumps off the bed, a bullet-shaped hole in the window. The phone rings again. 'I let you go this time,' the voice says. 'Next time, it'll be your skull.' As the composer stares, pop-eyed, the car pulls away in the background.

This scene is the first time the A-plot (the gang stuff) and the B-plot (Satya's relationship with Vidya) converge (in an earlier scene, Runu Sagar propositions Vidya when she auditions for a chance to sing in his film). It's also a comic version of the famous scene from *The Godfather* in which Hollywood producer Jack Woltz wakes up with his prize horse's severed head in his bed. That scene, like the one in *Satya*, is about the intimidation of a predatory movie mogul; it too begins with the camera advancing slowly towards a sleeping figure. And the capper – Sagar being threatened that his head will be next – is from another scene in *The Godfather*. At his sister's wedding, Michael tells his fiancée how his father, Don Corleone, helped out singer Johnny Fontane when he was having trouble with a band leader. 'Luca held a gun to the guy's head', Michael says, 'and my father assured him that either his brains or his signature would be on the contract'.

I hadn't noticed until Mazhar Kamran pointed it out, but this nearly minute-and-a-half-long scene is one continuous shot. Unlike the bravura single take when Satya meets the gang, this is a subtler one, without much camera movement. Varma and Kamran had obviously worked out that the most effective frame would be one that had both Sagar and the car. The absence of cuts strengthens this visual unity – the viewer can see cause and effect unfold in real time. Varma was so sure of this plan that he wouldn't allow Kamran any extra shots. 'I had lit up the street, and I wanted to take a shot of that,' the cinematographer chuckled. 'He just refused.' Kamran shot the scene two or three times the same way. He offered to shoot other elements – the van, perhaps, or the gangsters talking – which would give Varma some options to play with in edit. The director wasn't having any of it, saying, 'If it has to work, it has to work as a single shot.'

Several of my interviewees mentioned Varma's supreme ability to figure out what he needed from a scene, shoot what was necessary and move on. Classical Hollywood directors like John Ford and Alfred Hitchcock were known for 'cutting in the camera' – having a clear idea what each scene would cover and minimising extraneous shooting. That way, when studio heads sat down to recut their films, they just didn't have any surplus material. This sort of decisiveness was typical of Varma, Kamran said. 'Lots of filmmakers take options. But Ramu doesn't use any safety nets. That gives him a zen kind of thing.'

There's an amusing coda in the next scene. Runu Sagar turns up, flustered and obsequious, at Vidya's flat to tell her she has the singing job. He bats away her offers of tea and coffee and runs away, as if expecting gun-toting hoods to burst in at any moment. Chowta underscores his nervousness by hitting the same high-pitched piano key that plays when the bullet goes through Sagar's window.

In between shooting schedules and on off days, Hooper would head off with a camera and film whatever he found interesting. 'He used to just move out like a documentary filmmaker and shoot footage of Ganapati and the rains,' Bajpayee recalled. The B-roll he shot in the monsoon made up a large part of the opening montage. 'I remember it taking five to eight hours to walk home one day, water up to our thighs,' Hooper said (I can personally attest that even 10 minutes on a flooded Mumbai road, with electrical wires and uncovered manholes hidden by muck and rain, is a uniquely unnerving experience).

—

As a recent resident of Mumbai and a lifelong watcher of Bollywood films, Varma spoke adequate Hindi by the time *Satya* was made. Still, there were phrases, idioms that eluded him. Sometimes, when the director vetoed a line, the writers would try and sneak it back in, hoping he wouldn't notice. Varma knew how to read a crowd, though. Kashyap said that because Varma didn't always understand the humour, he'd get them to read the scene aloud and see how the people around them were reacting.

One bit of writing that emerged from this unique screening process was the 'Ram-Shyam' joke. Bheeku, Satya, Yeda and Chander are sitting along with a few other gang members in a room in an under-construction building. Malhotra, the builder whom Kallu Mama had threatened over the phone, has gone to his car to get the money he owes them. While they wait, Chander offers to tell a joke. By the time he's reached the punchline, Bheeku's doubled over with laughter. No one notices they've been ambushed till a shot is fired.

'I want some lines to be written for the construction site, just before the gunshot kills one of them,' Varma told Kashyap on the morning of the shoot. The writer remembered a bawdy joke* a friend had told him and, figuring it might be the sort of thing gangsters enjoyed, mentioned it to Varma, who asked him to narrate it to a small audience – apparently to cloak the fact that he didn't understand the Hindi punchline. Everyone cracked up, and the director asked Kashyap to get it down on paper.

Varma remembered the day almost identically – minus the language problems. 'I wasn't interested in what the lines were,' he said. 'I just wanted to divert the audience's attention, so that when the gunshot comes, it'll be a shock.'** Anurag has a habit while narrating, he'll get very emotional and speak the lines the way the character should speak. When he wrote and narrated it to me, I wasn't even listening to the lines actually, I was seeing Anurag's face. My mind was preoccupied with where to put the camera and when the gunshot should come, but I registered that he was enjoying. I thought, more

---

* Ram and Shyam are in bed with a married woman when her husband turns up. The two of them manage to hide. The husband starts to sweet-talk his wife, asking if she'd like a TV, a fridge. Each time she says, '*Ram dega ji*' – Ram (the god) will provide. The third time, Ram jumps out and demands to know that if he is paying for everything, will Shyam be getting her for free?

** In this he was entirely successful. Shukla remembers watching the scene in a Delhi theatre. When the bullet hit, he said, a man in the row behind, who'd been giggling at Chander's joke, jumped out of his seat, cussing.

or less this will work.' He said he only understood the joke later, during the edit.

Through design and luck, planning and instinct, things started to cohere. Frequent rewrites and additions to the script meant the actors could hardly look rehearsed even if they wanted to. They were encouraged to improvise, so they added tics and phrases that seemed right in the moment. The writers weren't old pros, so they were happy to have their words played around with. The camerapersons worked quickly, determined not to slow the actors down, bottling whatever lightning was on offer. Varma talked to everyone, considered what they said and took what he needed.

Then there was the location shooting. Apart from the realistic visual qualities this lent the film, it also tied in philosophically with everything else that was going on – the natural flow of dialogue, the minimal use of artificial light, the fluid approach to scene-building. As Hooper said: 'I think the idea of placing realistic characters in realistic scenarios, realistic settings – all of this accumulates in a certain shared aesthetic among everybody.'

'The only thing I was really conscious about was that we should stay true to what I was hearing from (these) sources,' Varma said in an interview in 2018. 'The fact that we took the decision to shoot in real locations made a difference … If we spent a lot of money and made a proper production design and location, I doubt the film would be the same.' The absence of studio sets must have helped to relax the actors, most of whom were struggling and broke, and therefore lived in places similar to the ones shown in the film. The characters seem to blend into their surroundings, whether it's Mule, inscrutable, leaning against a blank blue wall, or Satya and Vidya, looking out at the rain from their respective flats, her view open and green, his through the jail-like bars found on the windows in most middle-class Mumbai homes.

'This film is integrated in the DNA of the city,' Asrani said. 'It's in the construction of the city. It's locked in there.'

The set didn't have a lot of visitors. Word on the circuit was Urmila Matondkar had 'de-glammed' for the role, and no one was lining up – then, as now – to get a glimpse of Manoj Bajpayee or Chakravarthy. Occasionally, there'd be an infusion of celebrity from outside the unit. One day, Sabir Masani was waiting outside Baba Bungalow in Bandra. He was feeling a bit short-changed – here he was, shooting his first Hindi movie, but where were the stars? Someone walked up to him and asked in a heavy voice, '*Ramu kidhar hai*?' (Where's Ramu?). Masani looked up. It was Sanjay Dutt.

—

Most people, even those aware that *Satya* had two cinematographers, assume the film was shot primarily by Gerard Hooper. Yet, in final cut percentage terms at least, this was not the case. Hooper was certainly hired as head cinematographer. In the time he and Kamran worked together, he was principal director of photography – the one in charge. 'I like to think that maybe I was instrumental in creating the look of the film,' Hooper said. 'But it was very much a shared understanding and aesthetic between us. I liked Mazhar a lot, we had a good working relationship.'

Kamran's role wasn't defined clearly in the beginning. He worked as a lighting cameraperson, second in command to Hooper. Both said it was an easy collaboration. It helped that they came from documentary cinema, and were in agreement as far as the overall aesthetic was concerned. Kamran does suggest he pushed for even less artificial light in some scenes than Hooper was willing to risk, but there was an affinity in the way they both saw the task. 'We were very collaborative, in terms of lighting decisions also,' Kamran said. 'He was very open-minded.'

Hooper thinks he stayed in India for about three months; how much of this was before shooting started, and how much was eaten up by delays during production is anyone's guess (Kamran remembers Hooper being there for the first month of shooting). The American doesn't seem to have asked Varma beforehand how long the shoot was likely to last. And even if he had, he probably wouldn't have accounted for the many breaks that put *Satya*'s production on pause. At any rate, there came a stage, with the shoot either one-third or half done depending on whose memory you trust, when Hooper had to return to his teaching job at Drexel University.

Hooper's decision to leave coincided with a break in shooting. Kamran didn't know it then, but Varma was mulling over whether to entrust the shooting to him. It doesn't seem to have been planned – Varma told me he only asked Kamran because Hooper was leaving. Eventually, yet another leap of faith was taken and Kamran was informed he would be the lead cinematographer for the rest of the film. He still remembers the first scene he shot as head DoP, with Shukla and Bajpayee in a bungalow near Mehboob Studio in Bandra. 'I can never forget that day,' he said. 'It's like I was put in the driver's seat. It's quite a feeling to do your first big film like that.'

Kamran believes he ended up shooting two-thirds of the film. Varma, too, figured that Mazhar shot 70 per cent. Kashyap said Hooper shot most of the film. Hooper made no guesses, but told me that when he left, 'there was a lot that still had to be done'. If most of the film was actually shot in chronological order – a big if – one could hazard a guess as to when Hooper may have handed over the reins to Kamran. Hooper remembers shooting the sequence with Satya and Vidya on the roof, which is close to the one-hour mark. Kamran was definitely in charge by the time of the killing of Guru Narayan on the bridge, 90 minutes in. The switch might have happened on one of the scenes between these two points in the film. Everyone agrees the transfer – a potentially debilitating moment – was seamless.

This kind of handover, from one cinematographer to another in the middle of a shoot, wasn't without precedent. In fact, some of the most visually arresting films ever have been shot by multiple cinematographers. Haskell Wexler took over from Néstor Almendros on Terence Malick's *Days of Heaven* (1978) when the Spanish cinematographer left to shoot another film. Christopher Doyle was the cinematographer on Wong Kar-wai's *In the Mood for Love* (2000), but when the film ran over schedule and he had to leave, Hou Hsiao-hsien's long-time collaborator Mark Lee Ping-bing completed it. Closer home, Kamal Amrohi's *Pakeezah* (1972) saw a handover necessitated by the death of veteran cinematographer Josef Wirsching, with the film only partially shot. A dream team of substitutes, including V.K. Murthy (*Pyaasa*), R.D. Mathur (*Mughal-e-Azam*) and Fali Mistry (*Guide*), stepped in to help finish the film.

———

Amod Shukla is at home with his wife and daughter. Khandilkar is there too, watching a news report on TV about the killing of an ordinary citizen mistaken for a gangster at the hands of the police. Shukla's wife asks her husband if the story is true. He says it is, then gives a short speech about the media caring more about the rights of criminals than public safety. '*Kasaai bhi bakra tab kaat-ta hai jab log usse khaate hain*' (A butcher only slaughters a goat when it's to be eaten), he says. He then heads out. Khandilkar moves to follow, but Shukla's wife wants a word with him. A second later, they hear a loud gasp. The commissioner is leaning against the wall, a bullet hole in his chest.

Varma grimaced slightly as he watched the scene. 'It's lecture-ish, but I wanted something like this because Paresh was the best-known actor in the film, and I wanted to register him strongly before killing him. I didn't know what else to do with him.' Confusingly, the gunshot sounds only after we see the cop wounded. Varma was surprised when I pointed this out; he didn't remember the sound being there in the original cut, and speculated that someone might have added it later (how that would have happened, and how it made its way onto the Blu-ray of the film, is anybody's guess).

Bharat Shah was a supportive financier, but Shukla's death had him confused, then rattled. Both Barnali Ray and Varma remembered Shah turning to the director during a trial screening and saying, '*Kya ... Paresh Rawal ko maar diya?*' (What ... you killed Paresh Rawal?). You have to feel for Shah. Here he was, financing a film with hardly any known actors and minimal commercial prospects. He'd already had to wrap his head around the idea that the one bona fide star, Urmila Matondkar, would be shorn of glamour and play what was essentially a supporting role. Rawal was the only other actor the public would recognise, and here he was being bumped off after a couple of scenes. What the hell kind of film did Varma think he was making?

There's another *Godfather* reference at this point. The crackdown on the gangs after the killing of a police captain by Michael Corleone as described in Mario Puzo's book is almost the same as the police retaliation for Amod Shukla in *Satya*. Varma writes in *Guns & Thighs* that the voiceover after Shukla's murder was 'directly lifted' from this passage.

Bheeku had to go too. Though his death comes in the 151st minute of a 167-minute film, it still feels like a carpet being yanked from under our feet, perhaps because we half-hope he'll survive till the end, but more because of the manner in which it happens. Varma asked Kashyap and Shukla to each write a version of how Bheeku might die. He didn't like either. So he gathered the actors – Bajpayee,

Shukla, Deshpande, Namdev, Banerjee – and laid out the scene himself. The commissioner is dead, he said, you're together in victory. People will be expecting another fun song to happen. Talk over each other, as people generally do at parties. With that, he left the actors to improvise. No one knew what the other was going to say or do.

Varma told Namdev in private, 'Whenever you find the right opportunity, just take the gun and shoot him.' He himself wasn't sure what the actors would do, so he set up two cameras and waited. 'I was as surprised as anyone with the effect that came,' he told me.

In the aftermath of the election victory, Bheeku and Kallu have come to meet Bhau at his home. Mule is also there, as is Bhau's taciturn bodyguard. As Bheeku chatters away, Bhau walks over to the cabinet behind him. He makes himself a whiskey. Then, without warning, he turns and shoots Bheeku in the back of the head. Kallu Mama is frozen in his seat, eyes wide in shock. The bodyguard trains his gun on the fat man, just in case. For once, Varma cuts the background score. In a film as noisy as *Satya*, those few seconds of stillness are more dramatic than any sound effect or musical cue they could have used. 'During shooting, I remember there was a sudden silence after that gunshot,' Varma said. 'People were so shocked. There was so much of shouting in the film, and there's this one gunshot, and everyone is still. I wanted to recreate the same effect.'

Bhau takes off the garland Bheeku had placed on him, flings it away violently. 'I was waiting for the election, otherwise I would've finished him long ago,' he says and walks out. Mule comes up to Kallu, who has barely moved. There was no other way, he tells him. Bhau could be chief minister of the state one day – he would have welcomed Bheeku as his muscle, but he couldn't trust Satya and the hold he had over his protégé. '*Kaun hai yeh Satya?*' (Who is this Satya?), Mule asks with some violence, echoing, perhaps, the thoughts of the four people who'd created this cypher of a character. '*Maine bola tha usko,* *ek jayega toh sab jayenge*' (I'd told him, if one dies, they all die)*. Mule does tell Bheeku this just before the intermission, though at the time it doesn't seem particularly significant. Perhaps he's right – Bheeku might have been a fearsome gangster, but he never understood the business.

Kashyap was the only one who felt the scene didn't make sense. How could Bhau just turn and shoot him like that? He and Varma had a big argument. 'Only when I saw the impact on screen, I realised I was wrong,' Kashyap admitted. Bajpayee, though, was all for his character's sudden death. 'He doesn't move an eye,' he said approvingly. 'Like a bird that's been shot.'

Barnali Ray Shukla said the shoot lasted 110 days, spread over four months. Even if her estimate is off by a month, *Satya* must have wrapped up by the end of 1997. Not much seems to have been known in the popular press about the film. 'Verma (sic) is reluctant to admit anything beyond the fact that it is based on the underworld,' Rediff complained. It was rumoured that the film was about Dawood Ibrahim.

GANGSTER MUSIC

Before he became one of Hindi cinema's best-known composer–directors, Vishal Bhardwaj was one half of the duo who made it possible for '90s kids to yell '*Chaddi pehen ke phool khila hai*'

---

*   Varma told me this line – the way it arrives just before the interval – is his favourite in the film. 'It wasn't even in the scene,' he said. '(Deshpande) added it in the shoot.' Sandeep Chowta composed the ominous cello-led theme that runs through *Satya* with this scene in mind. During the mixing, Sridhar, the sound engineer, pushed the music volume up when Deshpande says the line. 'It gave me goosebumps,' Varma said. 'That groove for me was the underlying emotion of *Satya*.'

(A flower in underpants has just blossomed) on Sunday mornings without fear of parental reprisal. This was the chorus of the song that played over the opening titles of the *Jungle Book* (1989–90) animated series (a Hindi dub of the Japanese anime *Janguru Bukku Shōnen Mōguri*) aired on the national broadcaster, Doordarshan. The memorably silly lyrics were by Gulzar, whose partnership with Bhardwaj, which continues till this day, introduced the poet–director to a generation of viewers he might not have otherwise reached. Bhardwaj composed the music for Gulzar's film *Maachis* (1996), which earned him critical acclaim and his first hit, the Punjabi folk-flavoured 'Chappa Chappa'. Like most people in the industry, Varma was a fan. He invited Bhardwaj to compose for a Kannan Iyer-directed film he was producing. The music went unused, but Varma kept in touch with Bhardwaj and called on him a year later, with *Satya* half-shot, to write its songs.

I met Bhardwaj in his office in Andheri in late 2018. It was a typically busy year – he'd written and directed the Partition parable *Pataakha*, and worked on the stage adaptation of *Monsoon Wedding*. He had 45 minutes to spare before an appointment with the singer and lyricist of a new track he'd composed. 'Ramu was making *Satya* without songs,' he said. 'In the middle of it, he changed his mind. He came to me one day and said, my film is too violent, so you make it a little gentler with your music.' I asked Bhardwaj if Varma was under any pressure to add songs. He said he wasn't aware of any compulsion, and reminded me what a radical thing it was to have a songless film in those days.*

---

* Even Nagesh Kukunoor, whose cult indie, *Hyderabad Blues*, had no songs, included a soundtrack on his second film, *Rockford* (1999). Varma actually did make a songless film next, the single-location thriller *Kaun*.

The first track composed for *Satya* was 'Geela Geela Paani'. Bhardwaj already had an idea what the film would look like; he had visited the editing suite, with Asrani at work. Varma had in mind a scene not yet shot: Matondkar in the rain, splashing through a bazaar. Bhardwaj came up with a 'soft melody' as requested by Varma – a moody beauty built around Lata Mangeshkar's echo-y vocal, plangent guitars and the sampled sound of water dripping. Unfortunately for Bhardwaj, two things came in the way of the song being fully appreciated. The scenes with Matondkar in the bazaar were shot but never made it to the final cut; the six-minute song only lasts a minute and a half onscreen. Also, most listeners couldn't wrap their heads around Gulzar's curious turn of phrase – '*geela geela paani*' literally translates to 'wet wet water'.* 'Nobody talked about the melody,' Bhardwaj told me. 'I felt disturbed for many years about that.'

'Badalon Se' – another gentle number, my favourite on the soundtrack – followed. Unlike the other songs in *Satya*, this one isn't lip-synced by an actor. Instead, it plays over images of Satya and Vidya walking on the beach and in the marketplace, eating at roadside stalls and falling in love. This is how most Hindi films treat song sequences today, apart from big commercial vehicles and choreography-minded directors like Bhardwaj and Sanjay Leela Bhansali. At the time of *Satya*, though, the musical montage was still a rarity. As a result, this sequence feels modern in a way 'Geela Geela Paani' (lip-synced by Matondkar) or 'Tu Mere Pass Bhi Hai' (Matondkar and Chakravarthy) do not. The track was sung by the

---

* It's not so strange if you consider the next line: '*Paani, surila, paani paani*' (Water, melodious, water). I'd hazard that Gulzar is trying to evoke the various senses – touch with *geela*, sound with *surila*, sight ('*asmaan bhar gaya*' – the sky is full), taste ('*honthon ne chakha paani*' – my lips tasted the water).

deep-voiced veteran Bhupinder – perhaps Gulzar remembered his wonderful vocal on 'Do Deewane Shehar Mein' in *Gharonda*, a film he'd written. (Varma made one inspired choice as well. Bhardwaj told me 'Goli Maar Bheje Main' was initially sung by the popular playback artists KK and Sonu Nigam, but they sounded too polished. Varma suggested Mano, a Telugu film singer, who nailed the raucous vocal.)

One of Gulzar's phrases in 'Badalon Se' threw Varma off. For each song, the director would explain the narrative requirement to Bhardwaj, who'd then compose accordingly. This would be approved by Varma, only after which Gulzar would be approached. Varma had definite opinions and suggestions for the music, but didn't say much about the lyrics out of respect for Gulzar (and possibly because his grasp on Hindi poetry might not have been up to a debate). One day, the director came to Bhardwaj, looking confused. 'What has Gulzar *saab* written? The second paragraph says "*dekho yun khule badan, samundaron mein nahaya na karo*" (with so little covering your body, don't bathe in the sea). But I have a *sari*-clad heroine!' Bhardwaj called on Gulzar and asked why he had included such sensual phrasing. The poet was puzzled. 'But I've seen his previous films. In all of them, the heroines are bathing in the sea. I thought I'll give him an image for that.'

One of the unwritten rules of Hindi cinema is that any character, of any extraction, in any corner of India, can break into a Punjabi number. That said, there is an explanation (of sorts) for the Punjabi song at the Maharashtrian wedding in *Satya*. 'Sapne Mein Milti Hai' was originally composed for *Maachis*, a film set in Punjab. Gulzar, the film's director, heard the track and felt Bhardwaj could do better. The composer came up with 'Chappa Chappa' (both tracks are sung by Suresh Wadkar), which was used in the film and became a hit. When Bhardwaj was asked to write a Punjabi-style hit song by

Varma, he made him hear the discarded *Maachis* track. Varma loved it, brushing away Bhardwaj's concerns about cultural specificity. 'No one thinks about all this,' he told him. He's probably right – for years, it never seemed strange to me that a group of Mumbaiyya and Marathi speakers were singing Punjabi words like '*kudi*' and '*munda*' and '*gora-chitta*'.

Even before he came on board, Bhardwaj knew Bajpayee, Srivastava and Shukla from Delhi theatre, and a couple of others from struggler drinking sessions in Mumbai. He remembers his *Satya* stint as a time of camaraderie and genuine excitement. Like everyone else I talked to, he was impressed by Varma's ability to know when he'd heard or seen what he wanted for his film. 'He has very strong convictions about things,' Bhardwaj told me. 'He doesn't look (for assurance) in the eyes of the assistants.'

Varma's reaction to 'Goli Maar Bheje Mein', the last song to be composed, almost drove a wedge between him and Bhardwaj. With a brief from the director – party song, drunk men – Bhardwaj came up with a tune and dummy lyrics ('*Jab talak rahenge gham, tab talak piyenge hum, gham ke neeche bam laga ke gham uda de*' – As long as we're sad, we'll keep drinking, we'll place a bomb under the sadness and blow it away). When Gulzar heard it, he complimented the tune but said the lyrics were mediocre, and that he would write something else. He did a version which Varma didn't like. He then wrote another. Varma didn't like this one any better, but he could only reject Gulzar's writing so many times. So he told Bhardwaj in confidence that he wanted to record the song, but with his temp lines. Sure, Bhardwaj said, but you have to tell Gulzar. 'I'll tell him later,' Varma said. The composer insisted, saying Gulzar would feel betrayed otherwise. It came to the point where he refused to record the song. Varma was furious. 'I'll never work with you again,' he told him.

Eventually, the song was recorded with Gulzar's lines – *'goli maar bheje mein, ke bheja shor karta hai.'* Varma was convinced it had been ruined. 'Ramu was very angry,' Bhardwaj recalled. 'He stopped talking to me. He said, we'll keep it in the album, I won't shoot it.' Wiser heads prevailed, and a roughhouse sequence was shot in Kallu Mama's den. A year and a half after the film released, Varma turned up at Bhardwaj's house in the middle of the night with a bottle of vodka. 'I have to confess something,' he told him. 'Gulzar *saab* proved all of us wrong. I was so foolish rejecting those lyrics.'

Varma always had a fascination for film scores. He's written about watching *Alien* 17 times when he was in college – in three of the screenings, he closed his eyes and concentrated on the sound. On another occasion, he smuggled a portable player into a movie theatre to record the music of *Enter the Dragon*, since the soundtrack wasn't available on cassette. Asrani told me Varma had a library of classic Hollywood scores, which he would use as temp music while editing. In the early days of *Satya*, when the team was still being assembled, Varma met a promising young musician named Sandeep Chowta at Nagarjuna's home. Chowta, a jazz and fusion player who turned to film composing with the Nagarjuna-starrer *Ninne Pelladata* (1996), played the director a theme he'd been working on. Varma liked it so much he hired him on the spot to do the background score. Chowta's big, bold sound was integral to *Satya* and later Varma films like *Mast* (1999) and *Company*, though his popularity peaked with 'Kambakht Ishq', a floor-burner featuring Urmila Matondkar from the Varma production *Pyar Tune Kya Kiya* (2001).

The background score was recorded in Chennai, along with the rest of the mix. The sound design was by the talented H. Sridhar. 'We were doing foley, background, dubbing, all together,' Kashyap recalled. 'Two months non-stop inside the studio. We all lived in Chennai during that period, in one bloody room.'

I have mixed feelings about Chowta's score. Even as someone who watches Hindi films for a living, I find it incredibly loud. I wish director and composer had sprinkled a little silence here and there, but that's not the Indian way (and certainly not the Varma way). Yet, the score does drive the action effectively. The rapid percussion before the producer's killing ratchets up the tension, as do the sharp taps at a tabla when a miffed Bhau arrives at Bheeku's office. It can also be affecting, in particular the flute-driven themes marking Satya's arrival in Mumbai and his last few desperate moments.

Kashyap thought Varma used music and sound brilliantly in *Satya*. The in-your-face arrangements that seem dated now were then considered 'fresh', he said. Kamran was even more emphatic. He first saw the film, sans score, at one of the Bandra trials. Later, when Varma asked him what he thought, Kamran told him the film wasn't working. See it with the music, Varma advised. He did, and couldn't believe how everything seemed to come together. 'Something happened to the film,' he said. 'It wasn't a re-edit – music alone changed the whole thing.'

Varma is aware he pushes scores to their breaking point. 'When I see an old film of mine, I sometimes wonder, why the fuck did I put the sound up so loud?' he said. 'Then, at some other time, I think that without the score, this would look very dull.' He also does it because after the edit is locked and the dubbing is done, this is the only thing left to manipulate. 'By the time I reach the mixing stage, I've heard the dialogue so many times I'm bored with it, and the background score becomes new. So, like a kid in a toy store, I tend to play with that more.'

Among cast and crew, Hooper is a lone critic of the score, saying it yanked him out of the film (his tolerance for button-pushing

scores isn't high – he likened John Williams' buoyant soundtracks to
someone taking a hammer to the head). Shukla wasn't thrilled with it
either, but for a different reason – it drowned out his lines. The scene
on the bridge, with Bheeku yelling at Guru, had music turned up so
loud that people who saw the early cut complained they couldn't hear
what the actors were saying. Varma kept it in; he wanted to hear 'the
sound of rage'. 'I remember people telling me I should have put the
sound down,' he said. 'Govind Nihalani approached me after a trial.
He said, Ramu, I'm sorry to tell you, but you've screwed up the film
with the score. The film is dramatic in itself, why should you use so
much of background?' Nihalani changed his mind after *Satya* became
a hit, telling Varma the music was crucial to its success because it
lent the film a genre-appropriate directness and a mass appeal that a
subtler score might not have had.

Satya has five sung tracks, but, unlike Varma's first two Hindi
films, barely any choreography. We've seen how 'Goli Maar Bheje
Mein' came together minus a dance instructor or any attempts at
cohesion. 'Tu Mere Paas Bhi Hai' has a few half-hearted moves by
Chakravarthy and Matondkar. The slow shuffle of 'Geela Geela
Paani' and the yearning 'Badalon Se' don't lend themselves to
choreography, and Varma wisely desists. The only song that got the
Bollywood dance treatment was 'Sapne Mein Milti Hai'. Bajpayee
remembers it being shot fairly late in the schedule. In charge was
Ahmed Khan, who had reenergised Hindi film choreography
with *Rangeela*. Khan and his assistants arrived on set and started
explaining to the actors how they wanted them to move – the timing,
the marks they would hit. 'I developed cold feet,' Bajpayee said.
'How can Bheeku dance on 1-2-3 counting?' He spoke to Varma,
who asked Khan to work out something looser, less coordinated
than his usual style.

The result is less professional dance number than your drunk cousins and uncle and aunt at a wedding. It's a wonderful blur – Bheeku trying to embarrass his wife; Pyaari surprising everyone by cutting loose; Chander (it's his sister's wedding), Kallu Mama, Yeda, Mule dancing the bhangra with various level of competency. Satya, meanwhile, is looking at the bride and groom and imagining Vidya and himself in their place. We get a few shots of an incongruously glossy dream, with Matondkar decked-up like she's in *Hum Aapke Hain Koun*. The shift from wedding venue to this is jarring – and Mazhar Kamran knows it. It's the one scene in *Satya* that's lit the way a normal Bollywood film of the day would be. During the edit process, someone Varma showed the scene to asked, '(Your cinematographer) can shoot like that? Why doesn't he shoot the whole film this way?'

While shooting the sequence, Varma kept reminding the actors to remember who they were playing even as they danced, to 'improvise from within the character'. 'The idea was that it should look like the characters are dancing,' he told me. 'Kallu Mama will dance in his own way, Mule in his own way – that's how it is in real parties.'

THIRD TIME AROUND

Renu Saluja, one of the greatest film editors ever, and the glue that held together independent Hindi cinema in the '80s and '90s, once gave Saurabh Shukla a bit of advice. A film is written three times, she told him. You write with a pen and paper. You then write with your camera, which becomes your pen, and your actors, who become your words, your spacing. And you write it a third time during editing.* 'Till the time a film ends', Shukla told me, 'you shape it

---

* This is a popular maxim among cinema practitioners, often attributed to French director Robert Bresson.

through sound, lighting, camera movement, performance, colour, cuts, dissolves – this is all actually writing.'

The editing of *Satya* began parallel to the shooting. In 1997, Avid, the game-changing editing software, was just starting to be used in Hindi cinema. Varma was initially wary of switching to digital, so he ended up using both Avid and the traditional Steenbeck machine. 'No one was an expert in Avid then,' he said. 'It took me a certain amount of time to adapt.' He brushed off the suggestion that the new technology had any effect on how the film shaped up. 'See, that is just a technical thing. Editing is not about what equipment you use – Steenbeck or Avid or Final Cut Pro – it's about the sensibility of the person.'

Bhanodaya ended up cutting on Steenbeck, Asrani on Avid. The editing happened at Rakesh Roshan's Filmkraft Studio in Andheri. Asrani remembers Roshan's son, Hrithik, then an assistant director a few years shy of the spectacular success of his acting debut, *Kaho Naa Pyar Hai* (2000), hanging around and asking questions. 'It all came together on the table,' Asrani told me. 'Varma was very clear about some things. In one of our first conversations, he said he wanted Satya to be a man from nowhere. He wanted people to wonder what his past might be.'

When I asked Varma about the respective contributions of Bhanodaya and Asrani to the edit, it seemed to set him off. 'I don't understand what an editor does,' he complained. 'Editor as a technician is not a creative field. He is a machine.' He said he invited suggestions from his editors, as he did from all his crew, but what ultimately remained was his decision. 'Let us cut this scene there, it should not be so long – that is not editing, it is directing. Editing is the heart of the film, but editors don't really do it. I would like to believe that more than a director, I'm an editor.'

After months of working with the same people, Varma was keen to get an outside opinion on his film. He arranged a trial screening. The film didn't have a background score yet, but Varma said it was more or less a final cut in his mind. A motley group of about 25 saw it – a couple of Varma's friends, some cast and crew, a handful of industry people, Matondkar's father. 'Finished film *dekhne ki aadat thi, pehli baar* rough sound *ke saath dekh rahe the*' (We were used to seeing finished films, this was the first time we saw one with rough sound), Kashyap recalled. Varma, the writers and Bajpayee waited anxiously for the film to end. Then things unravelled.

Hardly anyone seemed to like it. Shukla's heart sank. *What we were having fun with turns out to be utter trash*, he thought. Sanjay Thakur, a friend of Varma's brother and unconnected to the movie business, handed the director a list of criticisms. Varma read it later. One of the notes pointed to a serious flaw: Satya's friendship with Bheeku wasn't getting established, which made his decision to go after Bhau alone at the end seem more suicidal than it already was. Thakur also pointed out an emotional glitch in the scene where Satya hears police sirens outside the building just after he tells Vidya they're moving to Dubai. In the original cut, he gives her the news, she goes to tell her mother, Satya sees the cops from the window and bolts. 'What kind of a bastard is he?' Thakur asked Varma. 'The moment the police comes, he forgets all his love talk and runs?' Varma took a close-up of Chakravarthy's indecision and helplessness by the window, and inserted it into the scene.

To bolster the credibility of the central friendship, Varma added two scenes – one by the sea, after Bheeku is done shouting, and one when Satya comes back from holidaying in Khandala and Bheeku yells at him like a frantic older brother. The scene in the jewellery store was shot later as well – another deepening of the Satya–Bheeku bond, with the gangster generously financing his friend's courtship. In Varma's recollection, there wasn't a lot of shooting that happened after the trial (Kashyap, naturally, said the entire second half of the film was reshot, a claim which didn't come close to surfacing in any of the other accounts). Yet, though they only filmed a few scenes over three or four days, Varma said these additions changed the film drastically. 'At the end of the day, you need to have feedback that can provoke you,' he told me. 'I give a lot of credit to Sanjay.' So next time you're watching *Satya*, remember there was someone named Sanjay Thakur, whom Varma didn't know well and who probably wasn't even specifically invited to that screening, who played a small but crucial part in the film turning out the way it did.

7

After Satya

'The world came close after Satya.*'*

– Anurag Kashyap

There's a photograph of the unit taken on the final day of shooting. It looks like an afterparty at a Hyderabad tech convention, all happy smiles and buttoned shirts and moustaches. But look at Varma at the back. He's staring straight at the camera, elbow resting on Mazhar Kamran's shoulder. He isn't smiling. It's the look of someone who's thinking, wait till they see what's in store, I'm going to knock them out cold.

Sriram Raghavan was a fan of Varma long before he had seen *Satya*. He liked all his films – *Shiva, Raat, Kshana Kshanam, Rangeela*. And he'd been hearing from his friend Anurag Kashyap that this was a *real* gangster film, not that Bollywood crap. So when he was invited for a trial at Famous Studios in Mahalaxmi, Raghavan was more than eager to attend. He remembered the preview being full of *hum jaise log* (people like us). The screening went like a dream. As soon as he got out, Raghavan bought a cigarette – he'd quit, but he suddenly felt he needed one. He shared a cab back with Tigmanshu Dhulia, who, as Shekhar Kapur's casting in-charge on *Bandit Queen*, had given Manoj Bajpayee and Saurabh Shukla their starts. The two budding writer–directors were silent on the drive home, reliving the film in their heads.

They weren't the only ones coming out of *Satya* stunned. With the kinks ironed out and the soundtrack added, the film was impressing whoever Varma showed it to. Even so, expectations among cast and crew were tempered. As everyone kept reminding them, you needed stars to open big, and they only had one (you also needed songs, and fortuitously, Vishal's music was catching on, especially the boisterous 'Goli Maar Bheje Mein' and 'Sapne Mein Milti Hai'). Those were the days when hit films ran for months. If *Satya* folded in a week or two, it probably wouldn't recover its costs.

Kashyap, Bajpayee, Sushant Singh and Kamran had moved on to Varma's next, the home invasion thriller *Kaun*. As *Satya*'s release drew near, how often did their discussions turn to the film's chances and the fallout of possible failure? They all thought they'd pulled off something special, but who could tell? *Is Raat Ki Subah Nahin*, for all its critical acclaim two years earlier, had sunk without a trace.

Sriram called his brother after the trial screening of *Satya* and said, 'Boss, I've seen one of the deadliest movies ever. I'll book tickets for us.' He was expecting a 'houseful' sign when he turned up for the first-day show on Friday morning at Anupam Cinema in Goregaon. Instead, there was hardly anyone outside the hall or crowding the ticket window, let alone touts selling in 'black'. He came away worried for the film's chances.

Satya opened on 3 July 1998, at a less-than-encouraging 50 per cent capacity. In those days, films generally weren't pulled from theatres in a hurry as they often are now. Nevertheless, Bajpayee felt the onset of panic – after all that hard work, he was back to square one. Outside Shaan theatre in Vile Parle, he met Ajit Dewani, who told him, '*Teri* film flop *ho gayi, doosri* film *jaa ke khoj*' (Your film is a flop, go find a new one).

Varma remembered trade analysts writing off his chances – *good film, but too intelligent, too intense.* Bharat Shah called him on the first night, saying, '*Thoda* disappointing *hai, dekhte hain*' (It's a little disappointing, but let's see what happens). The following night, Varma got another call. This time, Shah was excited. '*Ramu, bol rahe hain ki* picture *utaregi nahin*' (They're saying the film won't be taken off). 'I had zero expectations,' Kashyap said. 'I remember, first week was some 60–70 per cent occupancy. This went up to 90. Third week was 97. Then it was houseful. I was thinking, what the fuck is going on?' Kamran recalled a couple of them piling into Varma's car and driving from the suburbs to Churchgate, staring in amazement at one full house after another.

The gang wasn't sweating now. Instead, for the first time in their lives, they were getting recognised. Bajpayee heard 'Bheekubhai, Bheekubhai' wherever he went. Sometimes, people would come up and speak to him in Marathi, figuring he knew the language; he'd figure out the gist and reply with the few phrases he knew. Shukla got used to being called Kallu Mama by strangers (it's 'dark-skinned uncle' in Hindi). Doors they'd never dream of knocking on earlier were now miraculously open. Outside a washroom at a movie theatre, a few vodkas down, Bajpayee met his childhood hero, Amitabh Bachchan ('There was some ringing sound in my ears,' he recalled). Kashyap related a similar story. A frantic search party cornered him at a studio, saying Bachchan was on the phone. 'Literally, my hands were shivering. I took the call. His first line I remember: "*Atal Bihari ko dhoondna aasaan hai, aapko dhoondna bada mushkil hai*" (Tracking down Prime Minister Atal Bihari Vajpayee is easy, finding you is very tough).'

A couple of months earlier, Chakravarthy was in the edit room when Varma gave a peek of his film to a mystery guest. Sitting in a corner of the dark studio, Chakravarthy listened to the man praise the scenes and wondered why he sounded so familiar. 'One thing, though, Ramu,' the voice continued. 'Why did you cast the south Indian actor? You should have taken someone from here. If the film doesn't do well, it'll be because of him.' In that terrible moment, Chakravarthy realised the speaker was Anil Kapoor. Sometime after the release of *Satya*, Kapoor was in Hyderabad for a film shoot. Chakravarthy happened to be in the same studio, and went to pay his respects. He was surprised when Kapoor jumped up and hugged him. '*Kya kaam kiya!*' (Excellent work!), the *Mr India* star said. 'When I was shown your scenes, I told Ramu, if the film does well, it will be because of this guy.'

Some of the most enthusiastic reactions came from those who saw their rough lives playing out on the big screen. At one screening, Kamran and Bajpayee were approached during the interval by a tough-looking group. 'These guys came up – surely underworld people from the *chawls*,' Kamran recalled. 'They told Manoj, *kya kaam kiya, phaad dala* (great work, you tore it up). They talked to him like he was a *bhai*. I'll never forget that moment. You make a film, and the actual people from this life confront you.' On another occasion, outside a different theatre, a stranger put his hand on Varma's shoulder and said, '*Hum logon ke upar acchi* picture *banaya hai tu*' (You've made a fine film about people like us).

Film journalist Anupama Chopra had yet another story. 'Pappu Nayak is an underworld foot soldier,' she wrote in *India Today,* two months after the film's release. 'Solidly built, he walks with a swagger in Goregaon, Mumbai. Ostensibly he works in a dairy but actually he's the local fixer, working with fists and choppers, settling disputes, extorting money and fixing elections. Last Sunday, Nayak saw *Satya.* For the fourth time. "*Boley to, bahut real story bataya hai,*" he says. "*Bheeku Mhatre ke liye char baar dekha. Wo ladka agar ek do film mein jum jaaye to Nana Patekar ko thanda kar dega*" (They've told it the way it is. I saw it four times for Bheeku Mhatre. If that guy does well in a few films, he'll put an end to Nana Patekar).'

Indian movie fans being what they are, things got weird. Bajpayee got a fan letter, a five-page poem to be sung by himself and Matondkar, with a request to pass it on to Varma.

The film ran for 30 weeks at Eros, a 1200-seat Art Deco theatre in Churchgate. Today, in a landscape where big studio films corner the entire market and make their money back in the first week, a theatrical run this long is as quaint as hand-painted posters. Yet, it wasn't unusual in 1998, when it was a point of pride for producers and directors to be able to claim that their film ran for a hundred days, 25 weeks, 50 weeks.

To mark the silver jubilee – 25 weeks – Vishal Bhardwaj recalled being put on a bus with Bajpayee and Matondkar and the others and sent to movie theatres. During the interval, the cast would appear on stage. Footage from one such appearance, marking week 15 of the film's run, can be seen on YouTube. Matondkar, in a tracksuit, waves with both hands to the crowd. Shukla does a politician's namaste, hands folded above his head. 'We were following Ramu blindly,' Bhardwaj tells an interviewer. 'There was so much force in his conviction. He'd narrate a scene and we'd start sweating.' Bajpayee, never one to downplay his own struggle, says, 'This adulation came to me very late'. Matondkar says it's nice to be appreciated for trying something different. A relieved Bharat Shah calls it a superhit.

Satya was certainly popular. But was it a hit? The people I spoke to could only offer vague estimates of the film's budget and earnings. So I looked elsewhere, and ran up against Indian film journalism's biggest stumbling block – the lack of dependable box-office data (and the resultant proliferation of unverified collection numbers). I could only find details of Satya's performance on the film trade website Box Office India. The numbers seem reasonably accurate, and paint a picture of the film's steady rise.

Satya was released on 85 screens across the country, considerably less than the 185 for Ghulam (which starred Aamir Khan) and 240 for Kuch Kuch Hota Hai (which had Shah Rukh Khan and Kajol) that year. It had a worrying first weekend: 75 lakh rupees to Ghulam's 2.2 crore rupees. But from then on, the film had a steady run, collecting a crore every week for the following six weeks. A large percentage of the earnings were from the state of Maharashtra, and within that, from Mumbai – 9.2 crore rupees out of all-India nett earnings of 14.3 crore rupees. It was helped hugely by the Shiv Sena government, the reigning power in the state, declaring the film tax-free in its second week (after three months, with the limit about to expire, it was granted a second exemption). Gross earnings were 18.47 crore rupees. While this wasn't anywhere near the 80 crore rupees made by Kuch Kuch Hota Hai, Satya's modest budget – 2.5 crore, as per Box Office India – meant that it more than made good on its investment.

INFLUENCE

The first post-*Satya* gangster film was Mahesh Manjrekar's *Vaastav*. It opened in October 1999 and, on a budget of approximately 7.5 crore rupees, grossed 20 crore rupees, slightly more than Varma's film. *Vaastav* veered towards the mainstream where Varma's film had leant away – it had a big star in Sanjay Dutt, an item number, a classic *maa–beta* divide, and a love song shot in Europe. Yet, it was also a tough-minded gangster drama. Manjrekar was an actor, writer and director for Marathi stage and film before he reached Hindi cinema, which made *Vaastav* seem authentically Maharashtrian in a way that *Satya* wasn't.

Vaastav was in the early stages of production when *Satya* was being readied. If Varma's film had any influence on Manjrekar's, it might be in the framing of a couple of scenes. When Raghu (Dutt) and his friend Dedh Footiya (Sanjay Narvekar) shoot a man sitting across the table, the close-up on them is similar to Satya and Bheeku towering over Guru Narayan on the bridge. And the murder of Vitthal Kaanya (Ashish Vidyarthi) in his car by assassins who pull up alongside on a bike recalls the killing of the producer at the start of *Satya*. More conclusive signs of inspiration are from other films. There's the shadow of an earlier Dutt film, *Hathyar*, in which unemployed *kholi* youth while away their time playing carom, which they do in *Vaastav* too. Tellingly, the scene that marks a violent shift to a life of crime in both films is built around a roadside pav bhaji stall. In *Hathyar*, a desperate Avi watches a stranger eat and later tries to mug him. And in *Vaastav*, Raghu, armed with an enormous *bhaji* pan, attacks the customer who's bullying his friend. Dutt's character ends up killing for the first time in both scenes, which leads to him taking help from a gang boss and becoming a don himself.

Vaastav cherry-picks ideas from other seminal gangster films as well. The scene where Raghu, now a criminal, turns up with presents for his family and is admonished by his mother, Shanta (Reema Lagoo), is similar to the one in *Agneepath* where Amitabh Bachchan tries to buy his way into the good graces of his mother and sister, but is rebuffed. Manjrekar looks further back for his film's ending – Shanta shooting Raghu is a modern version of Nargis shooting her son in *Mother India*. Raghu falling for a sex worker with braids in her hair is an image straight out of *Nayakan*. There's a link to *Parinda* and *Is Raat Ki Subah Nahin* too – Imtiaz Hussain, dialogue writer on all three films.

The most gangster thing about Manjrekar's film, however, might be the 'produced by Deepak' title in the opening credits. This is unusual because, unlike lyricists and dancers in Hindi films, most producers aren't mononymous. But there's a reason Deepak Nikalje's name did not appear in full – the real estate-man-turned-politician was the younger brother of Rajendra Sadashiv Nikalje, better known as gangster Chhota Rajan, on whose life *Vaastav* was rumoured to have been based. Here, already, was the controlling hand of the underworld, trying to tell their own stories.

Despite *Ardh Satya*'s influence on Hindi gangster films, Govind Nihalani didn't make any himself before *Thakshak* (1999). The film was closer to the mainstream than anything he'd done, and the concessions were awkward – florid photography and a narrative unsettled by songs. But the setting was new. Ishaan (Ajay Devgn) and Sunny (Rahul Bose) are heirs to a Mumbai construction business, which is run like the mafia. These aren't the louts of *Satya* and *Vaastav*; they wear suits and work out in upscale gyms. But they're just as coldblooded, especially loose-cannon Sunny. Devgn's a bit too nice to be a convincing mob guy, but the mania of Sunny – no surprise he's named after the most volatile Corleone – adds a new dimension to the high-society gangster: not just a delegator but someone who'll actually go out and do the dirty work.

More than out-and-out gangster films like *Thakshak* and *Vaastav*, *Dil Pe Mat Le Yaar* (2000) might realistically be called the first post-*Satya* film. It shares with *Satya* a writer (Shukla), three actors (Bajpayee, Shukla and Srivastava), a composer (Bhardwaj) and an action director (Amin). Both are stories of immigrants who come to Bombay, with Bajpayee getting to play closer to his north Indian roots as a car mechanic from Uttar Pradesh who is forced to turn to crime. It arose from the same incident that took over Varma's imagination: the killing of Gulshan Kumar. Like Varma, *Dil Pe*'s director, Hansal Mehta, wanted to enter the minds of the two assassins. 'What were their compulsions?' he wrote on his blog. 'What was their motive? These questions kept plaguing me as I tried to visualize the murder.' Mehta first mentioned the idea to his friends Anurag Kashyap and Manoj Bajpayee when *Satya* was in production. By the time *Dil Pe* was ready, Bajpayee's rise in profile after *Satya*, *Kaun* and *Shool* was instrumental in securing a theatrical run (Mehta's first film, *Jayate*, never released).

Dil Pe Mat Le Yaar isn't concerned much with gangsters, but there's a lot of *Satya* in the frames. Like Varma, Mehta didn't want his Mumbai to come across as desirable. 'I wanted the film to look "dirty",' he wrote. 'I wanted the images to look carelessly framed and the camera movement to be minimal.' Characters from one film could easily walk into the other; I can picture the videographer Shukla plays in *Dil Pe* being hired by Chander to shoot his sister's wedding in *Satya*. There's a shared rhythm to the way the characters in both films speak. Bajpayee's soft-voiced Ram Saran is markedly different from the hot-headed characters he plays in *Satya* and *Shool*, but some of Bheeku Mhatre's mannerisms seem to surface in Bhaskar Shetty (Kishore Kadam), the belligerent gangster in Mehta's film. In a scene where he's pushing Ram to shoot someone, he says '*maar maar maar maar*' (kill him), exactly like Bheeku tells Satya in their jail fight (there, '*maar*' meant 'hit me'). The scene ends with Bhaskar saying '*accha hai*' (that's good), and laughing, much like Bheeku chuckling and saying '*dum hai*' (he has balls) when Satya bests him.

Towards the end of the decade, films like *Dil Pe Mat Le Yaar*, *Rockford* (1999), *Bhopal Express* (1999), *Split Wide Open* (1999) and *Snip* (2000) started sprouting up on the edges of the industry. These were mostly indies with difficult subjects and few commercial trappings or big stars, which is to say, films in the image of *Satya*. This was due in large part to PVR opening India's first multiplex in Delhi in 1997. These new theatres were small, plush, the tickets more expensive. This meant that an offbeat film had a greater chance of running for a week or two and making its money back with a multiplex release than it would on large single-screens. Multiplexes were initially limited to big cities, which made the imagined viewer easier to profile and target. Instead of a vague pan-India viewer, directors could now pitch their slick horror movie or noir comedy to an urban, educated, English-speaking person between 20 and 45. Producers could afford to take a few risks. For a few years, 'multiplex films' became industry shorthand for productions with small budgets and previously untenable ideas. In an interview in 2003, Varma said that multiplexes were changing the way he operated (this was back when there were only three dozen of them in the country). 'We had only emotional hits earlier', he said, 'now we can have mathematical hits.'

Vishal Bhardwaj watched *Makdee*, his debut feature as a director, 'first day, first show' in a single-screen hall in 2002. '*Uss samay* theatres *ka bahut bura haal tha*' (Theatres were in bad shape in those days), he told me. 'I was seeing the screen through the fan.' When his breakthrough film, *Maqbool*, released two years later, the premiere was in a multiplex. 'The face of the cinema changed because of the multiplexes,' Bhardwaj said. 'People had stopped going to the cinema because there were rats in the theatres and the air-conditioning and quality of the seats was appallingly bad. So people used to watch in their homes on pirated CDs. But when multiplexes came, that audience started coming to the theatres.' This multiplex audience was largely middle- and upper-class, a shift in viewer demographics that prompted the slow dilution of all-inclusive *masala* cinema, and the rise of a savvier, more targeted type of Hindi film.

———

Unlike *Satya*, Varma's second film on the underworld began with real-life gangsters in mind. From Hanif Kadawala – an accused in the '93 blasts – he heard the story of how Dawood Ibrahim and his one-time lieutenant Chhota Rajan fell out. 'They so desperately want to kill each other,' Kadawala says in *Guns & Thighs*, 'but Ramuji I am telling you this, even today if Dawood calls Rajan on the phone, if Rajan is smoking a cigarette he will drop it and say, "Haan! Dawood Bhai!"'[*] This became the kernel for *Company*. Ajay Devgn plays Malik, a Dawood-like don, who mentors Vivek Oberoi's brash street operator, Chandu, a stand-in for Rajan. Varma picked details from the gangsters' lives. Malik's flight to Hong Kong, from where he runs his empire by remote control, parallels Dawood's retreat to Dubai. Malik's lieutenant, Yadav, complaining to him about Chandu might be inspired by Chhota Shakeel and Sharad Shetty speaking against Rajan to Dawood. And the attempt on Rajan's life in Bangkok in 2000, which he evaded by jumping off the balcony of his first storey house, becomes a terrific rooftop chase in *Company*.

---

[*]   Kadawala was shot and killed in his office in 2001, allegedly on the orders of Chhota Rajan, though the gangster was acquitted in 2021.

Varma and writer Jaideep Sahni also turned a sardonic eye on convivial relations between the underworld and the film industry. In one scene, a beefy star in a baseball cap says he's being threatened by Chandu and demands police protection (he's a stand-in for Hrithik Roshan, whose father, actor and producer Rakesh Roshan, survived an attempt on his life by Abu Salem's men in 2000). The unimpressed commissioner of police, Srinivasan (Mohanlal), mentions that he's rumoured to be friendly with Chandu's former boss, Malik. The actor brushes it off, saying they're on 'hello-hi' terms. Srinivasan gives him a baleful look and delivers the film's best line: 'I have 42 tapes of your hello-hi.' Phone-tapping was in fact being used with some success by the authorities then. Over the past few years, the Mumbai police had recorded several conversations between Chhota Shakeel in Pakistan and Nazim Rizvi, Sanjay Dutt and other film industry folk in Mumbai.

Company was less concerned with how Mumbai gangsters carry out their hits than it was with those who give the orders. This again was new – Hindi gangster films had mostly been from the point of view of foot soldiers, not generals. The most significant departure from *Satya* was the way the film exchanged natural light and straightforward shooting for a supercharged style. Working with the talented cinematographer Hemant Chaturvedi, Varma cut loose from the (relative) restraint he'd shown on his first Hindi gangster film. *Company* was a funky jumble of canted angles and saturated colours, pitched somewhere between the techno-noirs of Michael Mann and the tripped-out sensory outbursts of Wong Kar-wai. You could argue that the repeated stretching and curving of the image is the director's way of suggesting a world built on skewed perspectives. My guess is it doesn't go that deep. *Company*, and most subsequent Varma films, look this way simply because he likes jarring, aggressive compositions.

Hindi gangster cinema was at its peak between 2002 and 2005. Not only were a number of crime films made, but many of them extended the genre in ambitious and surprising ways. If *Company* signalled a new kineticism, Sanjay Gupta's *Kaante* (2002) marked the upscaling of the genre. In this reworking of *Reservoir Dogs*, six criminals – played by Amitabh Bachchan, Sanjay Dutt, Suniel Shetty, Mahesh Manjrekar (the same one who directed *Vaastav*), Lucky Ali and Kumar Gaurav – come together to rob a Los Angeles bank. *Kaante* wasn't a particularly refined work, but it was flashy, had great competitive scenery-chewing by a tough-guy cast and took the genre for a rare jaunt outside Mumbai (and India). Dutt was in another gangster film that year, *Hathyar* – nothing to do with his 1989 film with the same title. This was Manjrekar's sequel to *Vaastav*, in which Dutt plays the slain Raghu's son, who, like his father, is forced by circumstances to take up a life of crime.

The gangster film began seeping into other genres. Two 2003 comedies were built around the Mumbai mafia – Kaizad Gustad's campy *Boom*, with Amitabh Bachchan as a white-haired don, and Rajkumar Hirani's smash hit *Munna Bhai M.B.B.S.*, in which gangster Munna (Sanjay Dutt) enrols in medical school to please his father (played by Sunil Dutt, Sanjay's father). The shooting of criminals by 'encounter specialists' like Daya Nayak and Vijay Salaskar – several of which were alleged to be pre-planned – became the basis for cop films like *Encounter* (2002), *Kagaar* (2003) and Shimit Amin's excellent *Ab Tak Chhappan* (2004). Shashanka Ghosh's madcap *Waisa Bhi Hota Hai Part II* (2003), was a successful hybrid – a comic thriller with the Mumbai underworld as a backdrop, Arshad Warsi playing an adman caught between rival crime lords Ganpat (Anant Jog) and Gangu (Pratima Kazmi as a rare female gangster).

Directors were really putting their own spin on the genre now. 2004 was a watershed year. There were the crackling debuts of Sriram

Raghavan (the noir thriller *Ek Hasina Thi*) and Shimit Amin (*Ab Tak Chhappan*, a hardboiled cop film) – both produced by Varma. The same year, Vishal Bhardwaj's shadowy psychological drama *Maqbool*, which played at the 2003 Toronto International Film Festival, released in India. The source material was Shakespeare's *Macbeth*, with the troubled general as the right-hand man of a mafia kingpin. Irrfan Khan plays Maqbool, whose affair with Nimmi (Tabu), mistress of the psychotic Abbaji (Pankaj Kapur), drives the couple to murder and madness. It's a remarkable film, not only finding ingenuous parallels to Shakespeare's text but infusing the gangster genre with a poetry it had never seen before. The witches are two corrupt cops with a gift for prophecy. The fatal omen of the Birnam woods is transmuted into the Arabian sea. It also builds bridges, as most of Bhardwaj's films do, between past and present Hindi cinema. There's Gulzar on songwriting duty, and the '*Billo meri aakhon ki kamini*' line in 'Ru Ba Ru' harks back to the loving use of the invective in his own *Ijaazat* ('*Badi kamini*,' Naseeruddin Shah tells Rekha in the 1987 film). Puri as a cop torturing a prisoner brings back memories of *Ardh Satya*. Kapur, a chameleon talent since the early '80s, was introduced to a new generation of viewers as the whispery-voiced, rheumy-eyed Abbu. There's also a touching shout-out to Varma – his name is mentioned by one of Abbu's men as a possible director for a film starring Nimmi.

That year, another *Satya* alum, Anurag Kashyap, took the gangster film for a long walk. *Black Friday*, based on S. Hussain Zaidi's non-fiction book, seems at first a straightforward look at the hunt for the perpetrators of the 1993 Bombay blasts. But Kashyap isn't just concerned with the procedural aspects, he wants to show the boredom of pursuit and flight, the false steps and stumbles. He deliberately allows the narrative to slacken, following gangster Badshah Khan (Aditya Srivastava) from one city to another. This quickening and slowing of pace is most clearly seen in an astonishing seven-minute chase, as a group of cops pursue a suspect on foot into the subway, across the railways tracks and through the narrow lanes of a slum (Danny Boyle spoke about its influence on *Slumdog Millionaire*). Kashyap also messes with conventional narrative structure: instead of keeping the reason for the blasts – the Babri mosque demolition in Ayodhya by a right-wing mob goaded on by politicians, and the subsequent riots in Bombay, in which the Muslim community bore the brunt of the violence – at the start of the film (as it is in Zaidi's book), he places it right at the end.

Black Friday's release in 2007, after a protracted legal battle, ended Kashyap's run of terrible luck. He was supposed to have directed *Shool* back in 1999, but disagreements with Varma resulted in E. Niwas taking over (Kashyap got a dialogue credit). His first film, *Paanch* (2003), got into trouble with the censors and never came unstuck. *Allwyn Kalicharan*, a thriller with Anil Kapoor in the lead, never got past the planning stage. But *Black Friday* showed audiences what industry insiders already suspected – that Anurag Kashyap had a director's eye. He hadn't quite found an authentic visual style yet – that would come when he partnered with Rajeev Ravi on *No Smoking* (2007) and *Dev.D* (2009). But he could tighten and release onscreen tension like a pro. He also had a way with performers, casting lesser-known actors in showy parts, just as Varma had done in *Satya*. Pavan Malhotra, an outstanding actor whose career never really took off, plays gangster Tiger Memon; Kay Kay Menon is magnetic as investigating officer Rakesh Maria; and, in one of several brilliant cameos before he broke out with *Peepli Live* (2010), Nawazuddin Siddiqui is a nervous suspect under interrogation.

It was with the release of *Sarkar* (2005) that the Mumbai gangster genre began to arc downward. Varma crossed *The Godfather* with the real-life example of divisive politician Bal Thackeray to tell the story of a crime boss who's also a civic leader. He pulled off a casting coup by signing Amitabh Bachchan as the ageing don and his son, Abhishek, as the film's Michael Corleone. *Sarkar* was slick, but it didn't propel the genre forward like *Satya* and *Company*. Still, no one could have guessed this would be the last Hindi film directed by Varma to receive positive reviews.

The gangster film started to head towards safer commercial ground. Just as *Company* and *D* (2005; produced and co-written by Varma) had drawn from real-life gang tales, so did *Shootout at Lokhandwala* (2007), thinly disguising a 1991 encounter between the police and gangster Maya Dolas. But Apoorv Lakhia's film pushed the genre into gratuitous macho territory. In place of the rough poetry of 'Goli Maar Bheje Mein', you had the bragging 'Ganpat', with its dumb chorus of 'We are the *bhais*'. *Once upon a Time in Mumbaai* (2010), Milan Luthria's retelling of the Haji Mastan–Dawood Ibrahim relationship, was just as commercially minded (though superior). It played like hopped-up Salim–Javed, with chewy dialogue, '70s fashions and lively turns from Ajay Devgn, Emraan Hashmi and Randeep Hooda.

FACTORY SYSTEM

There's a man by the name of Roger Corman, who made disposable movies but changed American cinema. His big idea was to hire bright kids out of college and get them to make movies on the cheap. He produced shoot-em-ups, exploitation quickies, creature features, biker films – whatever was hot at the time. These would play in drive-ins and seedy theatres, recover their meagre costs and sometimes get recut and spliced into new movies. No one remembers these films, and no one would remember Corman today if he hadn't given starts to Martin Scorsese, Jack Nicholson, Francis Ford Coppola, Jonathan

Demme, Peter Bogdanovich, Dennis Hopper, Bruce Dern, James Cameron, Ron Howard …

For a few years in the late '90s and early 2000s, Varma became a sort of Roger Corman for Bollywood. Just as Corman established his own bare-bones studio system, Varma willed into existence a network of young filmmakers and technicians. He called it the Factory. Varma was a much better director than the American, and the films he produced weren't trashy B-movies. Still, Corman and Varma had a lot in common. They dealt almost exclusively in genre cinema. Both presided over a succession of production houses. And both were a beacon for talented artists starting their film careers.

It began with the starts given in *Satya* to Kashyap, Asrani, Kamran and Singh, and a first brush with real fame for Bhardwaj, Bajpayee, Shukla and Chowta. Varma seemed to take the film's success as a sign, because he never stopped working with newcomers after that. With each new film, he'd introduce writers, directors, actors, cinematographers, editors, choreographers, composers. He gave Sriram Raghavan, who'd been futzing around the edges of the industry since the late '80s, the chance to direct his first film, *Ek Hasina Thi*. Raghavan has since become one of best-regarded directors in India, making the caper *Johnny Gaddaar* (2007), the acrid revenge film *Badlapur* (2015), and the Chabrol-esque *Andhadhun* (2018). Shimit Amit began by editing *Bhoot* (2003) for Varma, then directed his 2004 production *Ab Tak Chhappan*. He went on to make the highly rated *Chak De India* (2007) and *Rocket Singh* (2009) for Yash Raj Films (inexplicably, he hasn't directed since). Jaideep Sahni started his screenwriting career with Varma's *Jungle* (2000) and *Company* before finding mainstream success with *Bunty Aur Babli* (2005). He subsequently wrote the sparkling screenplays for *Khosla Ka Ghosla* (2006), *Chak De India* and *Rocket Singh* – the beginnings of a New Middle Cinema, a movement that's contributed the lion's share of noteworthy Hindi films over the last decade.

Hemant Chaturvedi shot *Company* and Bhardwaj's *Maqbool*, influencing a generation of cinematographers. Opportunities were given to directors Prawaal Raman (*Darna Mana Hai*, 2003) and Chandan Arora (*Main Madhuri Dixit Banna Chahti Hoon*, 2003), writer Pooja Ladha Surti (*Ek Hasina Thi*; *Naach*, 2004) and a first lead role to Randeep Hooda (*D*). Even Shankar–Ehsaan–Loy, Hindi film's most consistent hitmakers in the 2000s, got an early break through Varma, composing the songs for *Shool*.

For a few heady years, Varma seemed to be running a parallel industry within Bollywood. Occasionally, he'd work with an A-lister; Amitabh Bachchan was a frequent collaborator, despite their making only one somewhat satisfying film together. But he never cast Salman Khan or Shah Rukh Khan (or Aamir after *Rangeela*), Hrithik Roshan or Akshay Kumar, or next-generation stars like Ranbir Kapoor, Alia Bhatt and Ranveer Singh. Instead, like Subhash Ghai in an earlier era, he was seen as the director most likely to 'launch' new talent. There was a difference, though. If you were unknown and starring in a Ghai film in the '80s, it meant you had what it took to be a star. If you were in a Varma film in the 2000s, it meant you were talented.

Varma's eccentric nature informed the way the Factory was run. 'As long as the hits and flops even out and the balance sheet looks right at the end of the year, the occasional disappointments do not really matter,' he said in a 2004 interview. The haphazardness extended to hiring practices. Vishram Sawant was brought in to design the Factory office. He ended up being given *D* to direct, the third in a loose gangster trilogy after *Satya* and *Company*. 'Now, Vishram Sawant is a guy who thinks very, very wild,' Varma said in an interview. 'Like the decor of The Factory, I've never seen any decor like that, as an interior work. So if he wants to make a film, I would like to believe that it'd be so bizarre.'

It helped that Varma was easier to access than many of his industry peers. Rohit Jugraj recalled how he ran after Varma's car when he saw him on a film set one day. He caught up with the director, handed him four short films he'd made and expressed a desire to assist him. 'Till date, I don't know if he has seen them or not,' he told Rediff. But Chandan Arora recommended him to Varma, and he got a job as one of the 'last assistants' on *Bhoot*. Not long after, Jugraj was given the Varma production *James* (2005) to direct. E. Niwas became Varma's '12th or 13th assistant' after he approached him one day without much of a plan. 'He asked me questions like what an assistant director did,' Niwas said later. 'I was zapped. I did not answer any of his questions.' When Anurag Kashyap backed out of *Shool*, Niwas, then just 23 and with no prior credits to his name, took over (and did a respectable job).

By marrying hungry young talent with commercial material, Varma helped raise the profile of genre cinema in the country. His productions were usually gangster films (*Company*, *Sarkar* and its two sequels, *D*), horror (*Bhoot*, *Darna Mana Hai*, *Gayab*, *Darna Zaroori Hai*) and cop films (*Shool*, *Ab Tak Chhappan*). These were made on lean budgets with low overheads – mid-range stars, location shooting, inexpensive young directors. They were aimed at a multiplex audience who compared them to Hollywood genre films. Varma allowed directors to find their style – the no-frills Shimit Amin is entirely different from the stylish Prawaal Raman or the cinephilic Sriram Raghavan. But with the exception of Arora's sweet-natured *Main Madhuri Dixit Banna Chahti Hoon*, the material adhered to a type. 'As a producer', Lalitha Gopalan wrote in her article 'Bombay Noir', 'he was responsible for a cycle of films in which protagonists are crime bosses, gangsters, kidnappers, and femme fatales ... Productions from the Factory radiated a distinctive style and narrative mode whose imprint is still evident long after Varma folded his operations.'

CINEMA'S OWN CITY

As the gangster film took a backseat by the end of the 2000s, the Mumbai city film sprung to life. A key entry was *Slumdog Millionaire* (2008), a British film about a boy from the slums who becomes an unlikely winner on a quiz show. India has had a complicated relationship with Danny Boyle's film. Though it got great reviews and was a minor hit in the country, some felt the term 'slumdog' was derogatory and that Boyle had made what amounted to poverty porn. This criticism became more pronounced with the film's huge commercial success outside India and its eight Oscar wins, including Best Picture. *Slumdog*'s view of Mumbai might be a little wide-eyed, but it doesn't revel in poverty any more than *Salaam Bombay* (another film accused of serving up Indian woes for international prizes). Somewhere in the criticism was buried the grudging knowledge that Boyle had made Mumbai look more exciting than any Indian director had managed in a long time.

    Slumdog Millionaire is perhaps the only foreign film that owes a debt to *Satya*. Boyle credited it, along with *Company* and *Black Friday*, with shaping his view of Mumbai. He even brought a bit of *Satya* on board by casting Saurabh Shukla as Srinivas the cop. In a possible tribute to Varma's film, Boyle kicks off *Slumdog* with an extended torture scene, with Srinivas hanging Jamal's body from the ceiling just as Kallu Mama and his men had done with the rival gang member.

    When Kashyap asked Boyle for advice on how to shoot a drug scene in *Dev.D* – a Delhi film – the director recommended a camera he used on *Slumdog* that gave a trippy effect. Boyle's frenetic visual approach and manic energy also informed the zany Mumbai crime films of Raj and DK (99, 2009; *Shor in the City*, 2011). But it was a film in a vastly different tempo that suggested unexplored possibilities for the Mumbai city film. *Dhobi Ghat* (2010) was a mood poem, a rare foray into artiness by Aamir Khan. Directed by Kiran Rao, Khan's wife, the film's debt to arthouse cinema is evident not only in its unhurried pace and quiet observational style but also in Rao's decision to bring in composer Gustavo Santaolalla, who'd scored films for Walter Salles, Alejandro González Iñárritu and Ang Lee. This philosophical, contemplative approach to Mumbai was predated by Madhushree Dutta's documentary *7 Islands and a Metro* (2006), and later seen in global-minded films like Ritesh Batra's *The Lunchbox* (2013), which brought international attention to the city's ubiquitous *dabbawalas* (food delivery agents), and Ruchika Oberoi's surreal triptych, *Island City* (2015).

Meanwhile, Kashyap seemed to sour on the city. His loose Mumbai trilogy – *That Girl in Yellow Boots* (2010), *Ugly* (2013) and *Raman Raghav 2.0* (2016) – paints the metropolis as filthy inside and out. Down these mean streets walk mean people, a nightmare realisation of Johnny Walker's sung complaint in *C.I.D.*: '*Insaan ka nahin koi naam-o-nishaan*' (There's no trace of human feeling here). There are startlingly brutal moments, none more disturbing than the reveal of the rotting corpse of a young girl in *Ugly*. The bleakness threatens to overwhelm everything. The way Kashyap shows it, this is a city that has lost the moral right to exist but has continued regardless.* It's also possible to locate the traumatic aftereffects of the 2008 terrorist attacks on Mumbai in these chaotic, savage films.

---

* Kashyap added a fourth 'dismal Mumbai' film, *Choked*, in 2020. A black comedy about the demonetisation crisis of 2016, it's cynical but less nihilistic than the earlier ones.

While Kashyap was losing faith in Mumbai, Zoya Akhtar was still able to see it as a city of dreams. A fluent director with a light touch and a knack for choreography, she made a splash with her first film, *Luck By Chance* (2009), about strugglers in the Hindi film industry. After two films about the super-rich on holiday (*Zindagi Na Milegi Dobara*, 2011; *Dil Dhadakne Do*, 2015), she returned to Mumbai with *Gully Boy* (2019). The film, which tracks the rise of Murad (Ranveer Singh), a poor but talented rapper from the Dharavi slums, recalled Saeed Mirza's *Salim Langde Pe Mat Ro*. Both are about a working-class Muslim boy who's a hair's breadth from a life of crime, and the scene where Murad visits his volatile, proud friend in jail echoes another Mirza film, *Albert Pinto Ko Gussa Kyoon Aata Hai*. *Gully Boy* was also the most quotable Mumbai film since *Rangeela*. The soundtrack and dialogue were either originated or vetted by local rappers, so what you hear is close to actual street talk (the film's dialogue writer, Vijay Maurya, appears for a few seconds in *Satya*, in the scene where the gang is introduced). *Gully Boy* was a reasonable hit, but its real success was the manner in which it dominated the cultural conversation for a few hot minutes. What everyone missed in increasingly unfocussed debates on appropriation and representation was that the Mumbai city film had made yet another comeback.

The city film continues to find a way. Milind Dhaimade's *Tu Hai Mera Sunday* (2016) paid tribute to Mumbai's middle-class housing societies and weekend football games, while bemoaning the perennial lack of space. *Mard Ko Dard Nahi Hota* (2018) was a kung fu-powered ode to Matunga, the neighbourhood director Vasan Bala grew up in. Ritesh Batra's *Photograph* (2019) cast a loving eye on the mundane city – tourist site photographers, coaching classes, ancient soda pop factories. Atul Sabharwal's cop film *Class of '83* (2020) expertly blended old Films Division newsreel clips into the action to recreate the Bombay of the '80s. Bollywood directors have shown an increased willingness of late to set their stories in unexplored towns. But there's only one home. As long as Hindi films are made, Mumbai will be mined for stories.

—

In 2012, Kashyap premiered *Gangs of Wasseypur* at the Cannes Film Festival. It released in India soon after, and was as much a sensation as *Satya* was in its day. The two-part film, set in a small town in Jharkhand, overflowed with characters, vivid colours, strange sounds, references to cinema and politics and local arcana – as wild and loose as *Satya* was tightly wound. This was gangster film as history, as farce, as opera. It had a bit of *Satya* in it – the scene where a murder is being coordinated over multiple cell phones is reminiscent of the aborted attempt on Guru Narayan's life. Kashyap plucked Manoj Bajpayee out of actor's jail and gave him a part bankable stars would have killed for. But *Wasseypur* had more in common with the localised Tamil gangster films of the late 2000s, and with foreign films like Fernando Meirelles and Kátia Lund's sprawling *City of God* (2002).

By taking the gangster film out of Mumbai, Kashyap revitalised it. Now, he set his sights on an expansive period film. *Bombay Velvet* was to be his masterpiece. He had the backing of a big studio, Fox Star. He cast big stars: Ranbir Kapoor, Anushka Sharma. He recreated 1960s Bombay in Sri Lanka. Amit Trivedi worked for two years on the jazz-cabaret soundtrack. Thelma Schoonmaker, Martin Scorsese's long-time editor, worked on the international cut.

Everything came apart spectacularly. Kapoor, capable of great subtle work, was miscast as a hot-tempered street brawler who becomes a gangster, a character seemingly pieced together from half-a-dozen Robert De Niro turns. Sharma was almost catatonic as the ingénue singer. It was like a Warner Bros. gangster movie transplanted to Bombay – there were fedoras and Tommy Guns and we even see a clip of James Cagney. The superb soundtrack, which imitates the '50s sound of O.P. Nayyar, left everyone cold. The intricate politics, the context, was lost in the flash. *Bombay Velvet* bombed at the box office. It was as if everyone was waiting for Kashyap to fail. The director recuperated in 'cinema-friendly' France. His next project, the pitiless *Raman Raghav 2.0*, felt like a fuck-you to humanity.*

Kashyap is often credited with moving the gangster out of Mumbai with *Wasseypur*, but other directors had already begun the exodus. The Bihar-set Varma production *Shool* got the ball rolling. Tigmanshu Dhulia made *Haasil* (2003), a film on student politics and low-level gangsters in Allahabad; *Saheb, Biwi Aur Gangster* (2011), about decaying royalty in provincial Uttar Pradesh; and the Chambal-set dacoit film *Paan Singh Tomar* (2012). Kabeer Kaushik's underrated *Sehar* (2005) had Arshad Warsi as an honest cop battling gangsters in Lucknow. Varma's *Rakta Charitra* (2010), set in his native Andhra Pradesh, was sprawling, incredibly violent and immersed in the politics of the region – a proto-*Gangs of Wasseypur*, though nowhere near as brilliant. Vishal Bhardwaj's *Omkara* (2006), an adaptation of *Othello*, was set in small-town Uttar Pradesh, as were Abhishek Chaubey's *Ishqiya* (2010) and *Dedh Ishqiya* (2014). More recently, Chaubey used the Chambal ravines as the backdrop for his searing revisionist dacoit film, *Sonchiriya* (2019).

Today, long-form crime narratives have found a home on streaming platforms. *Sacred Games* (2018–), co-directed by Kashyap, did what *Bombay Velvet* couldn't – marry the story of

---

* It was '2.0' because Sriram Raghavan had made a film on Raghav, a real-life serial killer, back in 1991. Though it was never released, it became a calling card of sorts for the director, eventually reaching Varma, who produced his first feature, *Ek Hasina Thi*.

an individual hood's rise with the history of Bombay. *Mirzapur* (2018–), set in small-town Uttar Pradesh, was less intricate, but violently funny and crowd-pleasing. *Aarya* (2020–) broke new ground by placing a woman, played by Sushmita Sen, at the centre of a gangster drama. On the big screen, the most exciting development has been the Tamil and Malayalam crime films of the last decade – the noirish *Kammattipadam* (2016), directed by Rajeev Ravi, cinematographer on *Gangs of Wasseypur* and *Bombay Velvet*; Vetrimaaran's sprawling *Vada Chennai* (2018); Lijo Jose Pellissery's *Angamaly Diaries* (2017), the most kinetic Indian film in forever; Pa Ranjith's caste-system-flaying *Kaala* (2018). There hasn't been a game-changing Hindi gangster film in a while, though Ashim Ahluwalia's *Daddy* was a coolly amoral biopic of Arun Gawli, the Marathi don Varma so admired.

SATYA TODAY

Varma continues to be fascinated with gangsters. In 2017, he released a six-minute trailer for a series called *Guns & Thighs*, which promised a lurid take on the Mumbai underworld. When we met, he was excited about a series he was developing, which would chronicle the Mumbai underworld from 1997 to 2004, and focus on a different mobster in each episode. He announced another project after that – 'D Company', on Dawood's rise to fame. 'I understand (the underworld) much better now than I did when I made *Satya*,' he said. 'That was in the thick of things, and many people were reluctant to talk about it beyond a point. Today, people are opening up and telling me things they would never have dared to then.'

The problem is no one is fascinated with Varma anymore. The rot began with *Ram Gopal Varma Ki Aag* (2007), a remake of *Sholay* that ended up being one of the worst-reviewed films of the decade.

Nishabd (2007) was an undercooked adaptation of *Lolita*. The last Hindi film he made that was somewhat well-received was *Rakta Charitra*, over a decade ago. He's been active – a little too active – since, directing over 20 films of varying lengths, mostly in Telugu. But the projects have grown increasingly outlandish. *Satya 2* (2013) had nothing to do with *Satya*, besides being about a young man in Mumbai who becomes a gangster. In 2014, he directed the three-minute *A Day in the Life of Lakshmi Manchu's Feet* – the ultimate fetish short. His vocal appreciation for porn stars yielded two shorts – *Meri Beti Sunny Leone Banna Chaahti Hai* (2017), in which a girl tells her parents she wants to emulate Sunny Leone, who by then had moved on from adult entertainment to starring in Hindi kitsch; and the monumentally strange *God, Sex and Truth* (2018), in which adult star Mia Malkova spouts philosophy while assuming a series of explicit poses.

Things could get even more self-reflexive and weird if Varma's under-production projects see the light of day. There's *RGV Missing*, co-directed with Adir Varma, in which Ramu, playing himself, is kidnapped. He's announced films with the titles 'Arnab: The News Prostitute' and 'Kidnapping of Katrina Kaif'. Most frightening of all, there's a three-part biopic on his life in the works, with different actors playing him in the first two parts, and Varma playing himself in the third (he's also writing, though not directing, the films).

It seems unlikely that Varma will re-enter the filmmaking mainstream. Perhaps, if the ambition is still there, and if there's a partner to rein him in, he might create something of note for a streaming platform. Yet, even if he doesn't, he's done more to change Hindi cinema than most directors of his generation. Look at the long list of people who owe their careers to him. Then look at his own films. *Rangeela*, *Satya* and *Company* will endure, perhaps *Siva* and *Raat* too. Three essential films, several excellent ones and the many fine films he produced – that's a staggering career. And few directors have ranged as far and wide as Varma – gangster film, horror, action, road movie, musical, psychological thriller.

Legacy is a heavy word, especially when applied to a small, scrappy production. But it's been 23 years since *Satya* released – long enough to be able to situate it in the firmament of Indian cinema. It's a forerunner of the new indie, or 'Hindie', movement – films that went against the *masala* grain. These films had *Satya* in their DNA. They were made by brash first-timers, film geeks, the children of Quentin Tarantino and Kamal Swaroop.

Varma's film was a challenge thrown to these younger directors: make the kind of film you would want to see yourself. 'Watching the kind of movies that were releasing earlier – I don't want to name names – I used to wonder: I don't like this, but the public seems to be enjoying it,' Sriram Raghavan said in an interview. 'Was I wrong? When *Bandit Queen* and *Satya* were loved by the public as well as me, I realised this is a path I can follow.'

Satya also represented a decisive break with the Parallel Cinema tradition – films that came up in the late '60s in opposition to commercial cinema. The movement was at its peak in the '70s, yielding socially minded films with some combination of Naseeruddin Shah, Shyam Benegal, Smita Patil, Govind Nihalani, Shabana Azmi, Farooq Shaikh and Om Puri. In the '80s, they were joined by Vidhu Vinod Chopra, Pankaj Kapur, Saeed Mirza, Renu Saluja and Sudhir Mishra. Their films were mostly funded by the government-run NFDC. Almost without exception, they had no box-office ambitions. Instead, the actors would occasionally work on commercial projects, collect their paycheques and return to do their little art films. Varma's film had no Parallel stalwarts in its cast or crew; the closest it came was Gulzar, whose sensitive, life-size films are better categorised as Middle Cinema. Nor did *Satya* traffic in social criticism, something the public was used to encountering in almost every Parallel film. It wasn't arty; there were no pregnant silences or poetic interludes. Instead, there were boisterous songs and fights and shootouts. Simply put, it was too much fun to qualify as a Parallel film. And it suggested a way forward that rendered this tradition unnecessary.

The most influential film of the '90s, by some distance, is Aditya Chopra's *Dilwale Dulhania Le Jayenge*. Its boy-meets-girl-then-meets-girl's-family structure is still being recycled two decades later, in everything from the action–comedy *Chennai Express* (2013) to the queer dramedy *Ek Ladki Ko Dekha Toh Aisa Laga* (2019). Also influential were *Jo Jeeta Wohi Sikandar* (1992), the film that kicked the youthful charge of the '90s into high gear, and *Rangeela*, the harbinger of MTV-style slickness. There's a case to be made for *Bandit Queen* as well. Its fingerprints can be seen on dacoit films like *Paan Singh Tomar* and *Sonchiriya*, and indirectly on *Satya*. It freed up language, and it allowed for a new kind of global Indian film – not stately, like the cinema of Satyajit Ray or Adoor Gopalakrishnan, but combustible, as *Salaam Bombay* was before it. Yet, *Bandit Queen*'s influence on Hindi cinema is limited by the kind of film it is. There is only so much a film this far from the mainstream, with no stars or songs or popular cinema tropes, can seep into the general consciousness. *Satya*, on the other hand, had guns, a hit soundtrack and a bankable heroine. Regular audiences watched the film, and it made money. All the people associated with *Satya* went on to work in mainstream cinema (though many have avoided the commercial heart of it).

Satya's influence is more felt than seen. There haven't been any straightforward remakes, like there have of *Dilwale Dulhania Le Jayenge*. Rather, its lessons have been absorbed to the extent that you might not always realise when you're watching an actor or a director inspired by *Satya*.

The visual schema, which we'll attribute to Varma, Gerry Hooper and Mazhar Kamran, has become commonplace through imitation. Any Indian cinematographer working wonders with cramped spaces – Rafey Mehmood in *Ankhon Dekhi* (2013), Mitesh Mirchandani in *Neerja* (2016), Pankaj Kumar in *Talvar* (2015) and *Daddy* – is continuing their legacy.

The realistic, scaled-down action worked out by Varma and Allan Amin was hugely influential, even as Amin (and Hindi film) headed off in another direction with the exploding cars and Michael Bay-inspired mayhem of *Dhoom* (2004).

'Badalon Se' didn't invent the romantic song montage, but did it better than anyone since Basu Chatterjee's 'Suniye Kahiye' (*Baton Baton Mein*, 1979) and 'Rim Jhim Gire Saawan' (*Manzil*). A decade later, this kind of sequence became a trademark of mid-budget Hindi cinema.

There's a bit of Bheeku in every hot-headed, large-hearted Hindi film hood in the last two decades, just as every inscrutable existentialist killer after 1998 owes something to Satya. Other performers have replicated Bajpayee's volcanic intensity (as has Bajpayee himself). But there's also the influence of the ensemble – all those unknown faces vying for the audience's attention. *Satya* taught young actors to value a few minutes in a good film over a bigger role in a star vehicle. It also heralded the boom in casting as a discipline, which has had a big impact on the Hindi cinema of the last 20 years. When Mukesh Chhabra cast over 300 speaking roles for *Gangs of Wasseypur*, it's a journey that started with Varma's cast of unknowns.

At a remove of 23 years, the legacy of *Satya* seems secure for now. But what of the long run? All the things that made it stand out on release make it a tough sell for the mannered Hindi film canon. It's not a pretty-looking film. You can't really watch it with the family. The ending is a downer. And action films tend to age worse than comedies or romances. *Satya*'s best shot at posterity might depend on whether its offspring – the people who worked on or were inspired by the film – continue to remind the public of its significance.

—

Every film is a documentary of its own making, the French director Jacques Rivette once said. From this, we might infer that a film, aside from being a visual record of performance and storytelling, is a record of the actors in it, and of those directing and photographing and writing lines, and everyone else involved with the production. With every film, you're watching the end result and part-witnessing, part-imagining the circumstances of its creation.

This is what *Satya* has become for me. I see Bheeku Mhatre yell and my thoughts drift to Bajpayee, desperate for success, throwing everything he has at the screen. Chander tells his Ram–Shyam joke and I imagine Kashyap writing the scene, chuckling to himself, *Ramu's going to like this*. Satya turns up onscreen with his sad eyes and I wonder if Chakravarthy felt a little lonely on set. I hear 'Goli Maar Bheje Mein' and I picture Varma – a man who didn't think twice before calling Amitabh Bachchan names – not being able to summon up the courage to tell Gulzar he doesn't like his lyrics, and sending his young writer into the breach instead.

This phantom *Satya* is interwoven with my memories of chasing its crew. Bheeku with a bottle reminds me of Manoj Bajpayee with a glass of red wine, reminiscing about the film over lunch, no recollection of me as the person who'd interviewed him for hours at his home a couple of years earlier for a newspaper profile. Vidya brings back memories of my trying (unsuccessfully) to sweet-talk

Urmila Matondkar's secretary into setting up an interview. Yeda growling 'Item *bahut bhaari hai*' reminds me not so much of my meeting with Sabir Masani in a coffee shop in Byculla, his flowing locks now down to stubble, but of Barnali Ray Shukla in a different coffee shop saying 'Sabir was half-*goonda* in any case.'

The documentary ends where it began – in Delhi. The book was conceived here, but written, rewritten, agonised over in the only place it would have been right to do so: Mumbai. I stayed in the city for almost six years, complained bitterly, detested the rain and the lack of space, grew to like *vada pav* and sunsets over the sea. *Satya* came alive only after I lived there. For this, among other things, I'm eternally grateful to the city.

——

After collaborating with him on *Satya*, *Kaun* and *Shool*, Kashyap fell out with Varma. Time healed the rift, and Kashyap never stopped crediting Varma with showing him what a film set with all its moving parts was like. I talked to Kashyap in 2018, in his Aram Nagar home. He was recovering from a fever, but spoke at length of his time on *Satya*, which he described as his 'whole film schooling'. After two hours had passed, I felt the conversation winding down. Then, all of a sudden, Kashyap picked up the phone and called Varma. 'It is 20 years of *Satya*,' he told the one man who couldn't care less.

I could only hear Kashyap's end of the conversation (how I wished he'd put on the speakerphone). But I imagine Varma was his usual dry self, insisting the film came together by chance. 'You didn't make it *galti se* (by mistake),' Kashyap said. 'We were all along for the ride.' He told Varma he now saw a mix of 'Gerry's documentary approach and your design' in the film. Varma said something about the bridge shootout, and Kashyap chuckled at how opposed he had been to the sudden death of Bheeku. 'I fought so much, after some time

even Makarand decided to ignore me,' he said. At this point, Varma
might have taken a dig at the younger man getting sentimental over
a 20-year-old film. 'That's why I was trying to call you,' Kashyap said.
'I'm in a space right now which you won't like. But once I recover,
let's get together for a drink and plan something.' They discussed
Kashyap's latest project, *Manmarziyaan* (2019), Varma asking who
was in it and what the title meant, Kashyap saying, touchingly, 'I've
made my *Rangeela*.'

With a promise to show Varma his new film, Kashyap hung
up. 'He hates it when you tell him you're sick.' He repeated, with
something like wonder, something Varma admitted during the
conversation. 'He said, *Satya* suddenly looks like I never made it.'

Bibliography

1. The Moment of Satya

Joseph, Manu. 'Eerie does it...' *Outlook*; https://magazine.outlookindia. com/story/eerie-does-it/222787 (2 February 2004).

Mehta, Suketu. *Maximum City: Bombay Lost and Found* (Random House, 2004).

Tandon, Vivek. 'Aamir doesn't just rely on his body, but his body of work: Kay Kay Menon'. *DNA*; https://www.dnaindia.com/mumbai/ report-aamir-doesn-t-just-rely-on-his-body-but-his-body-of-work- kay-kay-menon-2031362 (2 November 2014).

Varma, Ram Gopal. *Guns & Thighs: The Story of My Life* (Rupa Publications India, 2015).

Warshow, Robert. 'The gangster as tragic hero' (*The Partisan Review*, 1948).

2. Ten Scenes

'Bollywood blockbusters: The story behind Satya', a half-hour TV programme on the film. Broadcast on CNN-IBN (n.d.).

Brahmatmaj, Ajay. 'Anurag Kashyap se antrang baatcheet'. Chavannichap; https://www.chavannichap.com/2008/11/0-1993-0-0-0-1993-0-1995-0-0-0-0-0-0.html?m=0 (4 November 2008).

Creekmur, C.K. 'Bombay bhai: The gangster in and behind popular Hindi cinema'; *Cinema, Law, and the State in Asia* (Palgrave Macmillan, 2007).

Doctorow, E.L. *Billy Bathgate* (Random House, 1989).

Ghosh, Sankhayan. 'We didn't make the film, it made itself: Ram Gopal Varma on 20 years of Satya'. Film Companion; https://www. filmcompanion.in/features/bollywood-features/we-didnt-make-the-film-it-made-itself-ram-gopal-varma-on-20-years-of-satya/ (3 July 2018).

Kabir, Nasreen Munni. *In the Company of a Poet: Gulzar in Conversation* (Rainlight Rupa, 2012).

Kashyap, Anurag. 'Satya – The true story Part 1'. Passion For Cinema; https://passionforcinema-archive.blogspot.com/2018/01/satya-true-story-part-1.html (25 November 2006).

Pandya, Mihir. 'Hindi cinema mein shahar: 1988 se ab tak'. Doctoral thesis, Department of Hindi, University of Delhi (2015).

Rath, Basant. 'Anatomy of a tragedy: Remembering the victims of the Uphaar Cinema Fire'. *The Wire*; https://thewire.in/urban/victims-uphaar-cinema-fire (13 June 2019).

Vasudevan, Ravi S. 'The exhilaration of dread: Genre, narrative form and film style in contemporary urban action films'; *Sarai Reader 02: The Cities of Everyday Life* (October 2002).

Warshow, 'The Gangster as Tragic Hero'.

3. The Hindi Film Gangster

Abbas, K.A., audio interview by The Centre of South Asian Studies, www.s-asian.cam.ac.uk/archive/audio/item/interview- k-a-abbas-part-1/.

Baxter, John. *The Gangster Film* (AS Barnes, 1970).

BBC News. 'Indian movie mogul convicted'.http://news.bbc.co.uk/2/hi/south_asia/3151036.stm (30 September 2003).

Biswas, Moinak. 'Mourning and blood-ties: Macbeth in Mumbai'. *Journal of the Moving Image* (Jadavpur University, 2006).

Daniyal, Shoaib. 'Forgotten fact: Most Mumbaiites are breaking the law when they grab a drink'. Scroll; https://scroll.in/article/727053/forgotten-fact-most-mumbaiites-are-breaking-the-law-when-they-grab-a-drink (17 May 2015).

Film Companion. 'Dibakar Banerjee & Tigmanshu Dhulia | Bandit Queen | FC Director's Choice'. https://www.filmcompanion.in/interviews/bollywood-interview/dibakar-banerjee-tigmanshu-dhulia-bandit-queen/ (9 December 2014).

Filmindia. 'Kismet provides a schoolroom for criminals.' Vol. 9 No. 7 (July 1943).

Kabir, Nasreen Munni. *Talking Films: Conversations on Hindi Cinema with Javed Akhtar* (Oxford University Press, 1999).

Koppikar, Smruti. 'Desperate for funds, underworld dons extort money from Bollywood'. *India Today*; https://www.indiatoday.in/magazine/cover-story/story/19970825-desperate-for-funds-underworld-dons-extort-money-from-bollywood-831993-1997-08-25 (25 August 1997).

Outlook. 'The Sanjay Dutt tape'; https://www.outlookindia.com/website/story/the-sanjay-dutt-tape/216640 (29 July 2002).

Raghavendra, M.K. *50 Indian Film Classics* (HarperCollins, 2009).

Rajadhyaksha, Ashish and Paul Willemen (eds). *Encyclopaedia of Indian Cinema*, revised edition (Routledge, 1999).

Rediff. 'The predator as prey'; http://www.rediff.com/movies/dec/27sat.htm (27 December 1997).

Sahani, Alaka. 'Double indemnity: What's common between Anurag Kashyap and Sriram Raghavan?'. *The Indian Express*; https://

indianexpress.com/article/entertainment/bollywood/double-indemnity-whats-common-between-anurag-kashyap-and-sriram-raghavan-2834858 (6 June 2016).

Sardesai, Rajdeep. 'Was Sanjay Dutt a terrorist? It's grey, says Rajdeep Sardesai as he recalls Mumbai's '92-'93 trauma'. *Scroll*; https://scroll.in/article/885790/was-sanjay-dutt-a-terrorist-rajdeep-sardesai-recalls-10-facts-about-mumbais-trauma-in-1992-93 (9 July 2018).

Schrader, Paul. 'Notes on film noir'. *Film Comment*, Vol. 8 No. 1 (Spring 1972).

Singh, Jai Arjun. 'Revisiting J P Dutta's Hathyar (and reflections on the bad old 1980s)'. Jabberwock; http://jaiarjun.blogspot.com/2014/04/revisiting-j-p-duttas-hathyar-and.html (12 April 2014).

The New York Times. 'Two Thugs'. https://www.nytimes.com/1931/04/24/archives/two-thugs.html (24 April 1931).

United Nations. 'Population growth and policies in mega-cities: Bombay'. Department of International Economic and Social Affairs, Population Policy Paper No. 6; https://population.un.org/wup/Archive/Files/1986_Bombay.PDF (1986).

Zaidi, S. Hussain. *Dongri to Dubai: Six Decades of the Mumbai Mafia* (Lotus Roli, 2012).

4. Bombay on Film

Anand, Dev. *Romancing with Life: An Autobiography* (Penguin Random House, 2011).

Bhatia, Sidharth. *Cinema Modern: The Navketan Story* (HarperCollins, 2011).

Chandra, A. 'Mani Ratnam's film 'Bombay' incenses Muslim leaders of city'. *India Today*; https://www.indiatoday.in/magazine/indiascope/story/19950430-mani-ratnams-film-bombay-incenses-muslim-leaders-of-city-808273-1995-04-30 (30 April 1995).

Chatterjee, Shoma A. 'Desh Mukherjee'. Upperstall; https://upperstall.com/profile/desh-mukherjee/ (n.d.).

Gopalan, Lalitha. 'Bombay noir'. *Journal of the Moving Image*; https://jmionline.org/article/bombay_noir (2015).

Kapoor, Coomi. 'Fury of communal violence burns 80 km stretch from tip of South Bombay to Bhiwandi town'. *India Today*; https://www.indiatoday.in/magazine/indiascope/story/19840615-fury-of-communal-violence-burns-80-km-stretch-from-tip-of-south-bombay-to-bhiwandi-town-803038-1984-06-15 (15 June 1984).

Mazumdar, Ranjani. 'Figure of the tapori: Language, gesture and cinematic city'. *Economic and Political Weekly*, Vol. 36, No. 52 (29 December 2001–4 January 2002).

———. *Bombay Cinema: An Archive of the City* (University of Minnesota Press, 2007).

Miguel, Helio San (ed.). *World Film Locations: Mumbai* (Intellect Books, 2012).

Swami, Praveen. 'A searing indictment'. *Frontline*; https://frontline.thehindu.com/the-nation/article30161873.ece (29 August 1998).

Varma, *Guns & Thighs*.

5. Getting the Team Together

Brahmatmaj, 'Anurag Kashyap se antrang baatcheet'.

Ghosh, 'We didn't make the film, it made itself: Ram Gopal Varma on 20 years of Satya'.

Khaleej Times. 'Ram Gopal Varma: 'Who will stop me? No one can''. https://www.khaleejtimes.com/wknd/bollywood/ram-gopal-varma-who-will-stop-me-no-one-can (21 October 2016).

Mehta, *Maximum City*.

Rediff. 'The films that scared Ram Gopal Varma'. https://www.rediff.com/movies/2008/jul/28sld1.htm (28 July 2008).

Varma, *Guns & Thighs*.

Varma, Ram Gopal. 'Ram Gopal Varma Blog #216. A(aa)ging SHOLAY'. RGV–Ram Gopal Varma Blog; http://rgv-ram-gopal-varma.

blogspot.com/2013/12/ram-gopal-varma-blog-216-aaaging-sholay. html (n.d.).

6. Making the Film

Ghosh, 'We didn't make the film, it made itself: Ram Gopal Varma on 20 years of Satya'.

Kamran, Mazhar. 'The light behind the king of Mumbai'. *Outlook*; https://www.outlookindia.com/magazine/story/the-light-behind-the-king-of-mumbai/300371 (23 July 2018).

Kashyap, Anurag. 'Satya: The true story'. Passion For Cinema; https://passionforcinema-archive.blogspot.com/2018/01/satya-true-story-part-1.html (25 November 2006).

Kothari, Jigna & Madangarli, Supriya. *Gangs of Wasseypur: The Making of a Modern Classic* (HarperCollins, 2013).

Kumar, Amitava. 'Writing my own Satya'. *The Popcorn Essayists: What Movies Do To Writers*, edited by Jai Arjun Singh (Tranquebar Press, 2011).

Mohamed, Khalid. 'Shot by shot'. *DNA*; https://www.dnaindia.com/entertainment/report-shot-by-shot-1041912 (15 July 2006).

Patil, Vimla. 'A role to remember ...' *The Tribune*; https://www.tribuneindia.com/1999/99jan24/sunday/head9.htm (24 January 1999).

Rangan, Baradwaj. 'Interview: Ram Gopal Varma'. Baradwajrangan. wordpress.com; https://baradwajrangan.wordpress.com/2008/08/14/interview-ram-gopal-varma (14 August 2008).

Rediff, 'The predator as prey'.

Singh, Jai Arjun. *Jaane Bhi Do Yaaro: Seriously Funny Since 1983* (HarperCollins, 2010).

Taliculam, Sharmila. 'A film has to touch the audience somewhere'. Rediff; https://www.rediff.com/movies/1999/oct/13ramu.htm (13 October 1999).

Varma, *Guns & Thighs*.

Varma, Ram Gopal. 'Ram Gopal Varma Blog #131. The Psychological aspect of background music'. RGV–Ram Gopal Varma Blog; http://rgv-ram-gopal-varma.blogspot.com/2013/12/ram-gopal-varma-blog-131-psychological.html (original post's date unknown).

7. After Satya

'Bollywood blockbusters: The story behind Satya', a half-hour TV programme.

Ahmed, Zubair. 'Bombay's crack "encounter" police'. BBC News. http://news.bbc.co.uk/2/hi/south_asia/3786645.stm (9 June 2004).

Aiyar, V. Shankar & Raval, Sheela. 'Desperate underworld targets Bollywood, muscle their way to larger share of profits'. *India Today*; https://www.indiatoday.in/magazine/cover-story/story/20010101-desperate-underworld-targets-bollywood-muscle-their-way-to-larger-share-of-profits-776082-2001-01-22 (22 January 2001).

Bamzai, Kaveree. 'Boom time for Bollywood as new directors, niche films, multiplexes bring in fresh change'. *India Today*; https://www.indiatoday.in/magazine/cover-story/story/20030929-boom-time-for-bollywood-as-new-directors-niche-films-multiplexes-bring-in-fresh-change-792137-2003-09-29 (29 September 2003).

Box Office India. https://boxofficeindia.com/movie.php?movieid=2555.

Chatterjee, Saibal. 'Bollywood's new badshah'. *The Tribune*; https://www.tribuneindia.com/2004/20040606/spectrum/index.htm (6 June 2004).

Chopra, Anupama. 'After Satya success, Manoj Bajpai-Ram Gopal Varma hold promise for the future'. *India Today*; https://www.indiatoday.in/magazine/society-the-arts/films/story/19980831-after-satya-success-manoj-bajpai-ram-gopal-varma-hold-promise-for-the-future-827001-1998-08-31 (31 August 1998).

Ghosh, 'We didn't make the film, it made itself: Ram Gopal Varma on 20 years of Satya'.

Gopalan, 'Bombay Noir'.

Jha, Subhash K. 'Web series are a marathon in story telling, says "your honor" director E, Niwas'. *National Herald*; https://www.nationalheraldindia.com/entertainment/web-series-are-a-marathon-in-story-telling-says-your-honor-director-e-niwas (23 June 2020).

Jog, Sanjoy. 'State exempts Satya from entertainment tax again'. *The Indian Express*; https://web.archive.org/web/20121010043103/http://www.expressindia.com/fe/daily/19981010/28355364.html (10 October 1998).

Katakam, Anupama. 'An acquittal in Mumbai'. *Frontline*; https://frontline.thehindu.com/other/article30219531.ece (24 October 2003).

MacInnes, Paul. 'How Slumdog Millionaire is changing film-making in India'. *The Guardian*; www.theguardian.com/film/2009/jun/04/slumdog-millionaire-india (4 June 2009).

Mehta, Hansal. 'Dil pe mat le yaar (2000)–Not so funny!' Hansalmehta.com; https://hansalmehta.com/2011/08/25/dil-pe-mat-le-yaar-2000-not-so-funny (25 August 2011).

Patcy, N. 'I ran after Ram Gopal's car …' Rediff; https://www.rediff.com/movies/report/rohit/20050919.htm (19 September 2005).

Rediff. 'Dalit protests in Mumbai: Chhota Rajan's brother listed accused'. https://www.rediff.com/news/2006/dec/01dalit.htm (1 December 2006).

Sahani, 'Double indemnity: What's common between Anurag Kashyap and Sriram Raghavan?'.

Sen, Raja. 'Ram Gopal Varma and his Al Qaeda'. Rajasen.com; https://rajasen.com/2010/02/19/ram-gopal-varma-and-his-al-qaeda/ (19 February 2010).

Varma, *Guns & Thighs*.

Index

Aag (2007), 209

Aakhri Khat (1966), 89–91, 94

Aar-Paar (1954), 52, 54–56, 86–88, 94

Aarya (2020–), 209

Aar Ya Paar (1997), 111

Aatish (1994), 72

Abbas, K.A., 104

Abraham, John, 44

Ab Tak Chhappan (2004), 8, 197–98, 201, 203

Advani, Nikhil, 125

Advani, Pankaj, 121

Afsar (1950), 52

Agneepath (1990), 39–40, 73, 76, 192

Ahista Ahista (2006), 121

Ahluwalia, Ashim, 209

Ajit, 5, 61–62

Akalmand (1984), 111

Akhtar, Javed, 57, 62, 66; *see also* Salim–Javed

Akhtar, Zoya, 97, 206

Albert Pinto Ko Gussa Kyoon Aata Hai (1980), 82, 88, 96–97, 100–101, 206

Ali, Imtiaz, 123

Ali, Muzaffar, 86–87

Alien (1979), 67, 106, 178

Aligarh (2015), 7

Allen, Karen, 28

All the President's Men (1976), 71

Almendros, Néstor, 170

Alter, Tom, 98

Alvi, Abrar, 57, 86, 88

Aman, Zeenat, 111

Amar Akbar Anthony (1977), 63, 87

Amin, Allan, 30, 38, 79, 132, 153, 162, 193, 213

Amin, Shimit, 8, 197–98, 201, 203

Amrapurkar, Sadashiv, 65

Amrohi, Kamal, 170

Anaganaga Oka Roju (1996), 133, 182

Anand, Chetan, 52, 54, 58, 83, 89

Anand, Dev, 21, 43, 52, 57–59, 81, 83–85

Anand, Mukul, 39, 67, 73

Anand, Vijay, 48, 58–61, 111, 125

Andersen, Thom, 93

Andhadhun (2018), 201

Angaar (1992), 65, 73–74, 103

Angamaly Diaries (2017), 209

Angels With Dirty Faces (1938), 73

Ankhen (1968), 60

Ankhon Dekhi (2013), 213

Ankur (1974), 106

Ansari, N.A., 59

Antham (1992), 40, 110–12, 114, 119

Apocalypse Now (1979), 39

Ardh Satya (1983), 19, 65–66, 95, 98, 107, 114, 123, 192, 198

Arjun (1985), 23, 64, 66–68, 72, 74, 108

Arora, Chandan, 202–3

Arrival (1980), 96

Arvind Desai Ki Ajeeb Dastaan (1978), 95

A Streetcar Named Desire (1951), 134

Asrani, Apurva, 4, 7, 17, 41, 133, 155, 158, 168, 175, 178, 182, 201

Attacks of 26/11, The (2013) 159

Awara (1951), 43, 77

Baazi (1951), 43, 52–55, 57

Babri mosque, 102–3, 199

Bachchan, Amitabh, 3, 5, 10, 13, 39, 44, 48, 61–63, 70, 73, 87, 92, 95, 98, 100, 188, 192, 197, 200, 202

Bachchan, Jaya, 81, 92

Bachchan, Aishwarya Rai, 134

Bade Miyan Chote Miyan (1998), 3

Badlapur (2015), 201

Bajpayee, Manoj, 4, 7–8, 17–18, 22, 25–27, 30, 34–36, 78–79, 119–20, 122–27, 133, 137, 139, 141–45, 160–62, 168–69, 180, 186–90, 193, 213–14

Bala, Vasan, 206

Bali, Geeta, 53–54

Bambai Raat Ki Baahon Mein
   (1968), 104
Bambaiyya/Mumbaiyya, 63,
   86–89, 143–45, 177
Bandit Queen (1994), 76, 78–79,
   102, 119–20, 122, 125–26,
   130, 132, 139, 146, 186,
   211–12
Banerjee, Dibakar, 12, 38, 78,
   150, 172
Barot, Chandra, 62
Baton Baton Mein (1979), 93
Batra, Ritesh, 205–6
Becker, Étienne, 127
Bedi, Bobby, 212
Benegal, Shyam, 106, 211
Better Tomorrow, A (1986), 72
Bhanodaya, 9, 11, 133, 141, 182
Bhansali, Sanjay Leela, 175
Bhardwaj, Vishal, 4, 6–8, 10, 12,
   23, 173–78, 189, 193–95, 198,
   201–2, 208
Bhattacharya, Aditya, 99
Bhave, Sumitra, 130
Bhiwandi riots, 101
Bhoot (2003), 201, 203
Bhopal Express (1999), 194
Bhosle, Asha, 115
Big Sleep, The (1946), 57
Bir, A.K., 94
Biswas, Moinak, 76

Bitter Rice (1949), 57
Black Cat (1959), 59
Black Friday (2004), 6, 104, 109,
   159, 198–99, 204
Blackmail (1973), 61
Blow Out (1981), 113
Bluff Master (1963), 82
Bogdanovich, Peter, 201
Bokade, Sudhakar, 45
Bombay (1995), 104, 115, 119
Bombay Cinema, 70, 82
Bombay Talkies, 48
Bombay to Goa (1972), 87, 107
Bombay Velvet (2015), 207–9
Bonnie and Clyde (1967), 71
Boom (2003), 197
Border (1997), 2, 31–32, 135
Bose, Rahul, 192
Boyle, Danny, 199, 204
Breathless (1960), 85
Brij, 59–60
The Brothers (1979), 72
Bunty Aur Babli (2005), 201
Burman, M.K., 56
Burman, S.D., 52

Cagney, James, 51, 73, 208
Call Northside 777 (1948), 59
Cannes Film Festival, 52, 101,
   207
Carpenter, John, 69, 112–13

censorship, 7, 49, 76, 78–79, 146, 199

Chak De India (2007), 201

Chakori (1992), 130

Chakra (1981), 97

Chakravarthy, J.D., 9–10, 16–17, 25, 30, 35, 39, 51, 68, 93, 107, 110, 132, 140–42, 144, 147, 168, 175, 180, 183, 188

Chandra, N., 64, 68

Chandra, Vikram, 44

Chandragupta, Bansi, 97

Chase, James Hadley, 40, 111, 119

Chatterjee, Basu, 90, 92–95, 116

Chaturvedi, Hemant, 8, 202

Chaubey, Abhishek, 78, 208

Chaudhry, Mahima, 132

Chennai Express (2013), 212

Chhel, Sanjay, 88, 121

Chhota Rajan. *See* Nikalje, Rajendra Sadashiv

Chhoti Si Baat (1976), 92

Chhupa Rustam (1973), 61

China Town (1962), 59

Chitchor (1976), 93

Chopra, Aditya, 146, 212

Chopra, Prem, 61, 66

Chopra, Vidhu Vinod, 69, 211

Chopra, Yash, 62, 65, 92, 99

Chori Chori Chupke Chupke (2001), 47

Chowta, Sandeep, 4, 11, 16, 27, 38, 41, 153, 165, 178–79, 201

C.I.D. (1956), 52, 56, 97, 205

Cinema of Interruptions, 77

Citizen Kane (1941), 144

CityLights (2014), 95

City of God (2002), 207

City on Fire (1987), 72

Company (2002), 6, 12–13, 45, 56, 109, 138, 150, 157, 178, 195–97, 200–204, 210

Contempt (1963), 151

Copland, Aaron, 16

Coppola, Francis Ford, 61, 67, 201

Corke, Vernon, 83

Corman, Roger, 200–201

Coutard, Raoul, 85

Craven, Wes, 33

D (2005), 6, 45, 200, 202–3

Dabi, Snehal, 18, 89, 144

dacoit/daaku films, 47, 76–79, 212

Daddy (2017), 44, 213

Dagdi Chawl (2015), 45

Darna Mana Hai (2003), 202–3

Darna Zaroori Hai (2006), 203

Daud (1997), 2, 4–5, 112, 117, 120–21, 123–24, 133, 139, 182

Dayavan (1988), 64, 68

D-Company, 46, 117, 154; *see also* Ibrahim, Dawood

D-Day (2013), 45

De, Shobha, 5

Dedh Ishqiya (2014), 208

Deewar (1975), 7, 44, 57, 62–63, 70, 72, 76, 92

Delhi theatre, 119, 125, 153, 161, 177

Denzongpa, Danny, 111

Deol, Sunny, 23, 66, 98, 108

De Palma, Brian, 69, 73, 113

Desai, Manmohan, 63, 92

Desai, V.H., 49

Deshmukh, Riteish, 158

Deshmukh, Vilasrao, 158

Deshpande, Makarand, 4, 11, 17–18, 44, 131, 161–62, 172, 216

Dev.D (2009), 199, 204

Devgn, Ajay, 192, 195, 200

Devi, Phoolan, 76, 79, 125, 146

Dewani, Ajit, 47, 119, 138–39, 147–48, 187

Deyyam (1996), 140

Dhaimade, Milind, 206

Dharavi (1992), 103, 128

Dharmaraj, Rabindra, 97

Dharmatma (1975), 7, 63

Dharmendra, 60, 72, 81, 111

Dhawan, Dilip, 82, 95–96

Dhobi Ghat (2010), 205

Dholakia, Arvind, 117

Dholakia, Mahesh, 117

Dhoom (2004), 213

Dhulia, Tigmanshu, 186, 208

Dil Chahta Hai (2001), 149

Dil Dhadakne Do (2015), 206

Dil Pe Mat Le Yaar (2000), 193–94

Dil Se (1998), 3, 119

Dilwale Dulhania Le Jayenge (1995), 13, 114, 212, 212–13

Disha (1990), 97

Dixit, Madhuri, 68, 70, 73, 98, 103

Dolas, Maya, 30, 200

Don (1978), 63, 92

Dongri to Dubai, 111

Dr Babasaheb Ambedkar (2000), 134

Duggal, Mukesh, 45

Dutt, Guru, 52, 55–56, 86

Dutt, Sanjay, 4, 46, 71, 73, 98, 114, 117, 168, 191, 196–97

Dutt, Sunil, 59, 77, 197

Dutta, J.P., 31, 64, 69, 77
Dutta, Madhushree, 205

Easy Rider (1969), 14
Ek Hasina Thi (2004), 8, 198, 201–2
Ek Ladki Ko Dekha Toh Aisa Laga (2019), 212
Encounter (2002), 197
Enter the Dragon (1973), 178
Europe '51 (1952), 127
Exorcist, The (1973), 113

Factory, The, 8
Feroz, A.K., 22
Film and Television Institute of India (FTII), 130, 151
Filmindia, 48
Ford, John, 164
Foreign Correspondent (1940), 67
Fountainhead, The, 136–37

Gaayam (1993), 33, 114
Gaman (1978), 86–87, 94, 97
Gandhi (1982), 106
Ganga Jumna (1961), 77
Gangs of Wasseypur (2012), 7, 33, 207–9, 213
Gangster (2006), 7
Gardish (1993), 74
Gawli, Arun, 44, 47, 148–49, 209

Ghai, Subhash, 45, 64, 155, 202
Gharonda (1977), 93, 95, 176
Ghatge, Vijayendra, 116
Ghosh, Shashanka, 197
Ghulam (1998), 3, 58, 87, 104, 146, 190
Ghulami (1985), 77
Gilda (1946), 53
Godard, Jean-Luc, 1, 85, 151
Godfather, The (1972), 11, 39, 61, 63, 67, 70, 74, 137, 162–64, 171, 199
Godfather, The: Part II (1974), 39
God of Small Things, The, 2
Goodfellas (1990), 19, 29, 122, 137
Govinda, 3
Govinda Govinda (1993), 114, 133
Great Train Robbery, The (1903), 16, 51
Griffith, D.W., 1, 50
Guddi (1971), 81
Guide (1965), 170
Gully Boy (2019), 98, 206
Gulzar, 22–23, 93, 174–78, 198, 211, 214
Gulzar, Meghna, 174
Guns and Thighs 11, 80, 93, 118, 154, 156, 171, 195, 209

Guns of Navarone, The (1961), 17, 162

Gupta, Sanjay, 46, 72, 197

Gustad, Kaizad, 197

Haasan, Kamal, 44, 68

Haasil (2003), 208

Haider (2014), 7

Halloween (1978), 113

Hammett, Dashiell, 110

Hashmi, Emraan, 200

Hathyar (1989), 46, 64, 69, 71–72, 77, 99–100, 191, 197

Hattangadi, Rohini, 113

Hawks, Howard, 50, 57

Hayworth, Rita, 53

Hazaaron Khwaishein Aisi (2003), 125

Hecht, Ben, 50–51, 155

Highway 301 (1950), 56

Hill, Walter, 69

Hingora, Samir, 46

Hirani, Rajkumar, 12, 71, 197

Hitchcock, Alfred, 27, 55–56, 67, 106, 164

Hooda, Randeep, 8, 45, 200, 202

Hooper, Gerard, 9, 17–18, 37–38, 128–29, 131, 149–52, 159, 163, 165, 168–69, 179, 213, 215, 128, 169, 167–68

House No. 44 (1955), 43, 52, 56–57

Howrah Bridge (1958), 59

Hsiao-hsien, Hou, 170

Hum Aapke Hain Koun (1994), 102

Hussain, Imtiaz, 125, 192

Hyderabad Blues (1998), 3–4

Ibrahim, Dawood, 5–6, 44–46, 103, 117, 154, 173, 195, 200, 209, *see also* D-Company

Ilaiyaraaja, 68

India: Matri Bhumi (1959), 127

In Search of Guru Dutt (1989), 86

In Which Annie Gives It Those Ones (1989), 3, 98

Irani, Aruna, 107

Ishqiya (2010), 208

Island City (2015), 205

Is Raat Ki Subah Nahin (1996), 6, 53, 75, 85, 104, 124–26, 146, 186, 192

Iyer, Kannan, 79, 120, 128–31, 149, 174

Jaal (1952), 57–58

Jaane Bhi Do Yaaro (1983), 14, 95, 98, 158

James (2005), 203

Jatin–Lalit, 117

Jeeva, 18
Jewel Thief (1967), 60
Jog, Anant, 197
Johar, Karan, 2
Johar, Yash, 132
Johnny Gaddaar (2007), 111, 201
Johny Mera Naam (1970), 60
Jo Jeeta Wohi Sikandar (1992), 102, 212
Joshi, Rajesh, 18, 159
Jugraj, Rohit, 203
Jungle (2000), 201
Jungle Book (1989–90), 174
Jurassic Park (1993), 15, 145

Kaala (2018), 209
Kaante (2002), 197
Kadam, Kishore, 193
Kadawala, Hanif, 45–46, 195
Kagaar (2003), 197
Kagti, Reema, 25, 75
Kajol, 2, 190
Kala Bazar (1960), 52, 58
Kammattipadam (2016), 209
Kamran, Mazhar, 10, 12, 17, 22–23, 29–30, 36, 38, 79, 129–31, 150–51, 157, 164, 168–69, 179, 181, 185–86, 188, 201, 213
Kapoor, Anil, 69–70, 148, 188, 199

Kapoor, Raj, 43, 52, 54, 57, 77–78, 97
Kapoor, Ranbir, 202, 207
Kapoor, Rishi, 45
Kapoor, Shammi, 59–60, 82
Kapoor, Shashi, 62
Kapur, Pankaj, 100, 198, 211
Kapur, Shekhar, 76, 78–79, 119–20, 125, 130, 186, 212
Kartik, Kalpana, 52–53, 83–84
Kar-wai, Wong, 170, 196
Karz (1980), 64
Kashyap, Anurag, as director 200–1, 206–7, 209–10; pre-*Satya*, 123–24, 154; writing *Satya*, 89–90, 143–46, 163–65, 167–68
Katha (1983), 98
Kaul, Awtar Krishna, 94
Kaul, Mani, 96
Kaun (1999), 5, 8, 134, 181, 186, 193, 215
Khal Nayak (1993), 46, 73, 114
Khan, Aamir, 3–4, 8, 25, 87, 98, 100, 102, 104, 116, 121, 145–46, 190, 202, 205
Khan, Ahmed, 22, 115, 180
Khan, Amjad, 63, 78, 87
Khan, Farah, 21
Khan, Feroz, 3, 63, 68
Khan, Irrfan, 8, 198

Khan, Kader, 63, 65, 73, 87

Khan, Mazhar, 74

Khanna, Rajesh, 90

Khanna, Vinod, 68

Khan, Rashid, 52–53

Khan, Salim, 62, *see also* Salim–
   Javed

Khan, Salman, 98, 102, 202

Khan, Saroj, 21

Khan, Shah Rukh, 2, 21, 73, 98,
   102, 124, 134–35, 190, 202

Kharbanda, Kulbhushan, 64

Khatri, Rattan, 63

Kher, Anupam, 66, 70

Khosla, Raj, 52, 56

Khosla Ka Ghosla (2006), 201

Kismet (1943), 43, 48–49, 54

Koirala, Manisha, 47, 104, 119

Kshana Kshanam (1991), 112,
   117, 133, 185

Kuch Kuch Hota Hai (1998), 2,
   142, 190

Kumar, Anoop, 85

Kumar, Ashok, 43, 48, 59, 85

Kumar, Dilip, 52, 58, 65, 73, 77

Kumar, Gulshan, 47, 155–57,
   159–60, 193

Kumar, Kishore, 58, 85

Lagoo, Reema, 192

Lakhia, Apoorv, 200

Lala, Karim, 44, 62, 73

Lee, Bruce, 10, 107, 109, 136,
   140

Leone, Sergio, 27, 69

Little Caesar (1931), 50

Los Angeles Plays Itself (2003), 93

Love, Sex Aur Dhokha (2010),
   150

Love Sonia (2018), 8

Luck By Chance (2009), 206

Ludhianvi, Sahir, 52

Lunchbox, The (2013), 205

Maachis (1996), 174, 176–77

Mackenna's Gold (1969), 17, 136

Madhubala, 45, 59, 81, 85

Maine Pyar Kiya (1989), 98, 102

*Main Madhuri Dixit Banna
   Chahti Hoon* (2003), 202–3

Majboor (1974), 23

Malhotra, Manish, 142

Malhotra, Pavan, 100, 131, 199

Malhotra, Sidharth, 51

Malini, Hema, 63, 128

Malle, Louis, 127

Mangeshkar, Lata, 175

Manjrekar, Mahesh, 46–47,
   191–92, 197

Manmarziyaan (2019), 216

Mano, 23, 176

Manzil (1979), 92, 95, 213

Maqbool (2003), 6–7, 76, 194, 198, 202
Mard Ko Dard Nahi Hota (2018), 206
Masani, Sabir, 17, 22, 37, 129, 132, 139, 145, 147–48, 157–58, 168, 215
Mashaal (1984), 65
Mast (1999), 178
Mastan, Haji, 44, 62, 200
Matondkar, Urmila, 8, 11, 20, 27, 40, 93, 110–11, 114–15, 117, 124, 132–33, 142–43, 146–48, 168, 171, 175, 178, 180–81, 189–90, 215
Maurya, Vijay, 206
Mavani, Raju, 30, 132
Maximum City, 5, 118
Mazumdar, Ranjani, 70, 82, 85, 88
Mean Streets (1973), 61
Mehboob, 58, 77
Mehmood, Rafey, 213
Mehra, Prakash, 62–63, 92
Mehta, Hansal, 41, 95, 123, 193
Mehta, Suketu, 5, 118
Meirelles, Fernando, 207
Memon, Ibrahim 'Tiger,' 46, 199
Memon, Yakub, 46
Menon, Kay Kay, 8, 176, 199
Middle Cinema, 92–93, 116, 202, 212

Mirzapur (2018–), 7, 209
Mirchandani, Mitesh, 213
Mirza, Saeed Akhtar, 64, 88, 95–97, 100–101, 206, 211
Mishra, Sanjay, 20, 159, 161
Mishra, Sudhir, 6, 75, 98, 103, 124–26, 211
Mistry, Fali, 170
Mohamed, Khalid, 132, 158
Mohan Joshi Hazir Ho (1984), 96
Mohanlal, 196
Money (1993), 114
Mother India (1957), 58, 77, 192
Mr India (1987), 64
Mudaliar, Varadarajan, 44
Mukerji, Rani, 2, 25, 104
Mukherjee, Desh, 92
Mukherjee, Gyan, 48
Mukherjee, Hrishikesh, 81, 92, 116
Mukherjee, Indrani, 90
Mukhtar, Sheikh, 59
multiplexes, 4, 194–95
Mumbai/Bombay, landmarks 81–82, 85–86, 100, 104; language 87–90, 144–47; trains 95, 100; 1992–93 riots 46, 102–3, 105; 1993 blasts, 46, 103, 118, 200; 2008 terrorist attacks 160, 207
Munna Bhai M.B.B.S. (2003), 7, 197

Muqaddar Ka Sikandar (1978), 63, 70, 87

Murthy, V.K., 55–56, 170

Musketeers of Pig Alley, The (1912), 50

Nagarjuna, 40, 107–8, 111, 114, 178

Nair, Mira, 99, 101, 128

Nair, Shashilal K., 73

Nair, Shivam, 121, 123

Namdev, Govind, 28, 39, 79, 141, 161, 172

Narayan, Udit, 115

Nargis, 58, 77, 192

Nath, Prem, 5, 60–61, 63–64

National School of Drama, 125

Navketan, 48, 52, 54, 56, 58–59, 70, 83

Nawaz, Shah, 49

Nayak, Daya, 197

Nayakan (1987), 16, 44, 68, 70, 104, 140, 150, 192

Nayyar, O.P., 57, 208

Neecha Nagar (1946), 52

National Film Development Corporation, 42, 158, 211

Nightmare on Elm Street, A (1984), 33, 113

Nihalani, Govind, 64–66, 122, 180, 192, 211

Nikalje, Rajendra Sadashiv (Chhota Rajan), 6, 45, 118, 192, 195

Ninne Pelladata (1996), 178

Nishabd (2007), 210

Nishant (1975), 123

Niwas, E., 199, 203

No Smoking (2007), 199

Oberoi, Vivek, 195

Omkara (2006), 7, 208

Once upon a Time in Mumbaai (2010), 6, 200

On the Waterfront (1954), 3, 35, 70, 104

Paanch (2003), 199

Paan Singh Tomar (2012), 208, 212

Pahwa, Manoj, 152–53, 161

Palekar, Amol, 92–93, 116

Pandey, Nirmal, 119, 126

Parallel Cinema, 94, 99, 211

Paranjpye, Sai, 64, 98

Parashar, Pankaj, 67

Parinda (1989), 5, 16, 64–65, 69–71, 73–75, 95, 99–100, 122, 125, 146, 150, 192

Parvarish (1977), 78

Pataakha (2018), 174

Patekar, Nana, 5, 65, 73, 159, 189

Patil, Smita, 65, 96–97, 211

Peepli Live (2010), 199
Pellissery, Lijo Jose, 209
Phantom India (1969), 127–28
Photograph (2019), 206
Piya Ka Ghar (1972), 92
Pocket Maar (1956), 43
Post Box 999 (1958), 59
Pradhan, Binod, 70
Pran, 23, 44, 61–62
Priyadarshan, 74
PVR, 4, 194
Psycho (1960), 38, 113
Public Enemy, The (1931), 50, 60, 117
Pulp Fiction (1994), 27
Puri, Amrish, 64–65
Puri, Om, 19, 65, 103, 113, 211
Puzo, Mario, 19, 171
Pyaar Kiya To Darna Kya (1998), 3
Pyaar To Hona Hi Tha (1998), 2–3
Pyaasa (1957), 67, 87, 170
Pyar Tune Kya Kiya (2001), 178

Qayamat Se Qayamat Tak (1988), 98, 102

Raakh (1989), 53, 99–100, 128
Raat (1992), 33, 75, 112–13, 185, 211

Radio Ceylon, 83
Raghavan, Sridhar, 122, 178, 186
Raghavan, Sriram, 8, 12, 78, 111, 121–22, 185–86, 197–98, 201, 203, 211
Raghuvaran, 65, 107–8
Rahman, A.R., 8, 114–15, 124
Rai, Rajiv, 45, 155
Raiders of the Lost Ark (1981), 28, 67
Raina, M.K., 94
Rajnigandha (1974), 93, 116
Rakta Charitra (2010), 7, 106, 208, 210
Raman, Prawaal, 202
Ramani, Sheila, 83
Raman Raghav (1991), 121–22
Raman Raghav 2.0 (2016), 75, 205
Ram Jaane (1995), 73
Ram Lakhan (1989), 98
Rand, Ayn, 10, 124, 136–37
Rangeela (1995), 2, 4, 8, 13, 80–82, 88, 93, 113, 116–17, 121, 132–33, 143, 145–46, 148, 180, 202, 206, 210, 212, 216
Ranjith, Pa, 209
Rao, Nitin, 17
Rao, Rajkummar, 7, 25, 35

Ratnam, Mani, 3, 16, 68, 104, 114, 135
Ratra, V., 52–53, 55–56
Ravi, Rajeev, 199, 209
Rawail, Rahul, 66–67
Rawal, Paresh, 31, 66, 68, 112, 120, 124, 133, 171
Ray, Satyajit, 97, 129, 212
Rehman, Waheeda, 58
Reservoir Dogs (1992), 27, 197
Robinson, Edward G., 51, 59
Romancing the Stone (1984), 124
Romancing with Life, 84
Roshan, Hrithik, 46, 182, 196, 202
Roshan, Rakesh, 182, 196
Roy, Arundhati, 2–3

Sabharwal, Atul, 206
Sacred Games (2018–), 7, 44, 208
Saheb, Biwi Aur Gangster (2011), 208
Sahni, Balraj, 53, 59
Sahni, Jaideep, 8, 196, 201
Salaam Bombay (1988), 82, 98–99, 101–2, 128, 204, 212
Salaskar, Vijay, 197
Salem, Abu, 46, 119, 154, 196
Salim–Javed, 62, 111, 200, see also Akhtar, Javed; Khan, Salim

Salim Langde Pe Mat Ro (1989), 88, 98–101, 131, 206
Saluja, Renu, 71, 181, 211
Samanta, Shakti, 59–60
Sanam (1997), 46
Sangram (1950), 43
Sankat City (2009), 121
Sarkar (2005), 6–7, 106, 114, 150, 157, 199–200, 203
Sathyaa (1988), 68
Satya 2 (2013), 210
Sawant, Vishram, 144, 202
Scammell, Roy, 67
Scarface (1932), 39, 50, 60
Scarface (1983), 39, 73
Schoonmaker, Thelma, 207
Scorsese, Martin, 11, 19, 61, 94–95, 200, 207
Scott, Ridley, 106
Sehar (2005), 208
Sen, Mrinal, 90
Sen, Sushmita, 209
7 Islands and a Metro (2006), 205
Shaan (1980), 64
Shah, Bharat, 15, 25, 32, 47, 133–35, 142, 151, 171, 187, 190, 196
Shah, Naseeruddin, 96–97, 198, 211
Shah, Shefali, 24, 133, 144, 161, 195

Shahid (2012), 41

Shaikh, Farooq, 87, 211

Shakeel, Chhota, 46–47, 195–96

Shakila, 55, 57

Shankar–Ehsaan–Loy, 202

Sharma, Anushka, 207

Shiv Sena, 37, 101, 103–4, 141, 190

Sholay (1975), 13, 77, 106, 124, 129, 209

Shool (1999), 7–8, 66, 193, 199, 202–3, 208, 215

Shootout at Lokhandwala (2007), 6, 30, 200

Shootout at Wadala (2013), 44

Shor in the City (2011), 205

Shree 420 (1955), 43, 76, 97

Shroff, Jackie, 70, 73–74, 116

Shukla, Barnali Ray, 10, 89, 134, 152–53, 171, 173, 215

Shukla, Saurabh, 4, 7–8, 16–17, 23–24, 31, 34, 75, 125–27, 137–38, 141, 143–44, 152–53, 155, 161–62, 169, 171–72, 180–81, 186–87, 189, 193

Shyama, 55

Siddiqui, Nawazuddin, 35, 199

Singapore (1960), 59

Singh, Bhupinder, 91, 93, 176

Singh, K.N., 52–53, 56, 77

Singh, Ranveer, 202, 206

Singh, Sushant, 8, 17, 31, 134, 141, 153, 157, 161, 186

Sinha, Bhagwan, 52, 56, 83

Sippy, Ramesh, 62, 92, 106

Siva (1989), 12, 19, 65–66, 68, 72, 105, 107–9, 111–12, 114, 210

Sivan, Santosh, 100

Slumdog Millionaire (2008), 109, 127, 159, 199, 204

Som, P. Shekar, 130

Sonchiriya (2019), 78, 208

Split Wide Open (1999), 194

Sridevi, 98, 112, 114, 136, 148

Srivastava, Aditya, 4, 8, 16–17, 79, 141, 161, 177, 186, 193, 198

Streets of Fire (1984), 69

Subramaniam, Shiv, 122, 125

Sugandh, Harish, 46, 135, 156

Sugandh, Jhamu, 132, 135, 156

Surti, Pooja Ladha, 202

Surve, Manya, 111

Swaroop, Kamal, 123, 211

Talaash (2012), 25, 75

Talvar (2015), 213

Tarantino, Quentin, 27, 106, 211

Taxi Driver (1954), 52, 54, 57–58, 83, 85–86, 89, 91

Taxi Driver (1976), 94–95, 122

Teesri Manzil (1966), 60

Tehkikaat (1994–95), 125

Tendulkar, Vijay, 65–66, 123–24

Terror in the Aisles (1984), 33

Tezaab (1988), 64, 68–69

Thackeray, Bal, 104, 141, 149, 199

Thakshak (1999), 192–93

That Girl in Yellow Boots (2010), 205

Third Man, The (1949), 59

Thiruda Thiruda, 114

Thunderball (1965), 64

Touch of Evil (1958), 85

Trivedi, Amit, 207

Tu Hai Mera Sunday (2016), 206

Tyrewala, Abbas, 122

27 Down (1974), 82, 94

Ugly (2013), 205

Underworld (1927), 50

Untouchables, The (1987), 69

Uphaar Cinema, 2, 31–32

Urf Professor (2001), 121

Ustadon Ke Ustad (1963), 59

Vaastav (1999), 6, 46, 72–73, 191–93, 197

Vada Chennai (2018), 209

Varma, Ram Gopal, early life, 106–8; later films, 197–98, 201, 211–12; making *Satya*, 139, 155–59, 164–69, 172–75, 180–81, 184–86; as producer 203–6; in Telugu film, 108–18

Vetrimaaran, 209

Victoria Terminus/Chhatrapati Shivaji Terminus, 16, 81, 94, 104

Vidhaata (1982), 73

Vidyarthi, Ashish, 6, 75, 191

Vora, Neeraj, 28, 88, 121, 147, 154

Wahab, Zarina, 93, 116

Waisa Bhi Hota Hai Part II (2003), 197

Walker, Johnny, 85, 87, 96, 205

Warshow, Robert, 1, 13, 16, 37, 40

Warsi, Arshad, 197, 208

Way of the Dragon, The (1972), 66, 107

Welles, Orson, 85, 144

Wellman, William, 50–51

Willis, Gordon, 70–71

Wirsching, Josef, 170

Woo, John, 72

Yaadon Ki Baaraat (1973), 61

Yakeen (1969), 60

Yateem (1988), 77

Yes Boss (1997), 21

Zaidi, S. Hussain, 111, 198–99

Zanjeer (1973), 44, 61, 63, 70

Zindagi Na Milegi Dobara (2011), 206

Zulm Ki Hukumat (1992), 103

Acknowledgements

R am Gopal Varma, for making a film I can still tolerate after dozens of viewings.

The ones who supplied the stories: Allan Amin, Apurva Asrani, Manoj Bajpayee, Chakravarthy, Vishal Bhardwaj, Gerard Hooper, Kannan Iyer, Mazhar Kamran, Anurag Kashyap, Sabir Masani, Sudhir Mishra, Desmond Nazareth, Nitin Rao, Shefali Shah, Barnali Ray Shukla, Saurabh Shukla, Sushant Singh, Suparn S. Varma.

Mint Lounge, my home for the last six years, for publishing 'Who killed the Hindi gangster film?', a piece based on research for this book.

Gerard Hooper, for digging out and sharing photographs he took 24 years ago.

Sidharth Bhatia and Sriram Raghavan, for their unmatched knowledge of noir cinema.

Akshay Manwani, Shruti Rajagopalan and Tanul Thakur, for their expert help, encouragement and for exhibiting at all times more optimism about the enterprise than I was feeling.

Nasreen Munni Kabir, for her painstaking edits, sharp eye and generosity.

Jai Arjun Singh, for putting up with dozens of emails that began with 'I don't think this paragraph works', and for being a cheerleader of this book from the start.

Chitrita Ganguly, for tactfully pointing out countless errors, and for implacably handling six years of writerly complaints.

My parents, Eesh and Vijayalakshmi, for support and encouragement in all matters.

About the Author

Uday Bhatia is a film critic with *Mint Lounge* in Delhi. He has previously worked with *Time Out Delhi* and *The Sunday Guardian*. His writing has appeared in *The Caravan*, *GQ*, *The Indian Quarterly*, *The Indian Express* and *The Hindu Business Line*.